Reinventing Childhood

After World War II

Reinventing Childhood After World War II

Edited by Paula S. Fass and Michael Grossberg

PENN

UNIVERSITY OF PENNSYLVANIA PRESS

PHILADELPHIA

Published by
University of Pennsylvania Press
Philadelphia, Pennsylvania 19104-4112
www.upenn.edu/pennpress

Printed in the United States of America on acid-free paper

10 9 8 7 6 5 4 3 2 1

Library of Congress Cataloging-in-Publication Data
Reinventing childhood after World War II / edited by Paula S. Fass and Michael
Grossberg—1st ed.
    p.   cm.
  ISBN 978-0-8122-4367-3 (hardcover : alk. paper)
  Includes bibliographical references and index.
  1. Children—United States—Social conditions—History—20th century.
2. Children—United States—Social conditions—History—21st century. 3.
Adolescence—United States—History—20th century. 4. Adolescence—United
States—History—21st century. 5. Children—Sweden—Social conditions—History—
20th century. 6. Children—Sweden—Social conditions—History—21st century. 7.
Adolescence—Sweden—History—20th century. 8. Adolescence—Sweden—History—
21st century. I. Fass, Paula S. II. Grossberg, Michel, 1950–.
HQ792.U5 R374   2011
305.2309182'109045—dcc   2011021264

To our children

Contents

Preface

Since the early 1980s, historians have been discovering the centrality of children and childhood to many aspects of political, social, and cultural life. Focusing on children in history was not entirely new to this past generation of historians, and the subject had been anticipated by many excellent studies by social historians beginning at least fifty years ago. But the intensification of interest in children as historical subjects along with research in this area has grown enormously during this more recent period, not least because reflections on children's welfare are currently so important and widespread. As historians give voice to a more comprehensive range of historical actors and listen to contemporary social concerns, childhood has become an important subject of inquiry and offers many directions for study. Children have thus become important subjects in their own right, and we have come to recognize children and childhood as essential to understanding historical developments generally.

Historians of the contemporary United States and Western Europe have been especially active in this burgeoning enterprise, although the field of childhood history has by no means been restricted to the West and much important research has emphasized children and childhood at all periods of history and in all parts of the globe. In the Western world, the modern view of childhood as a protected space separated from both the developing market economy and the broader adult society, first became a dominant social vision during the nineteenth century. As a result, many of the West's sharpest portrayals of children in literature and the visual arts emerged at that time in both Europe and the United States and these continue to organize our perceptions and sensibilities. In many ways, therefore, modern childhood can be said to have been a creation of that world. Precisely because we have learned that the way we view children and understand childhood today is deeply embedded in the modern historical imagination, many historians of the nineteenth- and twentieth-century post-Enlightenment, postrevolutionary world have turned their attention to children as subjects of investigation, and the topic has been especially prominent among historians who study the contemporary world.

One of the revelations of this dynamic field of inquiry is the centrality of children and childhood to fundamental matters of law, social policy, politics and political symbolism, institutional life, and cultural production. This resulted from the experiences of children, the separate sphere of childhood that was increasingly inscribed in the modern vision, and the necessary protections of innocence and dependency by the state and civil society. Thus, as children became more generally viewed as needing protection, a large range of social and cultural institutions were created to that purpose. Some of these were essential components of the developing nationalism of the time; others resulted as byproducts of economic and cultural development as families, reformers, educators, and others sought to provide children with the childhood now understood to be best for them. In the United States, where the state has been the subject of deep suspicion even as all levels of government have grown, the modern vision of childhood has often developed more as a result of private initiatives fostered by a vibrant civil society, rather than via state directives. As the essays that follow make clear, the American variant of child welfare and changes in child life frequently rests on ambivalence toward state interventions that are taken for granted and vigorously pursued in other parts of the West. In the United States, policies relating to children have been the product of a shifting balance between government agencies and nongovernmental institutions.

The authors of this volume have been actively helping to create and define the history of children and childhood as part of Western historical development, and this book is an expression of the joint venture they launched to explore the subject in the recent past. We argue that even within the context of the modern world, the period since World War II has introduced major elements of change that have fundamentally altered both the lives of children and how we understand them through our conceptions of childhood.

Over the past several years, the seven contributors to this volume have worked together, hosting and assembling conferences, and as a continuing small group seminar, in an effort to define, analyze, and chart how children's lives and childhood have changed since World War II. It is not too much, we believe, to describe this change as a reinvention of childhood, since the thoroughgoing alterations have affected so many arenas that impinge on the lives of children: law, government policy, family life, education, mass culture, and the definitions of age. The essays generated by our collaboration are varied and reflect our individual viewpoints and emphases, but they also demonstrate the two major commitments we all share: that studying children is crucial to understanding the complex developments of the period, and that the years since the end of World War II have together been a distinct and extraordinarily rich episode in that history in the United States specifically and in the Western world more generally.

Once we begin to list some of the social, political, and legal transformations packed into this relatively short period of time, the facts that frame the subject become obvious and the reasons for these essays clear: the massive expansion of schooling to older children and youth of many social backgrounds; the institutionalization of the welfare state; the explosion of consumer and popular culture and its penetration into children's consciousness; changing family dynamics that include much more effective contraceptives, dramatically new and varied kinds of assisted reproduction, the steep increase in divorce, and the normalization and spread of women's employment outside the household; the significant expansion of citizenship and civil rights to populations previously only marginally included; a newly globalized economy and the dynamic internationalization of culture, investments, and migrations that have accompanied it. These are among the fundamental alterations in private and public life into which Western children have been introduced in the postwar years and it is in this context, we argue, that childhood has been refashioned in consequential ways for the young and the society they live in. Indeed, we argue further that in the United States this period itself was significantly bifurcated into two eras: 1945 through the mid-1970s, and the late 1970s to the present.

It is our hope and expectation that these essays will result in serious discussion and bring about an engagement with the new field of children's history. We also look forward to having the matters we explore become the subject of exchange with our colleagues in other fields of history and other disciplines. As historians of childhood we are keenly aware of the interdisciplinary nature of our enterprise, that studying children necessarily involves conversations with other social scientists, educators, psychologists, policymakers, lawyers, teachers, social workers, and others. We are eager to inject childhood into a much larger discussion of the nature of the modern world that includes historical sources and contemporary forces that influence children's lives. We hope these essays will engage both scholars and students to think deeply about the areas we introduce and to include them in their studies of post World War II history more broadly.

We believe one way to encourage such reflection is to add a comparative perspective to our histories. Although six of the essays concentrate on the United States, the final chapter chronicles major child welfare policy changes in Sweden from the end of the war to the present. Our aim in including this chapter is to suggest that many of the developments that figure so prominently in the articles on American children were also part of the postwar Western experience more generally and indeed were experienced by all postindustrial societies. At the same time, we also want to contend that the United States produced a particular variant of Western conceptions of childhood and children's policies during these years.

In comments sprinkled through the chapters on the United States and then in the final essay, we offer Sweden as a singular but illuminating example of both commonalities and differences in Western children's policies, and indeed in conceptions of childhood itself. Any comparison would be useful, but Sweden provides a particularly revealing counterpoint to postwar American children's history because Swedes often devised very different solutions to similar problems. A national ban on corporal punishment that included schools and homes, the creation of children's allowances that gave young people a significant degree of economic independence from their families, and the determination not merely to ratify but to implement as completely as possible the 1989 United Nations Convention on the Rights of the Child are but some instances of the different path taken in Sweden and analyzed in the book's final chapter. As these examples suggest, the comparison demonstrates how children and adults in Sweden and the United States, as in other Western societies, experienced postwar transformations in the context of their own histories and through their own particular cultures. The Swedish example, above all, demonstrates the different results when the state takes a leading role. American ambivalence toward the state, and its reliance on civil society, had consequences that become quite clear in contrast.

The Swedish example brings into sharper relief several other findings that the authors of the essays on the United States share. As already noted, all the essayists on the United States found a distinct disjuncture in children's experiences and children's environments taking place sometime between the middle of the 1960s through the 1970s. No such break occurs in Sweden at this time. Instead, in the absence of Swedish participation in World War II, Swedish policies regarding children seem to have developed more gradually over time and to grow more evenly through the influence of the country's twentieth-century political values. Similarly, almost all the essays on the

United States observe a noticeable increase in concerns about children and childhood, especially since the 1970s. Americans have always worried about children and invested in them as symbols of hope and fear for the present and the future. But there is a palpable increase in the temperature of this anxiety and a sharp urgency in the expressed concerns about all the major institutions that deal closely with children and child welfare—schools, family, the marketplace, media, and the law. Certainly, Swedes too express anxieties about their children in the modern world, but this growing alarm seems not to have affected Swedes to anything like the same degree nor led them to act in the same ways as Americans.

As with any comparison, contrasting postwar histories of children and childhood in America and Sweden sharpens our ways of understanding what changed and allows us to ask more effective questions about why those changes took place. Adding a comparative dimension to a volume that concentrates on the United States is critical for another reason. It aligns our book with the internationalist perspective that has become a dominant—and welcomed—feature of children's history. Placing histories of children and childhood in a global context, even in the limited fashion employed here, demonstrates yet again that the very universalism of age as a category of experience and analysis means that an understanding of the distinctiveness of any particular cultural practice can surface only by placing specific developments in a broader explanatory framework. We hope that the book encourages readers to think about this aspect of children's history as well.

1

The Child-Centered Family?
New Rules in Postwar America

Paula S. Fass

"In America," Dr. Benjamin Spock told his millions of devoted readers, "very few children are raised to believe that their principal destiny is to serve their family, their country or God. Generally we've given them the feeling that they are free to set their own aims and occupations in life according to their own inclinations." This passage neatly summed up what Spock headlined as "Child-Centered America." The clinching line came in Spock's next paragraph: "The tendency is for American parents to consider the child at least as important as themselves—perhaps more important."[1] In stating the American dream in this way, that the child's destiny was not hindered by parents and past, Spock in the 1950s, 1960s, and even into the early 1970s was connecting the well-known American dream of future improvement to a particular view of the relationship between parents and children. That view of the critical connection between child rearing and American identity stretched back possibly as far as the American Revolution in the last third of the eighteenth century, and certainly to the 1830s when Alexis de Tocqueville made his cunning observations about their relationship. And then, as if by articulating it so bluntly for all the readers of *Baby and Child Care*, the parent-child experience he was testifying to began to disappear, replaced by a very different kind of child-centeredness.

The relationship between parents and children, and quite specifically among the significantly enlarged post-World War II middle class to which

America's most popular childcare manual was addressed, would change in important ways in the 1970s and 1980s. That change put parents much more firmly in the driver's seat, reduced the independence and autonomy of children, and made it hard for middle-class parents to imagine that their children's lives would be even as rosy as their own, let alone better.

By the late 1970s, commentators began to observe these changes. Christopher Lasch, one of the most perceptive, believed that middle-class families were beset by "warlike conditions" that affected marital relationships, the rearing of children, and the psychological dimensions of American happiness. Concerns about these conditions grew and became more intense as the end of the century neared. Some blamed it on the fallout from the Vietnam War or on liberated women, while others blamed Spock himself for helping to rear a permissive generation. But it was not necessary to place blame anywhere for most to recognize that American family life had been substantially refashioned. As we think about the changes after the 1970s, it is best not to embrace a mistaken nostalgia for an earlier time in what is often an illusion of a 1950s family high or an exaggerated jeremiad about what followed. Students of the American family have often adopted such polarizing perspectives, and some of the social commentators of the time were trapped in that duality.[2] Nevertheless, it is important to examine and contend with the very real changes in child rearing and in children's lives that took place in the half century following World War II, and to understand that the nostalgia was itself a symptom of just how wounding the perceived rupture with the past was.

A Backward Glance

American family life, and specifically the relations between generations, had always been multiform and complex. Composed of several very different regions and multiple racial, religious, and ethnic groups, no one pattern could do justice to the real pleasures, tensions, and conflicts that marked the relations between parents and children in America since its revolutionary beginnings. Historians are usually able to observe only general tendencies and certain consciously held beliefs that both natives and outsiders expressed when they reflected on America's particular cultural forms and social habits. Nevertheless, the vast and increasing size of the country, its free market, broad-based white male suffrage, and available land did set American experiences apart from those of Europeans (and almost everyone else) in the nineteenth century, and allowed a cultural style to develop that privileged the future, and with it the next generation.

This did not necessarily transform Americans into solicitous parents or protect children from harsh treatment and brutal household regimes. Rather, social and economic circumstances in the United States made it easier to transfer responsibility to the young, providing earlier autonomy to young people, whose own judgment would be required to wrestle with the open-ended conditions accompanying the economic potential and landed vastness. Ulysses S. Grant recalled in his memoirs that from the time he was eleven and "strong enough to hold a plow," until he was seventeen, he did all the work with horses on the land his father (a leather tanner) owned. In return,

> I was compensated by the fact that there was never any scolding or punishing by my parents; no objection to rational enjoyments, such as fishing, going to the creek a mile away to swim in summer, taking a horse and visiting my grandparents in the adjoining county, fifteen miles off, skating on the ice in winter, or taking a horse and sleigh when there was snow on the ground.

Grant loved horses, and by the time he was eleven he was allowed to trade horses on his own account. On one occasion, when he was fifteen, he executed such a trade seventy miles from home.[3] These long-distance travels were nothing new.

This independence was often described by foreign visitors as resulting in a laxness in children's manners and an unwillingness by parents fully to guide and correct the younger generation. Some thought American children were badly brought up, unruly, and discourteous to adults. But others, such as Polish count, Adam C. de Gurowski, understood that parent-child relations were the result of the special circumstances of American life; in his words, "the space, the modes to win a position by labor were unlimited, and thus children began early to work and earn for themselves. Thus early they became self-relying and independent, and this independence continues to prevail in filial relations." In 1857, the count concluded that children matured early and were early "emancipated . . . from parental authority and domestic discipline."[4] In this way, de Gurowski accounted for the observations so common at the time. "Children accustomed to the utmost familiarity and absence of constraint with their parents, behave in the same manner with other older persons, and this sometimes deprives the social intercourse of Americans of the tint of politeness, which is more habitual in Europe."[5] To some degree observations such as these from class-conscious European aristocrats, such as Alexis de Tocqueville and Count de Gurowski, were natural responses to a society without feudal traditions and its mannered courtesies. But, these views also registered the looser forms that governed the interactions between American parents and children and the greater responsibilities given children in a land of copious opportunities.

A half-century after de Gurowski's observations, some Americans were already attempting to find ways to encourage these traits of independence and autonomy in children; traits, they feared, were vulnerable as the circumstances that had encouraged them changed in the context of industry and city life. Thus, America's premier philosopher and educational reformer, John Dewey, tried to inscribe independence in a reformed schooling where children could actively participate in their own instruction, thus replacing an early independence in the world with a new active experience in school. In trying to create a school surrogate for active engagement early in life, Dewey sought in the "Child and the Curriculum" (1902) to restore to the branches of learning "the experience from which it had been abstracted." Dewey opposed the habits of schooling in which children were "ductile and docile." Of the child in this revised school setting, Dewey proclaimed at the end of his essay, "It is his *present* powers which are to assert themselves; his *present* capacities which are to be exercised; his *present* attitudes which are to be realized."[6] Dewey was well aware that schooling was itself locking children away from the very experiences that once assured their active independence. He thus sought a schooling that would create real experience, not just learned anticipation. Only in this fashion would children continue to be inducted into the American style of independence.

Dewey was responding to the major changes in American social and economic life at the turn of the twentieth century, when earlier natural potentials for autonomy and self-regulation were being slowly eroded through the advent of factories, tenements, and, yes, schools. For Dewey, America's changing institutions were making it harder to find ways of encouraging those traits in childhood that he, among others, assumed to be necessary components of American democratic character.

Another half-century later, Benjamin Spock brought these same issues into the nursery. During that half century of turbulent twentieth-century child-rearing debates, Americans had come to expect that the early years were fundamental to personality, so Spock's advice was planted in fertile ground.[7]

After World War II, Spock engaged in an attempt at early childhood psychological reconstruction much as Dewey had attempted a sociological renewal. Little wonder then that Spock would be accused of encouraging permissiveness, just as Dewey's "permissive" educational reforms were believed by some to undermine authority. Back in the nineteenth century the experience that these attempted reconstructions were meant to resurrect had made visitors, such as Harriet Martineau, respond with a similar kind of condemnation regarding America's ungovernable children, permissively brought up by their parents.[8]

By the time Spock tried to create the conditions at home to encourage an independent spirit in two-year-olds—through, among other means, toileting regimes ("He won't really have reached this last stage of training until *he does these jobs by himself*")—it was too late. Despite playful line drawings that emphasized the point, "Children want to do grown-up things,"[9] the changes in the American economy and institutional life that had been developing for over a half-century had overwhelmed the potentials for the kind of child development and intergenerational relationships Americans believed were a cultural inheritance. In place of early independence and a growing autonomy among children, the sociocultural context was re-creating intergenerational relations in ways that became clear only by the end of the twentieth century.

What Changed?

After World War II millions of veterans returned to a society that offered opportunities seemingly everywhere—in an expanding set of economic choices, new educational institutions, independent homeownership in fresh suburban enclaves, and a reinvigorated and more stable family life. These are matters that depression era and war weary Americans had hoped for. It seemed like a revival of opportunities and a renewed American dream. Historians have described these changes in some detail, and while many have been critical of continuing inequalities in an expanded consumer republic or the wastefulness of new suburban tracts, or the constrictions of women's choices in a family constructed in a cold war climate, most historians and other analysts have recognized that both the new standards of living and the new domesticity promised comforts if not palaces to many more Americans than ever before.[10] If nineteenth-century opportunities had created independent landowners and entrepreneurs, the postwar promised to create a republic based on an expanding middle class with open-ended possibilities for leisure, consumption, and personal self-realization.[11]

Indeed, the decade of the 1950s often appears to be the gold standard against which later marriages and families are judged. Divorce rates were low, mothers were at home caring for their children, and children attended well-run schools. Later changes in these domains are usually identified as the sources of the increasing difficulties faced by American children, as divorces skyrocketed in the late 1960s, local schools were disassembled and education was underfunded in the 1970s, and the explosion of women with young children in the workplace became alarmingly evident in the 1980s. In fact, however, the transformation of parent-child relations had already begun before these more obvious changes took place. And Benjamin Spock's insistence on the child's autonomy represents an alarm bell in the midst of the so-called stability of the domestic 1950s rather than a signal of its fulfillment.

The place to begin is in the schools. The attention to schools at mid-century were signs of an extensive economic transformation already underway, although it was hardly visible to most observers at the time. Americans had taken pride in their schools since the nineteenth century, when they had joined other modernizing states and industrializing societies in creating institutions to develop a literate citizenry. But classroom time for most American children was usually quite limited, usually no more than a few years of intermittent attendance for the majority, with only the very few who moved toward college experiencing a longer preparation.[12] The expansion of schooling that marked a profound shift took place in the first four decades of the twentieth century, as secondary schooling expanded enormously and enrollments skyrocketed. By the middle of the twentieth century all adolescents were spending serious time in high school, now a firm feature of the American landscape, indeed sometimes the most prominent landmark in towns and cities across the country. The United States was unique in this regard. In the first half of the century, Americans created comprehensive, publicly funded, widely available high schools for the masses. Organized in communities across the country, these schools were the result of unparalleled prosperity and made necessary by immigration.[13] Even the Swedes and Germans, highly committed to education, confined high school attendance to a small select few whom they isolated in institutions for the elite.

After World War II, high school attendance and graduation became an expected part of normal American adolescent experience and, by the 1950s, American educators were already beginning to measure the high school dropout rate and to worry about this as a sign of social failure, rather than celebrating the growing expansion as they had in the past. By 1960, almost 90 percent of seventeen- and eighteen-year-olds (upper high school years) were in school.[14] And the road into the classroom did not end there. Whereas only about 15 percent of young people eighteen to twenty-two went to college in 1940, on the eve of America's entrance into World War II, 53 percent did so by the early 1960s.[15] Schooling was now a standard part of the extended adolescence that prepared children for adulthood in the United States. This explosion in the institutionalization of American adolescents represented a critical transformation in social life. As social psychologist Arlene Skolnick has observed, "Today all roads to a successful livelihood lead through the classroom."[16]

As Dewey knew well, and as anyone who has been there can testify, schooling and adolescent classrooms in particular offer a peculiar kind of "experience." At once real life in a school peer culture, schools provide academic preparation for a very different future outside the classroom, while separating young people from their parents without giving them a sense of competence. And it comes in the midst of the tense process by which the two generations define the boundaries of separation that lead to independence. While it is a route to opportunity, it is a poor substitute for real life. The seeming independence of young people in high school is a mirage, as parental support, continuing residence at home, and peer conformity limit young people's horizons and direct their behavior. This was already clear to a host of observers in the 1950s, from Edgar J. Friedenberg to Paul Goodman and Kenneth Keniston,[17] who began to offer blistering criticisms of the lives of confined young Americans.

David Riesman was probably the most perceptive critic, as he described the results of a new social scene where the young learned not independence through the active creation of meaningful individual goals, but a glib conformity encouraged by peer pressure and initiation. No one who read *The Lonely Crowd* could mistake the point that lay behind Riesman's apparently neutral observations about the changes taking place around him and his team of researchers. The book was published in 1950, long before nostalgia for the 1950s had begun.[18]

In fact, throughout the 1950s, there was a haunting sense that American children and youth were being prepared for a transformation in adult experience while they were in the process of defining a new life phase. Underneath the seeming domestic retreat provided by the suburbs and the apparent confidence reflected in the marriage and birth rates, one can see the relationship between the generations being renegotiated in a changing economy. The new emphasis on extended schooling and competitive skills training, I would contend, was a response not so much to the Cold War as some historians have argued (although some Cold War competition was clearly at stake) as it was to an early sounding of a much longer-term transformation in global economics. The "postindustrial society," heralded by Daniel Bell in 1968, was underway as an earlier dominance of factory labor for the majority of workers or small-scale entrepreneurship gave way to a service economy and an international system of trade, capital exchange, and offshore production. When Japanese cars moved smoothly into United States markets after the first oil crisis in 1973, Americans were taken by surprise, but the Japanese automobile industry (and its underlying developments in steel and technology) had long been preparing for just such a shift. The decline of American industrial production (which had itself replaced the farm-based economy of an earlier century), and the factory work that allowed some to work from an early age (at least by our contemporary standards) and still participate in expanding opportunities, was already changing the urban landscape in Detroit in the 1950s.[19] Textile manufacturing was moving rapidly, first to the American South and then offshore. At the same time, the white-collar sector, both in managerial tiers and in lower-level forms, was growing rapidly, and with that came requirements for literacy and social behavior. If not every child who went to school was preparing to become a professional, many more were learning that the corporate office, not the shop floor, was their likely destination.

In the 1950s, therefore, alert middle-class parents and those eager to have their children join the middle class were already taking note and keeping their children's noses close to a bookish grindstone as they anticipated a transformation in rewards long before it was broadly advertised. These same parents exercised generational authority in a new way, and they did it long after most parents in the nineteenth century and many working-class parents in the twentieth were forced to give up because the economy loosened their grip. Indeed in Arlene Skolnick's words, the middle class was "the most revolutionary class insofar as the family is concerned. Our major periods of family crisis have occurred when the middle class has redefined the meaning of the family."[20] Although Skolnick attributes that change to the period after the 1960s, I think it is wise to see its early manifestations in the 1950s. Children who were being directed toward schooled success, not only spent more time in school, they dated less, rarely went steady, married later, and were supported by their parents through their college years.[21] These patterns would become very familiar by the end of the century, but in the 1950s they were still quite new.

We can also see some of the ways in which families in the 1950s anticipated later experiences by examining the shift of married women with children into the workforce, a movement often associated with a much later time. Many married women with children entered the work force in response to the new office work that called on their literate skills. But it was also linked to the increased schooling of their adolescent children. American women had always gone to work in emergencies, during wartime, and when their husbands were laid off or died. At the height of the single-income household ideal in the 1950s, married women in an expanding middle class went to work when there was no war or emergency. This time they went to supplement family incomes in order to raise their class profile through consumption or, if they were especially alert to changing opportunities, to allow their children to stay in school longer. Women with children went to work because their children no longer could. All children were required to stay in school longer, as they began to train for the rewards of the changing economy, and many women went to work to help them through college. This shift from children's work to the work of women in the 1950s had revolutionary consequences since it accustomed Americans to meeting adult middle-class women in the workplace, but also because it meant that the expectation that middle-class women with working husbands and with children might work prepared the way for the surge in female employment after the 1970s.[22]

When observers such as Skolnick and Lasch attributed the huge change in family dynamics to the period after the so-called social revolution of the 1960s when women left the home, they are certainly correct, but that change was already well underway in the 1950s, before the women's movement gave voice to growing sentiments about inequality. What was new and important after the emergence of an articulate feminist movement was the willingness of women (more or less) to have their *younger* children in the care of others. Whereas women went to work in the 1950s as their children reached high school or college, starting in the 1970s they did so earlier and earlier in their children's lives. This not only flew in the face of Dr. Spock's best advice about child rearing, but overturned over a century of historical experience where young children were expected to remain in the care of their mothers. We will return to this matter later.

One other aspect of the 1950s that is critical to our understanding of the changes in the relationship between parents and children, and one that comes from an unexpected quarter, is rock 'n' roll music. Before we yield to an unrealistic image of domestic harmony in the 1950s, it is useful to listen to the music of the time. No parent who lived through the mid to late 1950s and whose children were entranced by and danced to the music of Elvis Presley, Bill Haley and the Comets, Jerry Lee Lewis, and the many others whose music permeated the radio airwaves, could imagine that the period was peaceful or conflict free. Long before the Beatles and Bob Dylan, American adolescents were expressing their irritation at the parental restrictions placed on their freedom in songs such as "Yakety Yak," "Rock Around the Clock" (tellingly taken from the dark high school movie, *Blackboard Jungle*), and "Charlie Brown."[23] Parents were often simply absent from the songs' lyrics, but the musical taste itself manifestly set the generations apart. In his defense of teenage rebelliousness, Edgar Freidenberg suggested that the pugnacious attitude that teenagers often expressed and that can be heard in the music of the time, was a necessary part of their self-definition.[24] Rock 'n' roll, one is tempted to argue, was a substitute for real autonomy, a realm of free expression that grew up to siphon off the desire for other kinds of independence. Music was a symptom of the tightening and lengthening of parental controls over children's lives.

It is not coincidental that rock 'n' roll is so closely identified with the 1950s high school, since it was after school that teenagers hurried home to watch *American Bandstand*. Part of this association has become the basis for our nostalgia for the period, but beneath this longing lies a reality that should be taken very seriously as expressions of real tensions and deep changes in traditional beliefs and practices affecting American generational relationships.

The changes were clear enough by the mid-1950s to propel into prominence one of America's premier public intellectuals, the neo-Freudian psychoanalyst Erik Erikson. Erikson became famous for coining the term "adolescent identity crisis" and for demonstrating that many conflicts related to earlier phases of parent-child relations came to a head during that difficult transition. Erikson argued that adolescence did not ease the relationship between the generations; rather, it intensified earlier conflicts. It was only after resolving these crises, Erikson argued from his perch at Harvard University, that American youth could move into adulthood.[25] The need for a new and widely popular concept is always worthy of our attention and, in this case, it was not only Harvard students or their parents who were listening to this new way of understanding youth. Behind 1950s youth, especially the ones who stayed in school longer, lay altered family dynamics in which parents were newly, if sometimes reluctantly, more in charge for longer periods and in more detail. Indeed, Erikson, like other intellectuals, was listening to changed tones in the relations between parents and children and observing tensions as adult supervision over adolescents lengthened and tightened.

After the Earthquake: Leaping into the Future

Seeing the 1950s in more complex terms does not deny the genuine and dramatic shifts that took place afterward. Starting in the late 1960s and then accelerating steadily, American intergenerational relations experienced a series of shocks that resulted from what Daniel Moynihan called "an earthquake" of family changes.[26] These included important new gender roles, sexual behaviors and mores, marriage patterns, divorce trends, and birth rates. It also included a youth rebellion that took even seasoned social observers by surprise. These all took place in a highly compressed period of time, from about 1963 to 1973. By 1972 its consequences were already drawing the attention of, among others, the Carnegie Corporation, which created the Carnegie Council on Children and asked psychologist Kenneth Keniston to lead a group of noted scholars in investigating what the changes meant for children.[27]

It is my argument that starting in the mid-1960s, the middle-class family began to crack down on its kids, consciously (if not completely successfully) circumscribing their range of choices, patrolling their behavior, and supervising their activities. The tremors I have noted that began in the 1950s burst into the open and now created a clear rupture with the past. The change was not visible until the 1970s and 1980s, in part because the post-1960s birth rate plummeted and the immediate post-baby boom generation was quite small. As a result, childhood matters were not high on the social agenda before the 1980s. Within another decade, however, observations about the changes in the lives of children began in earnest. Children of middle-class parents by the late 1980s and 1990s had perceptibly less freedom of physical movement and less room to explore alternatives to the success-driven futures their parents designed for them. The reasons for this combined economics and psychology in a potent blend of fear and hope that began to define child rearing from then on. In so doing, the earthquake of changes finally ended the commitment to an American pattern that had been dominant for over one hundred and fifty years and which was still struggling to survive in the 1950s and 1960s: a pattern where children were deemed more important than their parents. Clearly, some families continued to provide their children with the conditions that encouraged their autonomy and independence, but the cultural conditions as well as the socially approved signals were turning in a completely different direction.

One way to understand the youth revolt in the 1960s is that it anticipated this crackdown. Indeed, once it took place, the revolt may even have alarmed parents and authorities enough to enforce a more restrictive regime in the next generation of families. Thus, one might argue that among a small group of well-educated young people who grew up in the 1950s, the increased exercise of parental authority helped to fuel a revolt. One way of understanding this revolt is to use the terms that the young chose themselves: they were in revolt against their buttoned-down, gray-flanneled parents. Those parents, some newly arrived in the middle class after the Second World War, did guard their propriety as new, solid, citizens by expressing this through external restraint and workplace conformity. In rejecting their parents' attitudes and behavior (with a little help from their friends), and striving to define themselves, 1960s youth were fulfilling the role that Spock, Friedenberg, Erikson, and an entire previous history of U.S. generational relations laid out for them. They sought to find their own voices in an exaggerated tradition of American independence. Of course, not all 1960s college and high school youth followed this path and many were quite ready to adopt their parents' guidelines and follow in their footsteps. It was the minority, however, who promoted and helped to ignite a sociocultural revolution that dominated the language of the time. These young people, as Beth Bailey has shown for even such a solidly middle American city as Lawrence, Kansas, precipitated a transformation in mores with regard to gender, sexuality, marriage, and language that had seismic consequences and created a genuine cultural rupture.[28] Regardless of whether we can find serious earlier manifestations of all the trends that became prominent by the late 1960s (declining births, later marriages, increased divorce, more promiscuous and varied sexual patterns), by the 1980s all the changes came to a visible climax as the 1960s generation matured and changed the way American children were raised. While some of those who had been in revolt may themselves have raised their children in accordance with their own experiences,[29] some even joining communal family structures and encouraging their young children to extreme nonconformity, the generation as a whole created a very different cultural configuration.

In 1970, to use one example, 33 percent of marriages ended in divorce. By 1990 (after the no-fault revolution), it had reached 50 percent, where it has more or less stayed ever since. Between 1950 and 1997, divorce increased by 67 percent. From 1960 to 1980, the number of women in the workforce doubled from 22 to 44 million. By the end of the century, 73 percent of couples were composed of two wage earners, effectively ending the single-earner model that had been a sought-after ideal for nineteenth-century workers and had become a twentieth-century norm. Most important for our purposes, the birth rate (in response to the sexual revolution midwifed by the birth control revolution) was cut in half, from 120 births per 1,000 women in 1960 to 60 in 1975, an extraordinary and unprecedented decline. It has subsequently risen, but has remained low. This decline enshrined new mores that sanctioned premarital sex.[30]

These matters finally all came together in the number of women *with children* who went to work. To appreciate this last change requires a longer historical view. In 1920, 9 percent of all mothers were working; in 1940, 15 percent; in 1973, 44 percent; and in 1985, 62 percent. That proportion grew steadily thereafter and included more and more women with younger and younger children. Initially statistics recorded only the percentage of women in the workforce whose children were under six (school age), but as statisticians kept pace with the social changes they began to record those with children under three (preschool age), and then one. Today it has become common to record the proportion of women in the workforce with children under six months of age. *This* was truly revolutionary.

A New Generation: The Anxious Dependents

Statistics are not history, but in the case of these statistics, they serve as the basis for understanding a significant historical change, since they telescope the underlying facts of the domestic transformation. In American households almost everywhere in the country in the last quarter of the twentieth century, women were having fewer children later in life, and leaving them with others at younger and younger ages while they worked outside the home. Many of these women were divorced and were raising their children on their own. Some working mothers with children had never been married. Figures published in the *New York Times* in 2009 show that 40 percent of all children born in 2007 in the United States were born to unmarried mothers.[31] And married women, as I have suggested, increasingly found that working was not a choice but a necessity.

As this happened, personal anxieties about children (and social anxieties about childhood) grew furiously. Indeed, one would be hard-pressed to find a stretch of time in American history in which anxieties about children were more intense than in the two decades from 1980 to 2000, and this includes periods of severe depression and long wars with serious ramifications for the civilian population.[32] Among these concerns, many addressed child safety. Parents now worried that their children were vulnerable to stranger abductions, predatory child-care workers, incestuous boyfriends, internet sex and pornography, murderous nannies—all related to fears about lack of adequate oversight by parents or care givers. Children were also seen as vulnerable to toxic vaccines, violence in the media, too much sugar in their diets, dangerous playground equipment, and bad schools—all related to inadequate community or governmental regulation and oversight. If the enormous generation born from 1945 to 1965 was the baby-boom generation, those born after that time had become the anxious dependents.

This anxiety has become the governing temper of American child rearing today, and it too has not so subtly changed generational relationships. To the commitment to schooling that middle-class parents began to adopt in the 1950s, which was already circumscribing the lives of their children through a more exacting attention to the future, parents now added anxieties about the adequacy of those schools and a drive for competitive schooling advantage that—at the extreme—is expressed in a hysterical desire to promote children into the most competitive colleges and universities, which often begin with correct preschool placements.[33] But this is only one narrow part of the picture. As mothers went out to work, tutorial services of all kinds moved in— SAT prep (already established in the 1960s); ancillary after-school education that grew up even in good suburbs in the 1980s; private tutors (once only the domain of the rich); culturally and academically enriching summer camps; private day schools. The period since the 1980s has seen an explosion in private schooling ventures of all kinds that service all sectors of the middle class, not just the rich. Lower-middle-class neighborhoods and strip malls today are dotted with school services to compensate for or augment public school instruction. In the public school realm, charter schools have exploded in popularity. Other parts of the day and week are just as closely monitored, and are filled with lessons in music, dance, and gymnastics, and myriad sports activities, creating highly regulated childhood regimes. All these helped to create the market for a new kind of car and a new voter designation as the minivan, and then the sports utility vehicle, became signs of the times.

All these expensive accouterments of growing up could never really become part of everyone's childhood. And that was part of their appeal. They provided real advantages to those who could afford them as wealthy middle-class parents attempted to shelter their children with the class privilege they bought, and less well-to-do members of the middle class struggled to keep up. Rather than liberate them into an independent future, parents chaperoned their every step. As these activities became the standard by which class status was passed on, less privileged parents tried to compensate through intense oversight and protectiveness to prevent their children from being drawn down into lower statuses where drugs, overburdened and chaotic schools, and general unpredictability threatened to define their children's future.[34] The concern about children's well-being is today in no way the exclusive preserve of privileged families, and while working-class parents do not exercise as much scrutiny, they are not thereby excluded from the general drive to exercise more control when they can. That this made children more, not less dependent, was hardly a consideration for parents who were both attuned to the new competitive requirements of a now manifestly globalized economy and eager to protect their children from the array of perceived social harms that seemed to loom everywhere as reported in the press and on television. These harms broadly advertised by sensational media increasingly emphasized parents' *private* responsibility to guard, promote, and channel their children.[35]

The growing dependence on schooling and the fear of harm also meant that parents had to circumscribe their children's behavior in new ways. If sitting still in a classroom was necessary for success, then parents, who might once have countenanced juvenile exuberance as a sign of spunky independence or a form of natural vitality, began to adopt the drug Ritalin as an aid to child control. Where in the past young children might be expected to outgrow their jumpiness, or parents accepted that they were not going to be successful in schooled activities, such unpredictability and its costs could no longer be patiently accepted since it was assumed that all children had to become successful on the same terms. In the words of a *Newsweek* article, "This is beyond question, an American phenomenon. The rate of Ritalin use in the United States is at least five times higher than in the rest of the world."[36] And the schools themselves, under new performance pressures, were only too willing to comply with parents' requests or to insist that parents adopt the drugs in order to keep their children in school.

Not everything revolved around schooling, but after the 1980s children's lives more and more revolved around organized activities. In fact, taken all together, children's lives were far more organized than ever before. This began with organized day care earlier and earlier in childhood, play dates and after-school sports, other after-school projects such as art and music, and more targeted summer camps that aimed at instruction far more than play.[37] A generation of parents, many of whom had been in revolt against the organization man portrayed by psychologist William Whyte in the 1950s,[38] helped create the organization child of the 1980s and 1990s, unwittingly reacting against the very changes they had helped to initiate.

What was lost in all this? As Howard Chudacoff has shown, a playful childhood, often composed of no more than periods of being alone doing nothing or hanging out with friends, was the first casualty.[39] Parental confidence in their children's competence at growing up and standing alone was also lost as middle-class parents began to expect, and even to fear, that their grown children would return to the parental home. Psychologist Jerome Kagan blames the child-rearing advice industry for part of this, since it makes parents imagine that their vigilance, and not the child's inner clock, is responsible for development.[40] But it is surely also a result of an uneasy perspective on the recent revolution in family life. I am not suggesting that the revolution was itself bad, only that the rapidity of the transformation, in combination with serious economic changes, has made us uneasy about our children. Today we are deeply anxious when we learn that even older children are left at home alone, and we imagine that they are not capable of coping. Often, indeed, poverty and other circumstances do endanger the latchkey child. But children have been left at home by themselves or with other children, or even on the streets, regularly throughout history. It is our anxiety about their welfare and our sense that they need to be constantly supervised and instructed that is different. This is partly a response to the fact that children today, more often than before, are either only children or have few siblings. Above all, however, it is an expression of a new sense of our inadequacy as parents and their helplessness as children.

Some concerns are justified. The growing sense that there is no one looking out for the interests of children, no watchful neighbor, few stay-at-home parents, no vocal reformers urging effective legislation to safeguard children's needs, is not entirely groundless. Our children do need to be cared for, but this could be accomplished without impeding their growth and independence. A good part of the change is the growing sense of the privatization of responsibility. With fewer neighbors in whom parents can trust, fewer community structures in which parents are personally invested,[41] and less trust in government regulation, parents of all classes feel they have been thrown very much on their personal resources. Perhaps, only the growing faith in religious life has moved in the opposite direction, providing Americans through church activities (not for the first time) with an effective buffer against isolation and a way to leverage faith into social capital. Not surprisingly, many American parents are turning once again to the churches for child-rearing advice.

Beyond this, modern parents, middle-class parents especially, are encouraged toward an illusion of perfection: If only they enrolled the child in the right program, or provided just the right medication, everything would work out well. If only they could withhold the tainted vaccine, their child could be assured of not becoming autistic. If only they lived in just the right suburb or the child went to just the right preschool, academic success would be assured. In the nineteenth century, when Americans had just become involved in their unusual adventure in intergenerational relations, Nathaniel Hawthorne wrote a haunting short story called "Rappaccini's Daughter." He described an Italian doctor made famous by his horticultural experiments. Dr. Rappaccini treated his beautiful daughter as his best, most treasured, and most highly cultivated plant. But in so doing he had kept her apart from society, sheltered in a fragrant garden, where nothing was left to chance. "Her experience of life had been confined within the limits of that garden," Hawthorne wrote (probably riffing on Rousseau). When a young student is beguiled by her and hopes to love her, the daughter realizes that she has become a poisonous lifeform, incapable of mixing with the world. She takes an antidote and dies.

Finding an antidote to the increasingly poisonous separation of children from their own actions and providing them with some control over their own future is hardly as simple, and one hopes that the cure will be less fatal. One reads op-ed pieces regularly that reflect the panic among parents trying to keep their children safe, together with accompanying fears that this protection will prevent them from growing up. A *New York Times* op-ed by Kaitlin Flanagan half seriously congratulates American children for staying home with their parents on Saturday nights and forgoing the pleasure of driving at sixteen years of age. "An American teenager is part wunderkind and part invalid, able to excel in obscure sports but needing his mother to rush the field with a jacket and Thermos of broth when he's finished."[42] The current hothouse environment has already resulted in an agonized assessment of our children's lives and serious concerns about the potential for American innovation in the future. While conditions in the United States have surely changed since the days of abundant and free land, survivalist techniques, and the open possibilities of the nineteenth century, the current tendency of parents to overcultivate their children as the middle class engages in warlike and competitive struggles, needs to find its own antidote. One of the most hopeful solutions could come through a more active engagement of the middle class with the cause of all children and the needs of the larger community. Another would be for Americans to reconnect with their own historical experiences and their cultural legacy and begin once again to trust their children and allow them to grow into their own futures.

2

Liberation and Caretaking: Fighting over Children's Rights in Postwar America

Michael Grossberg

Children's rights have been a critical but contentious issue in the United States since the late nineteenth century and the emergence of modern conceptions of childhood. Since then rights have assumed greater and greater importance as a primary way for Americans to determine the meaning of childhood. Nevertheless children's rights did not develop in a consistent or a linear manner. Quite the contrary; contests over children's rights were creations of particular periods in history. In no era was that reality more evident or consequential than in the second half of the twentieth century. Two stories illustrate how the focus of children's rights shifted dramatically during those decades.

In 1967, Mary Beth Tinker was a thirteen-year-old eighth grader at Warren G. Harding Junior High School in Des Moines, Iowa. On December 16, she, her older brother, and his friend decided to express their opposition to the Vietnam War by wearing black armbands to school. Mary Beth and the other two students were suspended, but remained convinced they had a right to express their political views at school. The teens turned to the law for vindication. Success came in the 1969 ruling, *Tinker v. Des Moines*, by the U.S. Supreme Court. Justice Abraham Fortas declared: "It can hardly be argued that . . . students or teachers shed their constitutional rights of freedom of speech or expression at the schoolhouse gate!"[1]

In 1994 Megan Kanka was seven years old and living in Hamilton Township, New Jersey, when tragedy struck. On July 29, Jesse Timmendequas, a violent sexual offender who lived across the street, kidnapped, raped, and murdered her. In response, Megan's parents asserted: "Every parent should have the right to know if a dangerous sexual predator moves into their neighborhood." The Kankas circulated a petition demanding immediate legislative action to protect other people's children. Over 400,000 signed it right away and a statute was passed in 89 days. New Jersey's Megan's Law required convicted sex offenders to notify the local police when they moved into a neighborhood and mandated that state officials maintain a registry of sex offenders. Very quickly it became a model for specific states and then the country as a whole when Congress passed a federal Megan's law in 1994 as well.[2]

These very different stories reveal two clashing conceptions of children's rights. The first grounds the rights of children in their fundamental humanity and asserts that the young, particularly as they age, should be granted significant self-determination, autonomy, and control over the decisions that affect their lives—much like adults. These rights can be asserted against the state, parents, and other adults. Mary Beth's claim that she had the right to participate in American politics through a war protest at her school represented just such an assertion of children's rights. The second story converts children's basic human needs into rights and is thus rooted in assumptions of children's inherent dependence and need for adult care and protection. Such rights are asserted primarily on behalf of children not *by* them. The demand of Megan's parents that children had the right to be protected from sexual predators vividly illustrates this version of children's rights. British political philosopher David Archard very usefully categorizes these two conceptions of children's rights as liberationist and caretaking. They are derived from contrasting conceptions of childhood, particularly differing understandings of children's competence, capacity, and maturity.[3] In the United States, liberation and caretaking aptly label the poles around which contests over children's rights have been fought for over a century. Each draws on the fundamental appeal and power of rights as a way for Americans to assert their individual and collective aspirations and identities. And yet the differences between them also reveal a persistent uncertainty and ambiguity about the very notion of the rights of children.

Both liberation and caretaking conceptions of children's rights expanded significantly after 1945 amid a national and global rights revolution. Expansion intensified the clashes between them as rights became an increasingly important vehicle for asserting and defending particular policies for children and particular ideas about the place of children in American society, especially adolescents under eighteen. However, the stories of Mary Beth and Megan tell us that the expansion of children's rights occurred sequentially during these years. Liberationist definitions of children's rights expanded significantly from the 1940s through the 1970s. Then, the last decades of the twentieth century witnessed a reassertion of a caretaking conception of children's rights. The shifting emphasis in rights represents changing understandings of childhood, particularly notions of children's competence, maturity, and capacity, as well as of the relationship between children, parents, the state, and civil society.

Liberation Rights

Mary Beth Tinker's war protest ignited a fight over children's political competence and capacity. She insisted that the decision to protest was her own and that she had a right to make a political statement at school. She rejected arguments that she lacked the competency and maturity to understand the issues posed by the war, that she was a tool of her parents or the American Civil Liberties Union (ACLU) that helped wage her legal fight, and that her age or her status as a student barred her from direct political action. Her understanding of childhood, particularly of teenage students like herself, included the right to express her political views publicly. Mary Beth's demand for adult-like rights was repeated by countless other youth in postwar America, pushing children's rights away from caretaking and toward liberation.[4]

Although caretaking has been the primary basis of children's rights since their first articulation in the late nineteenth century as part of modern conceptions of childhood, liberationist claims like Mary Beth's too have been made repeatedly since then. Examples from that time can be found in the experiential history of children's resistance to attempts by parents, the state, and private organizations to restrict their participation in the nation's social, political, and economic life: children resisted censorship enacted to protect their morals by flocking to nickelodeons and reading dime novels; they challenged controls on their leisure time by filling dance halls and skating rinks; they evaded compulsory school laws and child labor regulations by playing hooky and hawking newspapers in the streets; they filed lawsuits to challenge their classification as feebleminded or as wards of the state, and on and on. Each represented not merely an act of resistance by the young but an assertion of the right to participate more fully in the adult world by smudging if not erasing the bright legal line between childhood and adulthood. Each also demonstrated the lure of rights as a language and tactic of opposition by the powerless against the powerful.[5]

An evocative illustration of early twentieth-century liberationist rights consciousness comes from children who defied adult attempts to control their labor by forming their own unions. In 1902, the seventeen-year-old head of a Pennsylvania children's mine union lobbied her employers to have a disabled child miner assigned an easier job. When the boss refused, she expressed her faith in rights to rally her comrades: "Girls, shall we stand for it—we that believes in the rights of man? Shall we stand for seeing her growing up a cripple and the union not doing nothing nor reaching out no hand to help? I know that it's tough to strike now, because some of us is supporting our families, whose fathers is striking. Shall we stand for it?" No!, they voted unanimously. After a two day walkout the boss agreed to shift the girl's job.[6]

Rights claims like this one demonstrate how children in the past asserted their own sense of competence and capacity and challenged those who would limit their rights by labeling the children immature, innocent, and incompetent. They also underscore a critical point made by historians Joseph Hawes and Ray Hiner: "The individual and collective responses of American children to the demands of adults have shaped adult behavior and experience to the extent that it is impossible to construct an adequate history of American adults without a knowledge of the history of childhood."[7] Liberation rights claims are a vital and consequential, if little recognized, part of that history.

After 1945 liberationist rights claims by and for children gained new recognition and entered the formal discourse of American rights for the first time. They became both a source and a product of postwar versions of modern childhood. Adult advocates of children and children themselves argued that the lack of participatory and autonomous rights unfairly stigmatized and penalized the young. They demanded greater recognition of children's similarity to adults to counterbalance the emphasis on differences between the two fostered by caretaking conceptions of children's rights. Following the lead of civil rights movements that extended the rights of African Americans, women, and other minorities, children's rights advocates fought to include the young in the era's roster of self-determining persons who could make claims recognized by law. They also, as historian Rebecca de Schweinitz asserts, extended the liberationist past into their present: "the youth protests of the 1960s represented not so much a break with the past as the continuation and escalation of a militant youth organizing tradition."[8]

The liberationist argument for children's rights peaked in the 1960s and 1970s. The most radical advocates demanded the complete end of children's subordinated legal status. John Holt, for example, declared in 1974: "Much is said and written these days about children's 'rights.' Many use the word to mean something that we all agree it would be good for every child to have: 'the right to a good home' or 'the right to a good education.'" But he dismissed such caretaking conceptions of children's rights in favor of liberation: "I mean what we mean when we speak of the rights of adults. I urge that the law grant and guarantee to the young the freedom that it now grants to adults to make certain kinds of choices, do certain kinds of things, and accept certain kinds of responsibilities." And he criticized the modern tendency to separate children and adults; "this segregation is accompanied and reinforced by a false ideology of childishness."[9] Any legal policies based on this "childish" view of children, he maintained, were illegitimate. In 1980 moral philosopher Joel Feinberg argued that children had the "right to an open future," which meant that parental decisions and adult policies on education, religion, medical care, and methods of acculturation had to be designed in a way that preserved children's future choices as much as possible. Assertions like these challenged inherited assumptions that all children were too incompetent, incapable, and immature to exercise adult rights.

The most radical claims of liberationist rights for children never received wide support. Their conception of childhood granted the young far more independence and far less dependence than most adult Americans were willing to accept. Instead most children's rights advocates and most children themselves held a more conventional understanding of childhood as a separate and in many ways subordinate stage of life. Rather than transforming the place of the young in American society, they sought a new balance between liberation and caretaking that tilted toward greater autonomy and self-determination for the young. For instance, a 1977 Carnegie Council on Children report recognized that "The right of children to be viewed as legal persons capable of interests and deserving representation independent of their parents has emerged only recently." Attributing this development to the liberation movements of the era, eroding faith in parents and other figures of authority, and a greater belief in the capacity of children to govern themselves, the Council applauded the fact that "In recent years the legal trends have been decidedly in the direction of granting children greater legal rights and responsibilities both by statute and by court decisions."[10] The Council could have added that the trend was also fueled by the emergence of an increasingly separate youth culture and by the heated rhetoric of democratic citizenship and individual self-determination ignited by World War II and the Cold War.

From the 1950s through the 1970s, liberationist children's rights expanded, culminating in the 1971 passage of the twenty-sixth amendment that lowered the voting age to eighteen. As with the *Tinker v. Des Moines* decision, much of the growth occurred through the courts. In 1967, for instance, the U.S. Supreme Court not only granted juvenile offenders basic adult procedural rights such as the right to counsel, notice of charges, confrontation of witnesses, and the privilege against self-incrimination, but in a crucial contribution to the liberationist language of children's rights the court declared: "Neither the Fourteenth Amendment nor the Bill of Rights is for adults alone." Fifteen years later, legal scholar Frank Zimring summarized the consequences:

> Before 1966, the United States Supreme Court had never decided a case that could properly be filed under the rubric of "juvenile rights"; in the last fifteen years, adolescence has been a major concern of the Court. The United States Reports are filled with cases adjudicating the rights of adolescents in matters as diverse as abortion, school suspension, involuntary civil commitment, corporal punishment, jury trials in juvenile courts, and political demonstration. . . . Federal district courts are flooded with constitutional challenges to regulations of the young that have previously gone unchallenged. Legislative bodies, state and federal, are rethinking public policy toward adolescent work and wages, compulsory education, access to medical care, and the jurisdiction and mission of the juvenile court.[11]

A liberationist meaning of children's rights became evident in the seminal 1954 *Brown v. Board of Education* decision. Not only did the Supreme Court ban segregated schools, it voiced its decision in the rhetoric of children's rights, unlike previous schooling decisions that had only endorsed the rights of parents to control the education of their sons and daughters: "In these days it is doubtful that any child may reasonably be expected to succeed in life if he is denied the opportunity of an education. Such an opportunity, where the state has undertaken to provide it, is a right which must be made available to all children." Critically, African American children were primary actors in the era's fight against racial segregation and not simply the beneficiaries of adult civil rights campaigners. Thus in one of the cases that became part of *Brown*, Prince Edwards County, Virginia, high school student Barbara Johns ignored the objections of adults and led a student strike at the all-black Robert R. Moton High School. She and other students demanded improved resources at their school and sought to make it part of the NAACP lawsuit challenging segregation. Similarly, countless individual students like Elizabeth Eckford, who braved taunts and threats to attend all-white Little Rock High School, became the foot soldiers of integration.[12]

Mary Beth's antiwar protest added a liberationist component to the political rights of children. By ruling in her favor, the Supreme Court classified middle and high school students as persons who had fundamental constitutional rights of free expression and political participation. The resulting *Tinker* Standard balanced student rights with the needs of schools to maintain orderly and safe classrooms by preventing student disruptions. In this new balance of power, students could assert their rights to control some aspect of their education, instead of being mere subordinates. Revealingly, most attempts by students to do so involved disciplinary issues and dress codes, not politics. In 1975, for instance, the Supreme Court expanded students' educational rights in an appeal by three Ohio high school students who had been summarily suspended. The justices required hearings before the imposition of such severe punishments.[13]

No doubt in a surprising development for young and old alike, male hair length became one of the most contentious school rights contests of the era. Over a hundred teen hair cases were appealed to lower federal courts and nine to the Supreme Court. One of those litigants, Arizona high school student Wayne Pendley, contended that growing long hair represented his "choice" and constituted one of his "individual rights." Such arguments convinced some courts, including a federal appeals judge who supported the hair rights claim of a Texas teenager by arguing: "one's choice of hair style is constitutionally protected and . . . the State may invade this interest only upon a showing of compelling reason." However, in the *Tinker* decision Justice Fortas had included a crucial caveat: "The problem posed by the present case does not relate to the regulation of the length of skirts or the type of clothing, to hair style, or deportment." Consequently, courts around the country differed over the issue of whether hair regulations and other student appearance codes constituted a constitutionally justified restriction on students' rights and the Supreme Court failed to render a definitive ruling. However dismissive some adults may have been of these claims, there is no doubt that many adolescents believed that they had this right of self-determination.[14]

Clashes over male student hair length illustrate why the school remained a primary site for rearranging the balance between liberationist and caretaking conceptions of children's rights. According to a 1969 survey by the National Association of Secondary School Principals, 59 percent of high schools and 56 percent of junior high schools had recently experienced some form of unrest. As historian Gael Graham contends,

> Many high school activists were extremely critical of public schools, and they expressed their dissatisfaction through lawsuits, underground newspapers, strikes, and demonstrations. They attacked not only dress and hair codes but also other seemingly pointless regulations and restrictions on free speech, press, and assembly. . . . Rejecting their status as children, they argued that students should have a greater voice in the running of the schools.

Revealingly, as she points out, that same year a *Life* magazine poll of 2,500 high school students, parents, teachers, and school administrators across the country found that although only 20 percent of parents and 35 percent of teachers thought students should have a greater role in running their schools, fully 58 percent of students wanted that power.[15]

Clashes also erupted when adolescents claimed their own medical and reproductive rights. The contests focused on what came to be known as the "mature minor doctrine," an exception to the general rule requiring parental consent for medical treatment of their offspring. The doctrine granted that a competent minor had the right to receive beneficial medical treatment or emergency care without parental approval. Statutes and judicial decisions defined such care to include treatment for sexually transmitted diseases, substance abuse, mental health problems, and birth control and pregnancy.

Abortion became the most controversial application of the doctrine as increasing numbers of teens sought to terminate their pregnancies without conferring with their parents. Their actions raised the question of whether pregnant youth, like adult women, were individuals with a presumed right of reproductive autonomy or children subject to parental caretaking authority. An answer came in 1976 when the Supreme Court rejected a Missouri statute requiring parental consent to a minor's abortion. Justice Harry Blackmun argued that "constitutional rights do not mature and come into being magically only when ones attains the state-defined age of majority. Minors, as well as adults, are protected by the Constitution and possess constitutional rights." Three years later the Court struck down a statute as unconstitutional because parental notification or consultation was required "without affording the pregnant minor an opportunity to receive an independent judicial determination that she is mature enough to consent or that an abortion would be in her best interests." In yet another balance of caretaking and liberation, however, the justices made it clear that adolescents could be subjected to restrictions that would be unacceptable for adults since, as Justice Lewis Powell explained, there were "three reasons justifying the conclusion that the constitutional rights of children cannot be equated with those of adults: the peculiar vulnerability of children; their inability to make critical decisions in an informed, mature manner; and the importance of the parental role in child rearing."[16]

Children's rights conflicts broke out over censorship as well. Since the late nineteenth century, governmental officials and private organizations had advocated censorship to protect youthful innocence, a fundamental component of modern conceptions of childhood. Books, movies, radio shows, comic books, and television became subject to censorship on the assumption that obscene, pornographic, or violent images and words harmed the morals of innocent young readers, viewers, and listeners. Though always resisted by most children, the bans came under sustained attack in the second half of the twentieth century. The courts expressed increasing skepticism of the harm to minors rationale for censorship and struck down obscenity statutes as violations of adult First Amendment rights.[17]

In a telling example of shifting views on censorship to protect children, the American Library Association (ALA) changed its long-standing position and began campaigning for greater First Amendment rights for all readers, including children. Soon the organization found itself engulfed in the struggles over children's media rights as a result of its annual Newbery Medal, which honored the best English language children's book that showed "respect for children's understandings, abilities, and appreciations." Many postwar award-winning books advanced a child liberationist perspective and were banned by local authorities. With some justification, one critic complained, "not only are the child protagonists most often seen as autonomous individuals who are able to deal with life as they wish, but they are often placed in a position of responsibility which not only tests but demands that ability. . . . Remarkably few books . . . end leaving their child-protagonists still as children." Censored winners included most of Judy Blume's books, especially *Are You There God, It's Me Margaret*; Lois Lowry, *The Giver*; and J. D. Salinger, *The Catcher in the Rye*. And such books were indeed both sources and products of the popular culture that helped sustain this era of liberationist rights. The ALA responded to such criticism by launching "Banned Books Week: Celebrating the Freedom to Read" and opposing "all attempts to restrict access to library services, materials, and facilities based on the age of library users."[18]

Children, parents, and organizations like the ACLU joined librarians to fight efforts by school boards to ban books. In 1982 the Supreme Court heard a protest by Long Island, New York, high school students against the removal of nine books, including Richard Wright's *Black Boy*, Kurt Vonnegut, Jr.'s *Slaughterhouse Five*, and Piri Thomas's *Down These Mean Streets*. The school board called the books "anti-American, anti-Christian, anti-Sem[i]tic, and just plain filthy." Justice William Brennan disagreed, arguing that the school library should provide a special zone for free inquiry: "Students must always remain free to inquire, to study and to evaluate, to gain new maturity and understanding. The school library is the principal locus of such freedom." He distinguished the library from the classroom and insisted that schools had less control over bookshelves than over instructional materials and in doing so articulated yet another balance of liberation and caretaking. Justice Potter Stewart did the same in 1968 by upholding age limits on access to obscene materials: "I think that a State may permissibly determine that, at least in some precisely delineated areas, a child—like someone in a captive audience—is not possessed of that full capacity for individual choice which is the presupposition of First Amendment guarantees."[19]

There are countless other examples of the expansion of liberationist children's rights during this era. By the early 1980s it seemed as if that expansion would continue into the future. But that was not to be. The fate of the most comprehensive statement of liberationist rights suggests why. In 1989 the United Nations promulgated the Convention on the Rights of the Child. Like American law and policy, the Convention carefully balanced caretaking and liberationist rights. In an effort to secure United States support, it included many fundamental American children's policies, particularly the best interests of the child doctrine that had long been used by judges to balance claims of parents, children, and the state. However, other provisions in the Convention globalized key liberationist rights of self-determination such as the right of all children to free expression, peaceful assembly, freedom of thought, conscience, and religion, protection from parental abuse, medical care, and social insurance. By doing so, the Convention not only stirred up latent American opposition to international agreements that might infringe on national sovereignty, it espoused far greater autonomy and participatory powers for children and mandated far greater parental and state duties to the young than many in the United States were willing to accept then or since. As a result, the United States joined Somalia in being the only nations that refused to ratify the Convention. Indeed many countries, particularly in Western Europe, not only ratified the Convention but embraced its goals by significantly expanding children's autonomy through the conferral of new rights. In Sweden, to take the most stark contrast to America, the Convention became a touchstone for all discussions of children's rights and children's policies. In the United States, however, the limits of liberationist rights had been reached.[20]

Caretaking

The passage of the UN Convention on the Rights of the Child occurred just as caretaking reemerged to dominate American debates over children's rights. Megan's story became a central and revealing episode in that reemergence. Their child tragically silenced by her killer, Megan's parents voiced a children's rights claim in her name. Megan's law vividly illustrated the shift in emphasis in children's rights away from liberation and toward caretaking that began in the late 1970s.

Caretaking had dominated initial American understandings of children's rights in the late nineteenth century. It accentuated the differences between children and adults by lumping children together instead of dividing them by age, gender, maturity and other distinctive traits. And it rested on key tenets of the modern conception of childhood that presumed the inherent dependence, incapacity, and incompetence of the young and their need for adult care and protection as well as the primacy of family autonomy and parental authority.

In an 1892 magazine article Kate Douglas Wiggin, author of the best-selling novel *Rebecca of Sunnybrook Farm*, made the case for this version of children's rights: "When a child is born, one of his inalienable rights, which we often deny him, is the right to his childhood. . . . There is no substitute for a genuine, free, serene, healthy, bread-and-butter childhood." Those rights, she insisted, included the right to be "well born; to not be made a fashion plate, to get dirty, to real toys . . . a right to a place of his own, to things of his own, to surroundings which have some relation to his size, his desires, and his capabilities." Thirty years later, social reformer Raymond Fuller made the same point more succinctly: "out of the nature of children arise their needs; and out of children's needs, children's rights."[21]

A caretaking understanding of children's rights became the basis for numerous late nineteenth- and early twentieth-century American child welfare policies such as compulsory schooling, child labor regulation, censorship, and juvenile courts. Each policy targeted a critical concern spurred by the modern conception of childhood from the need to protect youthful innocence to the determination to segregate children from the marketplace. As we have seen, many of these new protections were resisted by children, particularly adolescents, who wanted to maintain their access to the adult world. Other protections, however, such as the prevention of physical and sexual abuse, were welcomed by the young. Critically, each policy was also asserted as a right that would buttress adult authority over children. In contrast to the affirmation of children's autonomous educational rights in the 1954 *Brown* decision, for example, a 1925 decision by the Supreme Court striking down an Oregon statute barring students from attending private schools vindicated the caretaking rights of parents: "The child is not the mere creature of the state; those who nurture him and direct his destiny have the right, coupled with the high duty, to recognize and prepare him for additional obligations."[22]

Caretaking dominated conceptions of children's rights until the years after 1945 when, as we have seen, American rights discourse began to emphasize liberation for the first time. But an updated understanding of caretaking resumed its dominance of children's rights in the late 1970s, propelled by a waning faith in the more autonomous conceptions of childhood that had prevailed in the liberationist era as well as new concerns among old and young alike about the vulnerability of children to a mounting number of risks: parental abuse, abduction, teenage pregnancy, sexual abuse, suicide, obscenity, gangs, and drug addiction. Examples abounded most dramatically fin de siècle revelations of mass child abuse by Catholic priests, and a rash of school shootings starting with the death of twelve students and a teacher at Colorado's Columbine High School in 1999 that made even the parish church and the school sites of child endangerment.

A turn to caretaking became a primary response to these mounting concerns. For instance, linking new policies of protection to individual instances of tragedy like Megan's murder continued a tactic that dated from the emergence of modern childhood and children's rights in the late nineteenth century. After the 1981 kidnapping and murder of his son, John Walsh turned Adam into a symbol of child abduction when he founded the National Center for Missing and Exploited Children and later secured passage of the 2006 Adam Walsh Child Protection and Safety Act that established a national registry of sex offenders. The 1993 kidnapping and murder of twelve-year-old Polly Klass led to the creation of a foundation bearing her name and the motto: "Making America Safe for All Children." The 1996 abduction and murder of nine-year-old Amber Hageman led to the swift creation of a national system of Amber Alerts that notified the public when a child had been kidnapped. These and countless other stories of brutalized youngsters not only helped shift children's rights back toward caretaking but demonstrated that children's rights themselves had become an inescapable part of any effort to create new policies for America's boys and girls. As a result in the United States, far more than in nations like Sweden, children's need for protection, not self-determination, began to dominate all rights talk and conceptions of childhood.[23]

Most adult proponents of caretaking were almost uniformly hostile to any recognition of children's autonomy and self-determination even for older adolescents. They sought domination, not simply a new balance between liberation and caretaking, and declared that liberation itself endangered the young. For instance, in 1976 law professor Bruce Hafen warned that "serious risks are involved in an uncritical transfer of egalitarian concepts from the contexts in which they developed to the unique context of family life and children." He argued that "the most harmful of the potential consequences is that the long-range interests of children themselves may be irreparably damaged as the state and parents abandon children to their rights."[24] In a declaration that revealed how necessary yet ambiguous children's rights had become, Hafen even asserted that the right not to be abandoned to their rights constituted the young's most basic right. A few years later, Edward Wynne charged lawyers and courts with harming children by fostering legalistic relationships in the home and school that destroyed the adult authority and sense of community children required. Returning to the children's needs in rights language of early twentieth-century child-savers, he insisted that children required "other rights which are not so subject to judicial enforcement: the right to have others care for us; the right to have some authority over, and responsibility to, others; and finally the right to live, work, and learn in a community instead of an impersonal environment." Wynne linked these caretaking rights to greater public regulation of the young by demanding the restoration of custodial policies that "subjected young persons to certain forms of more intense protection, scrutiny, and constraint."[25] By the early twenty-first century Martin Guggenheim, a long-time legal advocate for children and director of the child law clinic at New York University Law School, had become one of the most prominent proponents of the need to limit the use of children's rights as a check on parental control. He contended that children, especially the very young who were the primary subjects of his 2005 book *What's Wrong with Children's Rights*, suffered from too much law and too many lawyers as a result of the liberationist campaigns of previous decades. American children, he declared, needed better care, not more liberty.[26]

The growing opposition to adult-like conceptions of children's rights not only blunted the further expansion of liberationist rights but succeeded in rolling back some—but far from all—of the powers previously granted children. Tellingly, state legislatures and Congress not the courts became primary sites for change. As an example of the old adage that it is the exception that proves the rule, fear of juvenile "super-predators" helped spur get-tough on crime campaigns of the 1990s that excluded violent juvenile offenders from the caretaking being offered other youths. Where liberationist juvenile justice policies such as the *Gault* decision giving young offenders some adult due process rights had fit within the larger pattern of children's rights changes of that era, the new get-tough on crime policies were completely incompatible with the caretaking ethos that dominated late twentieth-century children's rights discourse. Criminal law reform turned violent juvenile offenders as young as thirteen into adults through state-sanctioned waivers that took them out of the juvenile courts and into adult ones and thus deprived them of the right to claim the status and protections given children. These policies also demonstrated some of the racial dimensions of the new caretaking regime since they affected African American youths more than any other group. These adolescents were assumed to be far less innocent and far more mature than other youths their age and thus beyond the bounds of childhood and its growing caretaker rights.[27]

Drinking laws also illustrate the impact of the new emphasis on caretaking over liberation. In 1971 Michigan had lowered the minimum age for purchasing alcoholic beverages from twenty-one to eighteen as part of a larger revision of children's rights with the new voting age of eighteen. Seven years later, though, Michigan voters reconsidered the issue and hiked the drinking age back up to twenty-one. And in 1980 they turned back a proposal to lower the minimum age to nineteen. That same year, two women whose children had been killed by drunk drivers formed Mothers Against Drunk Driving (MADD), an advocacy organization that made higher drinking ages a primary policy goal. In 1984, despite his opposition to centralized national authority, MADD convinced President Ronald Reagan to lobby Congress to use the coercive power of the federal budget to force states to raise their drinking age to twenty-one or lose millions of dollars in highway funding. Soon after the act passed every state adopted the policy. By the end of the century, MADD revised its goals to make child caretaking a priority: "The mission of Mothers Against Drunk Driving is to stop drunk driving, support the victims of this violent crime and prevent underage drinking." Efforts to reassert the dependent status of children and their right to more caretaking occurred across the spectrum of children's lives, often spurred by nongovernmental organizations such as MADD.[28]

A move away from the student First Amendment rights established by Mary Beth's victory in *Tinker* demonstrates how the resurgence of caretaking began to enlist the judiciary. In 1986 the Supreme Court turned back a freedom of speech claim by Matthew Fraser, who as a senior in a Washington state high school had nominated a fellow student for a school office with a speech filled with sexual innuendos, but not obscenity. Like Mary Beth, Matthew had been suspended and then turned to the ACLU to defend his rights. Chief Justice Warren Burger limited the reach of *Tinker*, arguing that sexually vulgar expressions were not protected speech and instead granting schools the power to deem them disruptive. Two years later the Court trimmed the rights of student journalists by upholding the authority of a Missouri high school principal to delete articles on contraceptives and teenage pregnancy from the student newspaper. Writing for the majority, Justice Byron White ruled that public school student newspapers were subject to a lower level of First Amendment protection than other forms of student literary expression, let alone the adult media. By holding that a public school did not have to tolerate student speech that conflicted with its "legitimate pedagogical goals," he tilted the *Tinker* Standard toward greater administrative control over students. And then in the 2007 "Bong Hits 4 Jesus" case, the Court upheld the suspension of Joseph Frederick for unveiling a fourteen-foot banner on a public sidewalk outside his Juneau, Alaska, high school. He sued, asserting his First Amendment rights under *Tinker*. The justices ruled that Frederick's free speech rights were not violated by his suspension over what the majority called a "sophomoric" poster. "It was reasonable for (the principal) to conclude that the banner promoted illegal drug use—and that failing to act would send a powerful message to the students in her charge," Chief Justice John Roberts wrote for the court's 6-3 majority. In dissent, Justice John Paul Stevens worried, "This case began with a silly nonsensical banner, [and] ends with the court inventing out of whole cloth a special First Amendment rule permitting the censorship of any student speech that mentions drugs, so long as someone could perceive that speech to contain a latent pro-drug message."[29]

Decisions like these and similar legislative and school actions shifted the principal meaning of student rights back toward caretaking. Each case also represented the defeat of a latter day Mary Beth Tinker asserting a liberationist claim; fewer and fewer such rights claims by children triumphed in the era, and indeed fewer and fewer may well have been made, as many if not most students acquiesced to the new caretaker regime. In a comparison of *Tinker* and *Fraser*, Hafen explained that they "reflect the divergence between the 1960s and the 1980s on a multitude of issues. They also echo a very old debate about the relationship between freedom and discipline in both educational processes and theories of personal and political development."[30] Accordingly, schools instituted new levels of surveillance such as security cameras in buses and in classrooms, random locker searches and drug tests, and security guards. "Zero tolerance policies" led to automatic suspensions and police involvement for students accused of plotting violence. The federal Gun Free School Act of 1994 reinforced those policies.[31] Schools also imposed new dress codes with some instituting requirements to wear uniforms. As with the revisions of *Tinker*, courts generally upheld these policies against student challenges as long as they could be deemed to meet pedagogical and school protection goals. As one federal judge put it in 1995: "Plaintiff ha[s] not shown that his wearing of sagging pants was speech protected by the First Amendment."[32]

The resurgence of caretaking also altered the balance in medical rights of the young. Though children, particularly adolescents, retained many of the rights secured during the liberationist years, a rising determination to protect children led to new adult controls on their medical and health decisions. Abortion continued to be the most contested issue. As part of a broader effort to restrict abortion and to increase the control of parents over the sexual decisions of their daughters, state legislatures passed increasingly stringent parental notification laws despite earlier decisions expanding teenagers' abortion rights. By 2008, thirty-five states mandated some form of parental involvement in a minor's abortion decision. Though the laws varied, most ordered pregnant teens to include one or both parents in the decision to terminate a pregnancy. They were premised on the conviction that teenage abortion was a family matter and not an individual right. In 1981 the Supreme Court ruled that parental notification laws were constitutional because the parent could not veto an adolescent's final decision to seek an abortion.[33] Two years later the Court accepted the constitutionality of parental consent laws as long as they allowed a judicial bypass when parents proved too recalcitrant.[34] Opponents of abortion and advocates of greater parental rights demanded still greater parental control over the abortion rights of teenagers. The results were mixed. Californians, for instance, defeated repeated initiatives that would have added parental notification to the state's constitution. And the Senate refused to consider House bills that would have restricted the ability of pregnant teens to cross state lines seeking abortions. Even so, parental notification laws elicited broad adult support; a 2005 Quinnipiac University poll found that 75 percent supported and only 18 percent opposed the restriction on minors' reproductive rights. The growing acceptance of parental notification laws was part of a larger effort to reassert adult control over children's sexuality, by curtailing juvenile autonomy through initiatives such as abstinence-only sex education.[35] A joke that circulated among frustrated sex educators in the early 1990s captured the new tenor of the debate: "Q: What is a conservative? A: A liberal with a teenage daughter."[36]

The resurgence of caretaking also led to renewed demands for censorship to protect children from immorality in the media. Adult fears about the harmful impact of popular culture on minors, particularly the seemingly rampant violence and sexuality in movies, television shows, music lyrics, and video games, revived deep-seated beliefs in innocence as a fundamental component and thus right of childhood. Law professor Kevin Saunders expressed those concerns in his 2003 book *Saving Our Children from the First Amendment*. He depicted a frightening world of adult media being forced on children, threatening their health and safety, and skillfully bypassing parental monitors. He argued that caretaking must be embraced by reinstituting censorship through parental and school controls that protected the innocence of the young through the creation of safe and secure media controlled places for children. Saunders dismissed children's media rights as an oxymoron since they assumed levels of rationality, competence, and maturity he thought were clearly lacking in most if not all children and teenagers:

Any separate claim by children that they should have access to materials that their parents believe to be inappropriate are issues to be
resolved by the parent and child. The recognized right of parents to
make child-rearing decisions should not give way to childhood attrac-
tions to pornography, violence, or hate-filled music. . . . While parents
may choose to make such materials available to their own children,
the children should not have the right to obtain the material contrary
to their parents' wishes, and distributors should have no right to sell
directly to other people's children.[37]

Sentiments like Saunders's encouraged both private and state censorship. The
movie industry imposed film ratings that excluded certain younger children
from theaters; company-imposed television and video game rating policies
aimed for the same result; congressionally mandated V-chip mandates em-
powered parents to regulate their children's television viewing choices, and
filtering software enabled them to impose similar restrictions on comput-
ers. Cities like St. Louis and Indianapolis instituted video game regulations.
The Federal Communications Commission (FCC) used its licensing power
to compel broadcasters to censor more material, particularly songs with drug
lyrics. Fears about children viewing obscene materials on the Internet led
to the Communications Decency Act of 1996 and Children's Online Protection Act of 1998. Though both acts were declared unconstitutional because
they contained vague and overreaching terms that threatened adult rights,
attempts to limit juvenile computer access continued even as children once
again resisted media censorship. Congress finally succeeded in 2000 when
the Children's Internet Protection Act passed judicial muster.[38]

These and countless other policies reinstituted the dominance of caretaking in American understandings of childhood and children's rights. Trans-
lating children's needs into rights without jettisoning children's dependent
status once again became the primary, though not the exclusive, way of defining children's rights. What remained unclear was whether liberation would
remain, as in the past, a subordinate understanding of children's rights or
whether in the future the emphasis in children's rights would again shift its
direction to create another period in which the young gained significantly
greater autonomy and self-determination as well as an increased ability to
participate in the decisions that affected their lives. To put it another way,
the changes in children's rights since 1945 raised the question of whether the
years of liberation represented a precedent for future periods of intergenera-

tional transformation or an aberrant era of youthful empowerment unlikely
to be repeated.

Conclusion

As the twenty-first century begins, the American debate about children's
rights continues to vacillate between liberation and caretaking. Both versions
of children's rights are creations of the past that are deeply embedded in our
understandings of children, childhood, and families; they are indispensable
and unavoidable components of any discussion of just and effective policies
for America's children. During the second half of the twentieth century each
became even more important in expressing the various experiences of children and adults and the equally diverse social constructions of childhood
made by young and old. However, the incessant and often shrill clashes over
children's rights during these years also revealed both the irresistible lure of
instituting a more uniform conception of rights rooted in either caretaking or
liberation, and the impossibility of doing so.

The repeated failure to establish a singular understanding of children's
rights tells us that we must accept calibrated conceptions of children's rights
that mix caretaking and liberationist in ways that balance children's need
for protection while granting them greater autonomy with increased competence, capacity, and maturity. Doing so would inevitably lead to disputes
over the proper moment at which children could claim a particular right and
with it more power to participate in the decisions that affect their lives. But
the past tells us that all efforts to balance liberation and caretaking will be
contested. Those contests represent crucial ways for children and adults to
determine the proper demarcations between the powers of the young and
their elders and thus the meaning of childhood.

The rights fights that erupted in the post-World War II United States also
demonstrate the ordering power of age to our understanding of American
public and private life. The interplay of governmental and nongovernmental
agencies, the power of sensational media stories and the social movements
they spark, and the impact of gender and racial beliefs on policymakers all
influence the history of children's rights and make it a particularly compelling
means of examining the construction of the polity, civil society, and family
life in the United States. And it compels us to recall and find meaning in stories like those of Mary Beth Tinker and Megan Kanka.

3

The Changing Face of Children's Culture

Steven Mintz

It's a common schoolyard game among six- to nine-year-olds. One child announces that another has "cooties," those imaginary contaminants with which a child—usually one of the opposite sex or one marginalized or stigmatized—is supposedly infected. Cooties can be transferred through touch (followed by the shout "You've got cooties") or guarded against (by pushing one's arms out), but the game is anything but harmless entertainment. "Cooties" is a pollution ritual, in which one child taunts friends or marks or labels outcasts. Through this game, certain children—usually unathletic or unattractive and often female—are treated as symbolically contaminating.[1]

Cooties is a game of surprisingly recent vintage. The word "cooties" only entered the English language during World War I, and while references to such a game appear intermittently, it apparently only became an integral part of children's culture after World War II. More than a game, cooties served as a way to reinforce gender boundaries, label and stigmatize difference, and affirm social hierarchies. It also reveals that the rituals of children's culture are not always innocent or playful. They can also be hurtful.[2]

If historians are serious about treating children as agents, with their own distinct voices, we need to recognize that, like other social groups, children create their own cultures, with distinctive slang, rituals, styles, tastes, and values. The study of kid cultures shifts our attention toward the cultural worlds that the young inhabit—including their collective activities, entertainments, meanings, and modes of expression—and the ways they perceive and interpret the adult world. No one would consider studying adolescence without paying attention to teen cultures; yet surprisingly few scholarly works have sought to reconstruct the history of children's cultures: the expressive and meaning-making activities that are an integral part of children's everyday lives. These include children's imaginative world, such as their folklore and humor; social relationships, including friendships and peer interactions; play, sports, and computer and video games; and consumption of commercial popular culture, such as children's books, television shows, and movies.[3]

The simplest perspective on children's culture grows out of structural functionalism. This approach looks at the roles and functions that children's culture serves. Their cultures are expressive, allowing kids to partake in youthful exuberance and vitality. These cultures are also developmental, allowing kids to grow aware of their bodies, play with language and social norms, and test their physical dexterity. In addition, the cultures are therapeutic, providing outlets for children's aggressive impulses, and compensatory, offsetting deficits and stresses in other realms of their lives. They can also be preparatory, grooming children for adult roles, but also resistant, caricaturing, challenging, and subverting adult values.

But a strictly functionalist perspective is inadequate in making sense of children's cultures. For one thing, a functionalist viewpoint ignores the most distinctive characteristic of children's culture: the blurred boundary between fantasy and reality. Without romanticizing children's culture, it is important to recognize that it diverges radically from the highly rationalistic outlook of adults, and incorporates magic, wonder, imagination, the fantastic, and the supernatural. A functionalist perspective also ignores the role of contestation. Children's cultures do not simply adapt to changing social and cultural circumstances. These cultures involve conflicts with adults who seek to regulate and direct kids' activities. As in every power relationship, we see a process of conflict, negotiation, and contestation.[4]

There is, of course, no single children's culture. Kid cultures vary widely along lines of class, ethnicity, gender, and other variables. Neither is children's culture autonomous. Kid cultures are heavily influenced by the instruments of commercial culture, although it is important to stress that children are not the passive recipients of external influences and adapt and reinterpret the influences that they receive.[5] Nor is children's culture static. Although there are certain continuities—especially in games, rhymes, and fairy tales—there are also profound transformations over time, depending on the demands children face and the world they are preparing themselves for.

This essay contrasts two distinct "regimes" of middle-class children's culture:

Cold War boyhood and girlhood and the very different children's culture that succeeded it. I will argue that the glaring contrast between these cultural worlds has had profound cultural consequences. Baby boomers and their parents have viewed the transformations that have taken place in children's culture since 1970 from a declensionist perspective: as evidence of cultural decline. Many of those who grew up in the early postwar era are convinced that they had lived through a golden age of childhood. Many believe that society was more child-centered then and afforded children many more opportunities for free, unstructured, outdoor play. Many worry that traditional childhood rituals and pastimes have faded and that childhood innocence has been exploited and corrupted by the instruments of consumer culture.[6]

Many adults point to the introduction of school classes in friendship as a sign that kids no longer know how to make or keep friends. Others lament the loss of older childhood rituals and pastimes, such as playing marbles, chasing fireflies, or indulging in "kick the can," activities that supposedly nourished children's imagination and taught them valuable social skills. Many worry that today's society, in its efforts to reduce risks of all kinds, has deprived middle-class children of opportunities for maturation and the acquisition of significant life experiences. Indeed a number of recent best-sellers, including *The Dangerous Book for Boys* and *The Daring Book for Girls*, and a television series, *Kid Nation*, have sought to exploit adults' desire to re-create a seemingly lost world of childhood as a time of playful adventure, risk, and discovery.[7]

It is easy to understand the appeal of the declension model. Unlike many golden ages that reside in a hazy, distant, and mythical past, many aging baby boomers can remember a childhood that seems much more innocent, slower paced, and more child-friendly than today's. The post–World War II era unleashed a torrent of iconic playthings, including the Slinky in 1945, Tonka Trucks in 1947, the Frisbee in 1948, Candy Land in 1949, Silly Putty in 1950, Mr. Potato Head in 1952, Play-Doh in 1956, the Hula Hoop in 1957, Barbie in 1959, and the Etch-a-Sketch in 1960. It also witnessed the appearance of the first children's television shows, beginning with *Howdy Doody*, which premiered in 1947, followed by *Captain Kangaroo* and *Disneyland*, which debuted in 1955.

Compared to today, the early postwar era seems much more child-centered and innocent, with clown shows, such as *Bozo the Clown*, created in 1946, and a profusion of child-oriented films, such as Walt Disney's *Song of the South* (1946), *Cinderella* and *Treasure Island* (1950), *Alice in Wonderland*

(1951), *Peter Pan* (1953), *Lady and the Tramp* and *Davy Crockett, King of the Wild Frontier* (1955), and *Johnny Tremain* and *Old Yeller* (1957). Reinforcing this image of a golden age of childhood was an outpouring of child-centered books, including Dr. Seuss's *Horton Hears a Who* (1954), *If I Ran the Circus* (1956), *Cat in the Hat* and *How the Grinch Stole Christmas* (1957), *The Cat in the Hat Comes Back* (1958), and *Happy Birthday to You* (1959), and children's foods, including Sugar Crisp (1949), Sugar Pops (1951), Frosted Flakes (1952, with advertisements featuring Tony the Tiger), Trix (1954), and Alpha Bits (1958).

But most dear to the heart of those who grew up in the 1950s are memories of a childhood that, in retrospect, seems far freer, less pressured, and less structured and hurried than childhood today. If childhood during the early postwar era was often filled with prolonged periods of boredom, many girls and boys, regardless of class and ethnicity, personally recall unsupervised play in vacant lots, fields, and streets, bicycling without helmets, and sandlot sports, unorganized by adults. This, many believe, was a childhood that encouraged imagination and creativity, a stark contrast to the seemingly overly pressured, overly structured, if also overly indulged middle-class childhood of today.

A Cold War childhood remains the yardstick against which Americans assess contemporary childhood. And according to that measure, contemporary childhood does not stack up well. Yet for all the appeal of the declension model, I will argue that it is fundamentally wrong. For one thing, nostalgia colors many of those fond memories. It is easy to forget the childhood-centered panics of the early Cold War era over comic books, strontium-90 in milk, and especially polio.[8] And affectionate memories also blind us to the race, class, and gender inequities of the era, the mistreatment of children with disabilities, the fistfights that were considered a normal part of boyhood, and the way boys teased and tormented girls and sometimes openly abused animals. The model of decline also misses the fact that changes in children's lives occurred incrementally rather than abruptly or disjunctively. Indeed, the roots of the commercialization and acceleration of childhood that many adults decry were rooted in the early postwar era. In addition, the underlying causes of change lie not in decaying values, but in structural shifts in demography, economics, and technology. There is no evidence that children's resourcefulness or imagination has diminished.

Still, specific historical moments give rise to distinctive children's cultures, and this was certainly the case in the early Cold War era. *Born on the Fourth of July*, the second film in Oliver Stone's Vietnam War trilogy, opens with a particularly evocative glimpse of middle-class boys' Cold War culture. A group of preteen boys play soldier in the woods near Massapequa, New York, one of the nation's booming suburbs. The film, which is based on the memoir of Vietnam vet Ron Kovic, who grew up in a lower-middle-class Roman Catholic family where his father was a manager of an A&P grocery store and his mother a housewife, lays bare the attitudes and experiences that led one young man to enlist in the military in a bid to fulfill his John Wayne-fueled fantasies of martial glory.[9]

The film's opening scenes bring to mind many of the defining characteristics of a Cold War boyhood: the ready availability of large numbers of kids to participate in play; the homosocial nature of most childhood play; the sizeable amount of undeveloped land where kids could roam free of adult supervision; the central place of team competitions in boys' sports and games; and the web of values and beliefs about patriotism that were hammered home through parades, war movies, and Westerns. And, we might add, the prevalence of gun play in Cold War boys' culture.

Other memoirs, like Homer Hickam's *Rocket Boys*, remind us of the importance of science, technology, and science fiction in boys' culture, evident in the significance attached to chemistry sets, model plane and automobile kits, homemade crystal radio sets, and rocket ships. It was also, as Hickam suggests, a culture of "packs"—of groups of boys that formed largely on the basis of geographical proximity, far larger than those formed by their sisters.[10]

Susan Allen Toth's *Blooming* and Wini Breines's *Young, White, and Miserable*, in turn, offer insightful glimpses into postwar girlhood. In her account of her Ames, Iowa, girlhood, Toth's focus is indoors rather than outdoors. She describes the sibling rivalry between herself and an older sister, slumber parties, finding refuge in a local library, and trips to a family cabin. Breines is interested in how a younger generation of girls raised to value domesticity and motherhood came, subsequently, to embrace feminism. She describes how she and many other girls chafed at the constraints and inequities that marked middle-class girlhood. The misery she describes in her book's title refers not only to girls' exclusion from sports and to inequities in assignment of household chores, but also the discontent with their lives that their mothers communicated to them. Breines's "sociological memoir" also looks at the contradictions that marked girls' socialization. For example, just as there was a latent conflict between the importance attached to marriage and the notion that girls should be able to support themselves, there was also a tension between an emphasis on virginity and a stress on appearance and sexual attractiveness. Barbie, the best-selling fashion doll introduced in 1959, highlights the contradictions in postwar girlhood. In one sense, Barbie places a premium on physical appearance, slimness, and attractiveness. But unlike earlier dolls, she also pursues a career outside the home, throwing into question the era's emphasis on domesticity and the belief that female happiness could only be achieved through marriage and maternity.[11]

Cold War middle-class kid culture was a largely sex-segregated culture, with friendships overwhelmingly homosocial. A culture of fun, children's cultural world delighted in subversive forms of humor. Popular reading materials—especially comic books and satiric, sarcastic humor magazines like *Mad*—underscored the gap between the culture of childhood and the culture of adulthood. It was also a culture filled with a rapidly increasing number of consumer items marketed directly to kids. In retrospect, it seems clear that Cold War children's culture sought to prepare the young for a particular conception of the future: a future in which boys would be prepared to defend the United States from threats to freedom, while girls would be readied for domestic responsibilities. Thus the emphasis in boy culture on mock gun-play and battles between cowboys and Indians, and in girl culture on doll play. But the most striking characteristic of Cold War kid culture, I would submit, was the self-conscious cultivation of childhood innocence. Pastimes like miniature golf, movies like *Bambi*, and especially television shows like *Lassie* and *Bozo the Clown* produced an innocent veneer, celebrating ingenuousness, cuteness, and childhood simplicity.[12]

Naming patterns are always fraught with cultural significance, and Cold War names and nicknames were at once highly value-laden and profoundly revealing. Compared to today, children's names, especially among white children, tended to be generic, drawn from a relatively small universe of common names. Informal, nonethnic names were widespread—highly appropriate for a culture of conformity. One-syllable names were especially common, like Steve, Sue, John, and Beth, as were diminutives: Tommy, Joey, Sally, and Judy. With few exceptions, names were rigidly sex-segregated, more dimorphic than those in the preceding generation, when names like Shirley were used by both sexes. This is a far cry from the formal, ethnic, gender neutral, idiosyncratic, and inventive names that have grown increasingly common.[13]

The middle-class children's cultures that arose beginning in the 1970s and 1980s differed profoundly from their predecessors. Several historical processes brought Cold War kid culture to an end. One was demographic. Beginning in the mid-1960s, birth rates plummeted, with far fewer families having three or more children. Especially striking was a dramatic increase in only children. The proportion of American women with just one child doubled in a generation, from 10 percent to 23 percent. Today, in many of the nation's larger cities, upward of 30 percent of children have no siblings, and very few contemporary kids have more than two brothers or sisters.[14] Although the older notion that only children are prone to various psychological disabilities (such as narcissism) has been thoroughly discredited, there can be no doubt that the dynamics in a household with one or two kids is very different from that in a larger family. For one thing, parents in smaller households devote more time and resources to their children. Parent-child relations tend to be more intense, and the kids receive more undivided attention. Only children also tend to spend more time alone.[15]

As family size shrank, so too did the number of children living in close proximity to one another. The rise of the "play date" is one consequence of the decrease in the number of neighbor children, as is the increase in structured, adult-supervised sports activities. At the same time, as the age of marriage and of childbearing rose sharply, and more mothers than ever before entered the paid workforce, there were fewer mothers present to informally supervise children's outdoor activities. As geographic mobility increased, fewer parents befriended neighbors, and they felt less comfortable letting their kids play unsupervised outside. Meanwhile, development and rising standards of legal liability meant that the empty lots where children previously played disappeared. A new kind of childhood, one that we might term "postmodern," arose.

Meanwhile, parents, recognizing the increasing value of education in a postindustrial society, wanted fewer but "higher quality" kids. Between 1970 and 2000 the real wages of high school dropouts decreased by roughly 20 percent while the real wages of college grads increased about 20 percent. As a result, much more was at stake in elementary and secondary education than in the past, and many middle-class parents responded by adopting a highly intensive form of child rearing that involved early cultivation of children's cognitive skills.[16]

Yet another force for change was technological. The electronic and information revolutions gave middle-class children ready access to information previously difficult to obtain and produced new kinds of toys and screen-based activities. In the late 1970s, new electronic games and communication technologies began to proliferate. Today, over a quarter of two-year-olds have a television set in their bedroom and half of all kids between seven and sixteen have a cell phone. We've moved a long way from a world where a child had to climb on a bookcase to sneak a peek at the erotic novel *Fanny Hill* or a father's collection of *Playboy* magazines. Now, pornography—and many other kinds of information—is found with a click of a mouse. At the same time, access to cable television channels, not subject to the same censorship rules that govern broadcast television, expose children to adult realities from an early age. Information about sexuality and exposure to violence is much more accessible to middle-class children than in the preceding generation.[17]

Attitudinal and ideological shifts accompanied these demographic, economic, and technological developments. These included the "discovery of risk." A new generation of parents, significantly older and better educated than their own mothers and fathers, worried intensely about their children's physical and psychological well-being and academic performance. Many felt responsible for ensuring that their children were not bored or unhappy. Anxiety became a hallmark of middle-class parenting. From birth, parenthood was colored by apprehension, from fears of Sudden Infant Death Syndrome and physical and sexual abuse, to more mundane problems such as sleep disorders and hyperactivity. Contributing to parental anxiety are three decades of panics over children's well-being. Since the early 1970s, there have been recurrent alarms over stranger abductions, poisoned Halloween candies, childhood obesity, and pedophiles luring children over the Internet. The mounting fear for children's safety led an increasing number of parents to embrace paid care and organized activities to structure and supervise their children.[18]

Especially important was the impact of feminism, which greatly increased mixed-sex play, gave girls new opportunities to participate in competitive sports, and threw rigid assumptions about gender roles into question. Sometimes, a profound social transition is evident in the disappearance of a previously widely used term. One example involves the fading of the word "tomboy," which, since it first appeared at the end of the sixteenth century, meant a girl who behaved like a spirited and boisterous boy. In recent years, that word has died away because the behavior has become normative among girls.[19]

The rebirth of feminism awoke many parents to gender inequities in childhood—such as an unequal distribution of domestic chores and the discouragement of girls from playing competitive sports—to which previous generations had been largely blind. It also encouraged a surge in the number of gender-neutral names. Some observers have concluded that the impact of feminism on children's culture was minimal, claiming that girls' culture still focuses on dolls, relationships, and grooming, while boys' culture continues to stress rough-and-tumble play, construction, superheroes, and physical competition. Yet this emphasis on continuity seems to be greatly overstated.

Although there continue to be some marked differences in boys' and girls' play and toy preferences, pronounced changes have occurred nonetheless, most notably in girls' increasing involvement in competitive sports. Cross-gender play has also multiplied, and the rigidly gender-segregated world of children's culture of the early postwar era has given way to something quite different. Interestingly, today's girls and boys are far more likely to play together in informal situations, outside of adult supervision, than in adult-structured situations, for example, in school classrooms or in team sports, suggesting that adults cling to outdated stereotypes that children have outgrown. Meanwhile, creative and imaginative forms of play are less gender-stereotyped than scripted play.[20] A similar pattern can be found in children's literature. Publishers, librarians, and educators tend to target distinct literary genres at girls and boys, with girls more likely to be recipients of books focusing on relationships and boys more likely to receive adventure books. When these children read for pleasure, however, they often read across those gender boundaries.[21]

As a result of these and other social and cultural transformations, children's culture changed dramatically. The geography of childhood grew more circumscribed.[22] There was a sharp decline in walking, bike riding, and time spent out of doors. With fewer friends nearby for children to play with, solitary play grew more common. So, too, did technologically mediated and adult-supervised and organized play.[23] More and more, children's leisure activities took place in the bedroom. No longer was a bedroom simply a repository for toys and other childhood artifacts, or a place where children could play with one another. It became a home entertainment and communication center.[24]

Two key touchstones for public concern over children's culture involve consumerism and video games. In each case, adults have found it increasingly difficult to serve as gatekeepers capable of monitoring and regulating what even young children consume. The commercialization of childhood has spawned intense anxiety. In recent years, a torrent of popular books—with titles like *Kidnapped: How Irresponsible Marketers Are Stealing the Minds of Your Children* and *Consuming Kids: The Hostile Takeover of Childhood*—have blamed unscrupulous marketers for a host of childhood ills, including unhealthy eating habits, wanton materialism, and the erosion of creative play. A barrage of aggressive and deceitful ads, we are told, do not simply promote expensive running shoes and logos on lunch boxes and T-shirts, they colonize children's imagination, distort their body image, and encourage precocious sexuality.[25]

During the first decade of the twenty-first century, according to one estimate, companies spent about $15 billion annually on advertising targeted at children under twelve, up from $7 billion a year a decade earlier. The average American child reportedly sees about 40,000 advertisements a year. Meanwhile, children wield more consumer power than ever before, receiving allowances that average more than $30 a week. According to a 1997 time use survey, kids spend two-and-a-half hours a week shopping, five times as much as they spend playing outdoors.[26]

There can be no doubt that the intensity and aggressiveness of advertising toward children has escalated sharply in recent years. Guided by the latest research in developmental psychology, marketers have devised sophisticated and irresponsible techniques to target child consumers. Key trends in marketing to children include age compression, targeting messages designed for older children toward ever younger children, and "trans-toying," turning everyday objects (such as shampoo or toothbrushes) into toys.[27]

It is mildly reassuring to note that the commercialization of childhood is not a new phenomenon. In fact, modern childhood and commercialization grew up hand-in-hand. Around the turn of the twentieth century, there was a proliferation of children's periodicals that contained advertisements—for bicycles, breakfast cereals, and other products—featuring child consumers. The Great Depression accelerated this process, as hard-pressed manufacturers promoted fantasy-oriented and licensed character toys drawn from the comic books, movies, and radio. The growth of television following World War II ratcheted up mass marketing of consumer goods to children. With the introduction of the first programming targeted directly at children, advertisers were able to hawk products directly to them year round.[28]

What, then, has changed in recent years? For one thing, children's spending increased dramatically. According to one study, kids aged four to twelve spent 400 percent more in 2002 than in 1989. At the same time, the deregulation of children's advertising during the 1980s, the proliferation of junk foods and advertising in schools, and marketing via the Internet have allowed marketers to penetrate spaces that were previously off-limits. Trusted organizations, including the National Boys and Girls Clubs, the National Parent-Teacher Association, UNICEF, and PBS partnered with commercial companies in aggressive marketing campaigns. Especially disturbing has been the commercialization of public schools. Today, roughly 12,000 schools receive Channel One, which provides television equipment in exchange for broadcasting 12 minutes of programming per day, including two minutes of commercials. In addition to posting ads in gyms and on buses and selling "pouring rights" to soft drink companies, schools accept sponsored educational materials, including a Revlon lesson "about good and bad hair days."[29]

The commercialization of childhood can be restrained. It appears that the most affluent, best-educated parents have been quite successful in reducing their children's level of consumer involvement. Their kids watch much less television and are much more engaged in noncommercial activities. Less affluent parents apparently have fewer opportunities to find alternatives to excessive television viewing and videogame playing. Evidence suggests that grassroots activism is also effective in combating the commercialization of childhood. Thanks to pressure from parents and activists, Kraft Foods eliminated in-school advertising in 2003; meanwhile, Channel One suffered a sharp decline in advertising revenue, which fell more than 12 percent in 2004.

Computer games, which are played regularly by some 80 percent of boys, have evoked particular alarm, and many recent criticisms echo those directed early at television and the movies: that video games desensitize children to violence, undercut their ability to distinguish between fantasy and reality, and diminish the development of imagination. Video games have been blamed for fostering hyperactivity among the young and diminishing social skills by isolating kids from one another. Adults fear that video games give even young children ready access to imagery that is more sexually explicit, misogynist, and brutally violent than that which was available to preadolescents in the past. Thus, for example, in one of the most popular video games, *Grand Theft Auto*, players can rape prostitutes and beat them to death with baseball bats.[30]

Video games' negative impact is easily exaggerated and their appeal too often ignored. They are not nearly as isolating as many adults fear. Not only do video-game players often compete against one another, but their game-playing experiences provide the basis for much of their conversation with friends. Other electronic media also help kids fulfill their needs for affiliation. At a time when individual households and neighborhoods have fewer children, cell phones, instant messaging, e-mail, and websites like YouTube provide ways for youth to form and maintain meaningful and supportive relationships and express themselves creatively. Meanwhile, video games enhance children's cognitive development, manual dexterity, and motor skills and foster visual acuity. These games are also cathartic, allowing kids to re-lease tensions and express feelings and impulses that are normally repressed. Video games give girls and boys a chance to master and manipulate reality, and create and control a fantasy world in which they can exercise power. Fur-thermore, the video game aesthetic is only one example of the highly stylized, hyperbolic forms of expression that pervade contemporary entertainment, allowing the young to embrace a distinctive cultural style. Still, it is not sur-prising that new media forms have aroused intense apprehension. Adults find it increasingly difficult to serve as gatekeepers capable of monitoring and regulating what even young children see.[31]

Kids are not passive receptacles of media, but active agents who play with and reinterpret what they see. Since the early twentieth century, children have constructed their identities and culture out of symbols, images, and stories from the raw materials provided by popular culture. While many adults as-sume that children's consumption of media is purely passive, mind-numbing entertainment, in fact many interactions with media are playful—spontaneous, unstructured, and exploratory. Much as Cold War children's culture sought to prepare the young for a particular conception of the future, so too does contemporary children's culture: a twenty-first-century world dominated by new technologies.

The media scholar Henry Jenkins has persuasively argued that video games serve a compensatory role in a society in which children's freedom to roam has been constricted by nervous parents, allowing "home-bound children . . . to extend their reach, to explore, manipulate, and interact with a more diverse range of imaginary places than constitute the often drab, pre-dictable, and overly-familiar spaces of their everyday lives." He maintains, convincingly in my judgment, that video games give expression to new kinds of narratives that are becoming increasingly common in various cultural genres, narratives that "lack the focus on characterization, causality, and lin-ear plot development which defines classical storytelling and instead focus on movements through and the occupation of narrative space." Jenkins has also made the valuable point that children's increasing engagement with electronic media has heightened adults' awareness of aspects of children's play and fan-tasy lives—especially the violent, the sadistic, and the scatological—which have long existed but were previously hidden from view. Since no V-chip or video game rating system can automatically preserve children's innocence, it makes sense to give the young the visual, technological, and media literacy skills that they need to use new media critically and safely.[32]

Historical change inevitably involves trade-offs, minuses as well as pluses, losses as well as gains. To be sure, the physical spaces of childhood have grown more circumscribed. Children spend much less time engaged in unstructured play and outdoor play, and geographical proximity no longer determines the way that playgroups form. Improvised playthings have been overwhelmed by commercial playthings and games with prepackaged scripts. But we need to appreciate the underlying structural shifts that contributed to these developments and must not give in to the nostalgia trap that assumes childhood is going to pot.

The fear that adults have taken the play out of childhood is greatly exaggerated. Children's play, despite changes in form, remains what it has always been: a way for kids to hone their physical skills, nourish their imagination, rehearse adult roles, conquer their fears, and achieve a sense of mastery. It still provides a space where children can learn to interact with others and formulate and follow rules. What has changed are the social and cultural contexts in which children play—as well as the future for which children are preparing themselves.

Although this essay criticizes the declensionist thinking that assumes children's culture is going to hell in a hand basket, those who criticize contemporary childhood do raise serious issues that American society has failed to grapple with adequately. Those who lament the passing of the Cold War children's culture are quite right to complain about the decline in free unstructured play and outdoor play, the increase in "screen time," and the colonization of children's imagination by a hypercommercial culture. A comparative perspective—contrasting Sweden and the United States—suggests that American society could do much more to provide an environment supportive of children's play.

Through public policy initiatives, Sweden has addressed issues that the United States has been reluctant to deal with: the commercialization of childhood, the uneven quality of childcare, and the decline in outdoor play. Sweden, for example, forbids advertising directed at children. It publicly funds and regulates small-family day nurseries in private homes. To ensure that playgrounds are widely accessible, it requires apartment complexes to provide outdoor play environments. And Sweden mandates that children spend part of every school day outdoors. Parents cannot and should not dictate children's culture. But as the Swedish example indicates, a society does have the ability to create an environment in which children's culture can flourish.

4

Ten Is the New Fourteen:
Age Compression and "Real" Childhood

Stephen Lassonde

In 1950 "Buck" Sledge, a locally prominent lawyer in Greensboro, Alabama, took his five-year-old son, William, to a patch of timberland beyond the town's perimeter to fire his automatic pistol. Planting his feet firmly behind his son's, Buck wrapped his long fingers around William's small hands so that when they pulled the trigger, the gun's kickback wouldn't knock the young boy to the ground. After the gun's first deafening round exploded, Buck calmly urged his son to try again. They fired the pistol over and over until William could hold and shoot the weapon safely without his father's help.

Even before he entered first grade, William learned how to handle guns and had crossed over into a world of boys apprenticing for manhood. "Guns," Sledge recalls, "were as much a part of boyhood in rural Alabama as playing football or working outdoors. . . . When we 'played war' we used pump guns and shot at each other with bee-bees. . . . Every boy fished, hunted, and practiced his shooting." Killing a deer, he reflected, was a rite of passage that ushered every boy to the threshold of manhood. "If you hadn't killed a buck by the time you reached adolescence, everybody thought there was something wrong with you."[1] Although he himself never hunted deer, like all the boys in his town Sledge became intimate with guns. By the time he was in high school he owned three pistols, two rifles, and a pair of shotguns.

Today, in most parts of the United States, the very idea of a five-year-old firing a handgun is disturbing. But Sledge and his boyhood friends all engaged in a number of activities at ages that confound contemporary attitudes about what children should or shouldn't be allowed to do. When Sledge was twelve, he says, he announced to his father that it was time for him to learn how to drive—and he did. By fifteen he was operating a harvesting combine on a farm. At sixteen he learned to fly and began practicing acrobatic tricks in his father's airplane. Sledge grew up in a place and time when the remnants of a looser, less articulated conception of growing up still guided parents' considerations about how to foster autonomy in their children. While the goal of encouraging children's independence has remained the focus of middle-class parenting in the United States, the wisdom of relying on improvised pathways to adulthood faded quickly among parents rearing children born after World War II.

During the second half of the twentieth century Americans increasingly looked to age markers as guides for bestowing specific privileges and obligations on children as they grew into adulthood. At six years of age a child began attending school, at sixteen he or she could drive a car. At eighteen a young person could vote and join the military, and at twenty-one—an "adult," under federal law—he or she could purchase alcohol and cigarettes.[2] These markers, while still evolving, began to be implemented as childhood was institutionalized over the latter half of the nineteenth century, when cultural, legal, institutional, and medical sanctions were created to promote a meaningful threshold between children and adults in American society.[3] Since then, the signposts of children's progression from infancy to maturity have multiplied. Childhood has been subdivided into numerous stages, chiefly due to the rise of the developmental paradigm during the twentieth century—a way of comprehending and forecasting the ordinary course of children's physiological, cognitive, moral, and psychological growth.[4]

The triumph of the developmental paradigm by 1950 greatly intensified the desire to understand and predict children's advance from one stage of growth to the next, and reflects the deepening conviction that children's psychological health was embedded in specific, chronological, sequenced maturation. Moreover, the two decades after World War II are popularly remembered as the golden age of family life and childhood in the United States. Indeed, it was during this era that the ideal of the "child-centered family" was enshrined by child-rearing experts, American social scientists, and the mass media. Though brief, the period stands out as the last in which there was broad agreement about the integrity and significance of the threshold between childhood and adulthood. By the end of the century historians had modified the image of postwar family life, distinguishing the gild of memory's haze from the reality of growing up during the baby boom. In Stephanie Coontz's pithy phrase, family life during the 1950s and early 1960s was "the way we never were." Even more damningly, social science of the period has been critiqued and discarded as "functionalist" for trumpeting the white, middle-class nuclear family as the most highly "adaptive" form of family organization in "modernized" societies.[5]

If, as Paula Fass points out, the child-centered family was predicated on the belief that one's children were more important than oneself, it also presumed the recognition of distinct roles for parents and children. Yet as middle-class Americans internalized institutional age markers, the need for paternal authority diminished and families could become more democratic.[6] One consequence was that the threshold between childhood and adulthood blurred almost as soon as it had been absorbed and diffused. Thus the last few decades have witnessed an increasing tension between the desire to "brighten" the line between childhood and adulthood, on one hand, and efforts to efface it on the other hand.

During the 1990s, U.S. marketers coined the term "age compression" to describe industry efforts to entice children or their parents to buy products formerly designed for adult use, such as lip gloss, popular music with sexually suggestive lyrics, and films depicting graphic violence. Examples of age compression abound and tend to arouse parental, and at times, even public alarm; and the fact that the progenitors of such dubious practices should invent a nomenclature for the very vulnerabilities they seek to exploit is alarming in itself.[7] Yet we might construe the idea of age compression more generally, and therefore more usefully, as *any* phenomenon that challenges commonly held notions about what people of any age should or should not do or experience at any point along the human life span. And of course, it is important to remember that concern about one age category pressing down upon, or pushing up against another assumes the existence, in the first place, of commonly agreed upon, well-maintained boundaries between age groups, when in fact the thresholds between and within age bands so readily recognized today are comparatively novel distinctions.

In fact, what emerges as we look back over the last half century are two very different but dramatic instances of age compression that complicate the very concepts on which distinctions within childhood and between childhood and adulthood are based. The parents of the baby boom and their children each upset the boundaries between adulthood and childhood, but in opposite ways: the generation that spawned the baby boom strove precociously for the trappings of maturity and embraced it as a social and cultural ideal. Their grandchildren, the generation born during the 1980s and 1990s, engage in behaviors and are exposed to activities, information, and media formerly reserved for adults. Baby boomers, by contrast, slowed the pace of growing up, distended its outer limits and postponed passage through the conventional rituals of adulthood, such as marriage, home owning, and child rearing to a degree unseen since the nineteenth century.

Before industrialization children's pathways to adulthood were much more varied than they have become, and there was certainly less consensus about what children's experiences should consist of since there were such marked differences in the ways experiences were structured from one social group to another. In what follows I will compare the cycle of age compression that occurred in the two decades immediately after World War II with current anxiety about age compression. Then I will speculate about the emerging role of age as a category for understanding the ways that power and social structures are reproduced in our own time.

Age Compression and the Developmental Paradigm in Historical Perspective

For most of human history the roles of adults and children have been partly overlapping, if not interchangeable. As Martin Kohli has pointed out, until industrialization the categories "adult" and "child" did not exist in forms we would readily recognize today. There were only household heads and everyone else: persons of all ages who were dependent on their household head for food and shelter.[8] While household members were *inter*dependent, to be sure, the idea of personal authority and autonomy arising from the mere passage of time in the individual's life was unknown. Functionally, the household head was an "adult" and his dependents were, relationally, all "children," regardless of their chronological ages.

Parents and elders were undoubtedly attentive to their children's growth, so we mustn't exaggerate the degree to which the conception of children as evolving creatures went unheeded. For millennia, children by about age six were considered socially and morally accountable for their behavior in ways that did not obtain earlier in their lives. During the Middle Ages, Shulamith Shahar has shown, the kind of physical and temperamental changes contemporary societies associate with puberty were well recognized.[9] It has only been during the last century or so, however, that childhood has become so freighted with meaning, and chronological age so broadly and permanently etched into the features of life in industrial and postindustrial societies. Heightened sensitivity to age has many sources, but the most sweeping was the establishment of compulsory school attendance laws in most of the United States during the latter half of the nineteenth century. Due to the large numbers of children forced to attend urban public schools, it became convenient to differentiate them cognitively and physically so that they could be taught more efficiently. This system was known as "age grading" and it helped to instill in schoolchildren an awareness of their comparative progress in relation to their chronological age peers.[10] The rationale for embellishing these distinctions was supplied by academic psychologists in the late nineteenth century, who theorized a predictable path of human maturation and ultimately erected the developmental paradigm.

A number of influences contributed to the rise of the developmental paradigm. The ground was prepared by a shift from the Victorian conviction that children were sturdy and would grow naturally into healthy adults, to a view of them as fragile, by the early twentieth century. According to historian Peter Stearns, two factors combined to promote this changing view and one compounded the effect of the other: the steady exit of grandparents from the household left fewer people present with the wisdom and experience to deal with children's everyday problems and left parents bereft of child-rearing know-how; moreover, the trend toward fewer children in the middle class meant that parents had more time to observe and worry over each child. A former belief in the emotional resilience of children, says Stearns, was replaced by nagging doubts about their capacity to confront and overcome fears.[11]

By the 1920s child-rearing guidance aimed at a mass audience stepped in to fill the gap between the enlarging sense of children's vulnerability and parents' seeming incapacity to protect them.[12] At the core of expert advice was the conviction that careful monitoring of the child could positively affect its future. The flip side of this belief was the fear that irreparable damage could be done to a child by an inattentive parent.[13] In the same decade, psychologist John B. Watson declared, famously, that children's emotional dispositions were "set" by the time they were three years old. Watson's assertion fed the fear of children's innate vulnerability and pointed to the need for further scientific study, which would be supplied by growing teams of academic researchers in the years to come.[14] Yet the impulse to document every forward movement of the infant from helplessness to autonomy has roots in mid-nineteenth-century Europe, where the first wave of "baby biographers" recorded minute changes in the physical and mental progress of their own children. Their successors in this tradition in the United States were G. Stanley Hall, who popularized adolescence as a phase in the transition from child to adult, and his student, Arnold Gesell. Gesell elaborated on Hall's innovative collection of parent reports of children's behavior to establish a systematic database documenting the normal sequence of children's physical, cognitive, and psychological growth.[15] Gesell's *An Atlas of Infant Behavior* (1934) and *The First Five Years of Life* (1940), posited his theory of maturation, or "development schedules." He asserted the importance of the biological aging process in children, offering a counterpoint to Watson's behaviorist orthodoxy a generation earlier. Gesell's insistence on the acceptance of children's "bad behavior" as natural and so resistant to correction urged parents to relax their vigilance around discipline.[16]

By the early 1940s, then, the stage had been set for a change in the tenor of child-rearing literature, according to psychologist Martha Wolfenstein, who analyzed advice to parents dispensed by the U.S. Children's Bureau's bulletin, *Infant Care*, between 1914 and 1951. Whereas the earlier literature was concerned with helping the parent master what she characterized as the infant child's "centripetal" tendencies—the impulse to get pleasure from its own body (through thumb-sucking and masturbation, for instance)—by the 1942 and 1945 editions a more "centrifugal" image prevailed: thumb-sucking and masturbation were now regarded as natural, ready resources for the child and worry about curbing access was dampened. Child training experts predicted that such formerly "dangerous" impulses would in any event become more diffuse means of gratification if the baby had other objects to play with. Earlier alarm that unchecked impulses in the infant would spread beyond control later in life gave way to what she called an emerging "Fun Morality" in American culture and the idea, eventually, that what the baby wanted was probably good for it. While Wolfenstein mildly approved of the change, she also worried about its implications as a child grew into an adult. Whereas pleasure and fun in American culture were previously regarded as potentially wicked, their rising valuation, she warned, may have created a condition in which "failure to have fun occasions lowered self esteem," feelings of inadequacy, impotency, and being unwanted by others.[17] While Wolfenstein's essay appeared after the publication of Dr. Benjamin Spock's *Common Sense Book of Baby and Child Care,* the sea change reflected in *Infant Care* by the early 1940s applied as readily to Spock, whose book sold nearly four million copies within a decade after its release in 1946.

Never before had there been so many well-educated women entering motherhood for the first time and thus, never were so many women capable of, and interested in, using child-rearing literature on such a vast scale.[18] Like Karl Menninger a decade earlier, and the Children's Bureau's experts by 1942, Spock stressed the importance of relaxing standards that had been applied all too rigidly by Watson's disciples, in a parenting style that regarded itself as "child-centered." Child-centered parenting transformed the popular prescriptive literature on middle-class parenting from an emphasis on enforcing regimentation and maintaining emotional detachment, to an attitude that both parent and child were creatures of nature endowed with untapped and underappreciated instinctual wisdom. But as Fass argues, child-centered parenting, which might appear to have eased the necessity for vigilance, actually had a contradictory effect by elevating children's needs above those of their parents.[19]

By mid-century four major influences had converged to establish the developmental paradigm as the new creed of parenthood into the foreseeable future: (1) the abandonment of faith in children's innate resiliency for one in which children were seen as fragile and requiring constant attention; (2) a growing body of research that mapped out the development of children by stages that built one upon the another with consequential outcomes, and which reinforced the importance of intervention at earlier ages; (3) the emergence of a corps of professionals—academic psychologists, psychiatrists, and pediatricians—who stressed the need for parental vigilance and; (4) an expanded, well-educated cadre of middle-class mothers eager to apply the lessons of the most up-to-date parenting techniques.

The Ideology of Postwar Age Compression

The generation that pioneered child-centered parenting boldly challenged the previous generation's conception of the upper threshold of youth by rushing into adulthood. Between 1946 and 1964 the average-age-at-first-marriage for both women and men sank to its lowest level in decades, while the birthrate soared, triggering the first of two eras of age compression during the second half of the twentieth century. As average family size swelled, "maturity" was cast as the proper object of every individual's self-actualization.[20] As a cultural ideal it exerted a positive pressure to marry, have children, begin a career, shoulder responsibility, and grow up faster. Home ownership was the most visible emblem of maturity and an important feature of what historian John Modell has called the distinctive commitment to the "family building" ethos of the 1950s: the belief that the height of personal satisfaction was to be achieved not just in marriage itself, but in child rearing.[21] The single-family dwelling permitted unprecedented privacy within families, as well as among the children in those households. Owner-occupied homes during the period shot up from 43.6 percent in 1940 to 61.9 percent in 1960.[22]

Maturity was to be accomplished for both men and women through marriage and child rearing, and was manifested in glaringly unequal and stereotyped notions of masculinity and femininity. This cultural orientation focused on adult sensibilities and values that had reigned for decades, but was only ever imperfectly fulfilled on a mass scale. During the 1950s, age and gender boundaries were re-straightened and seemingly re-solidified after decades of turbulence.[23] Because marriage had become so important in the attainment of adulthood, age compression in its postwar iteration effectively ostracized the unmarried and the childless.[24] This had serious and negative repercussions for anyone who forsook marriage—gays and lesbians, to be sure, but anyone who chose not to marry because of career ambitions or family obligations.[25] By extension, widows, widowers, and divorcees, having once attained adulthood, reverted to the social netherworld of the uncoupled; and since maturity could only be achieved and maintained through marriage, it left the unmarried in an ambiguous position at best.[26] Single and divorced people were, by axiom, considered unfulfilled and potentially mentally ill— "sick or immoral, too selfish or too neurotic to marry," according to a study conducted at the very apex of the baby boom, in 1957. This stigmatizing attitude toward the unmarried or divorced held up across gender lines and marital status, the study found, as even single and divorced women and men viewed their decisions not to marry or remarry as symptoms of their own abnormality.[27]

While spontaneity, impulsivity, and individual expression characterized what it was to be youthful or "immature," a desire to shoulder responsibility and to demonstrate independence and emotional strength was the goal of the growing male. Women's complementary role consisted of appreciating, supporting, and depending upon men for leadership, resolve, emotional restraint, and the necessities of life. It was an era when mass media promoted bold, action-oriented, if unexpressive males, and submissive, flirtatious, child-obsessed females.[28] Women in Cold War America, it has been argued, were "redomesticated" in ways that ultimately fed the rise of feminism by the late 1960s. But men experienced a kind of domestication themselves and began to chafe, as Barbara Ehrenreich has shown, against conventional outward displays of masculine identity, domesticity, and the quest for maturity.[29]

"Real" Childhood and "Middle Childhood"

As baby boomers came of age during the latter decades of the twentieth century, they looked back nostalgically on childhood during the 1950s. One consequence of this has been the idealization of their own experience as "far freer, less pressured, and . . . more innocent than childhood today," says Steven Mintz.[30] The association of childhood with innocence emerged during the late eighteenth century in Europe, but with the radical segmentation of children's developmental arc, innocence has come to be equated even more narrowly with the absence of sexuality in children. Authorities on childhood such as historian Howard Chudacoff have underscored this association by suggesting that the years between six and twelve are a time when "children are really children."[31]

Chudacoff's assertion finds a parallel in current academic and professional formulations of child development, which identify this phase as "middle childhood," or the "concrete operational stage," when important developmental work occurs. By the sixth year of life, they find, most children have developed a sense of empathy, have learned that they can manage their emotions, and begin to practice socially acceptable behaviors. In this stage their capacity for memory and logical abilities become much more powerful, and they can organize tasks to complete goals; they grasp the concept of time, and can comprehend different ways of understanding the same idea or phenomenon. By age six most children have acquired a core sense of gender and begin to "internalize" parents' and others' responses to their behavior; and by age eight they develop a sense of responsibility for their own actions.[32]

However, even the term "middle childhood" is not understood and deployed uniformly by child welfare professionals. The Centers for Disease Control and Prevention, of the U.S. Department of Health and Human Services, refer to the years from six to eleven as middle childhood, but further subdivide the group into ages six to eight and nine to eleven, lumping age twelve with "early adolescence." The American Academy of Pediatrics, on the other hand, defines middle childhood as age five to ten, and adolescence as eleven to twenty-one. Developmentalists, a diverse group that includes psychologists, anthropologists, sociologists, geneticists, neuroscientists, biologists, and educators define middle childhood as the "period from roughly age five to twelve."[33]

These differences in definition may be attributable to the medical profession's focus on physiological growth as compared with the attention that many developmentalists pay to the relationship of cognitive growth to social and cultural influences, as well as their reluctance to attach normative judgments to such definitions. Nonetheless, the more notable aspect of this age band is that it is during middle childhood that children are not yet (generally speaking) *active* sexual beings; and the awakening interest in sexuality is one of the critical markers separating children from adolescents.[34] Sigmund Freud described it as a period of sexual latency in human development: a time of physical, emotional, and psychological growth when the child's sexual impulses lie dormant. But it is also characterized by the "consolidation of psychosexual achievements from earlier periods," before the appearance of hormonal activity and the emergence of secondary and primary sexual characteristics in the young adolescent. As psychologist W. Andrew Collins has pointed out, "Freud's characterization of this period . . . has been widely misconstrued as indicating it is relatively insignificant, perhaps because the psychosexual events of earlier and later periods appear more dramatic in psychoanalytic thought."[35]

Freud's successors stressed an evolving "sense of industry" in middle childhood (Erik Erikson), and the ascending importance of interpersonal relationships (Harry Stack Sullivan). Jean Piaget, another major influence on the study of this developmental phase during the twentieth century, focused on the prominence of cognitive growth, and the ability to reason and solve problems systematically.[36] But again, it is the role of this stage in sexual development (or its apparent *absence*) that implicitly aligns middle childhood, both popularly and among some child welfare professionals, with nature. To say, then, that "children are really children" between the ages of six and twelve presents this phase as somehow more "natural," and thus an inviolable stage of life defined by its presumed innocence about sexuality. Further, it implies that childhood should be protected from the "unnatural" influences of culture, so it remains untouched by the experiences, images, messages, or knowledge intended for those who are not children.[37]

Age Compression Since the 1980s

Over the last three decades, anxiety about age boundary transgressions—particularly for children under the age of twelve—is most often fixed on fear of sexual predatorship and attempts to sexualize children, especially girls.[38] But these are only the most sensational elements of worry about the encouragement of behaviors across age boundaries.[39] A wide range of disturbing behaviors, purportedly now more common, are attributed to age compression: including earlier interest in sexuality and sexual activity among girls and boys; earlier experimentation with cigarettes, alcohol, and other drugs; an increase in violence and crimes by children; a rise in the rate of eating disorders at either extreme (anorexia and obesity); higher juvenile suicide rates; earlier identification by children with peer groups (in direct proportion to the decline of parental influence); heightened attention to consumer products; and attachment of self-esteem to consumption and the tokens of affluence.[40] Marketers are highly attuned to the profitability of blurring age boundaries between adults and children, as well as between preteens and adolescents, and have launched playful advertising campaigns that wink at the role-reversals produced by children who master new technologies before their parents.[41]

The most frequent and familiar incursions into children's psychic space come from representations of morally questionable adult behaviors in the mass media. The root of the problem, according to culture critics and media watchdogs, is parents' diminishing capacity (or will) to monitor their children's activities. Accurate or not, the problem is compounded, they maintain, by a society that lionizes conspicuous consumption, on one hand, and the bind that so many contemporary American families find themselves in when both parents (or the sole household head) must earn enough to afford the inflated standards of living they aspire to, on the other. Laboring outside the household limits parents' ability to regulate their children's activities, it is argued, compromising their control over children's exposure to potentially harmful influences.[42] More and earlier engagement with mass media of all kinds—movies, television, popular music, video games, and the Internet generally, but most insidiously, the interactive features of social cyberspace (chat rooms, YouTube, MySpace, Facebook, Instant Messaging, Twittering, e-mail, etc.)—make children and young people more vulnerable both to adult predators and to one another.[43] Children, moreover, have unprecedented access to forms of mobile, faceless interaction. Cell phones and text messaging, which elude adult surveillance, are made possible, ironically, by the very desire of parents to monitor their children effectively in the first place. Evidence of age compression is also visible in other spheres. Internet sites that enable young people to disclose the details of their private lives to wider audiences, for example, not only elicit fear for children's vulnerability, but encourage an unwholesome imitation of tabloid celebrity and unseemly narcissistic behavior.[44]

At the opposite end of the spectrum of worry about children "growing up too fast," is the desire to outfit children, early on, with the tools to get a head start on their age peers academically. This has increased apprehension about a growing emphasis on success and achievement at earlier ages, which, while not patently unwholesome, asks children to take on adult-like pressures nonetheless. Contemporary middle-class parents are, internally, deeply divided about what is "healthy," on the one hand, and how to ensure that their children get ahead, on the other. Thirty years ago pediatrician David Elkind expressed worry about what he called the "hurried child"—children pushed or impelled to achieve. These children, he observed, often experienced "responsibility overload," "change overload," and "emotional overload" and suffered, consequently, from hurried emotional growth. This phenomenon has only intensified as middle-class children since the 1980s have felt increased pressure to excel in school, compete in organized sports, or join multiple extracurricular activities.[45]

While the rest of the nation smirks about New Yorkers anxious to get their toddlers into the "right" nursery school, "Baby Einstein" is a national phenomenon, offering videos backed by the sounds of Mozart and Beethoven to stimulate brain activity in infants as early as three-months old.[46] By eight months, your toddler, according to educational psychologist Robert Titzer, can learn to read. Titzer taught his own child to read at nine months by creating a series of homemade videos in the early 1990s. He subsequently developed a slicker, professional edition called "Your Baby Can Read," whose promotional materials proclaim that children's brains reach 90 percent of their size between five months and five years old, so "Why . . . delay teaching a child to read when the most natural time to learn language is during the infant and toddler years?" And "why," asks an infomercial for the series more ominously, "let that window of opportunity close?"[47]

Examples such as these demonstrate the degree to which the developmental paradigm has escalated the anxiety over how much parents can actively shape their children's futures. The transmission of wealth generationally for middle-class Americans now depends largely on the attainment of increased levels of education. As a result, the enculturation of the child determines the degree to which socioeconomic status can be carried forward. The transmission of cultural competence—forming specific habits of mind that prepare the child to be not just successful at school and ultimately highly skilled, but also intellectually nimble, emotionally resilient, and socially competent—has become critical to the child's, and collectively, the family's future success.[48] Therefore, middle-class parents perceive the stakes of child rearing as correspondingly high. Their ability to help their children acquire the right set of tools for success in the marketplace, they believe, depends not only on optimizing their children's performance in school, but on their capacity to foster healthy psychoemotional growth as well.[49]

Age compression squeezes together and blurs normative age boundaries. In addition to fostering a long list of specific ills, say critics, it threatens to shorten the duration of childhood. As experiences once associated singularly with adolescence or adulthood "push down" into the consciousness of children, exposing them to attitudes and behaviors once reserved for people deemed psychologically equipped to resist or indulge them, it is said they invade the protective space that childhood was designed to be. Nonetheless, current discourse about "appropriate" experiences for children should be understood, at least in part, as the startling result of an offense against contemporary adult sensibilities—sensibilities formed in the light of personal experience. One's own childhood might provide a motive for reproducing a similar experience for one's own children, or its opposite—a desire to compensate for the childhood the parent never had.[50] This is not to say that adult ideas about what their children should hear, see, or emulate are irrational and unfounded, but rather that they must be understood as historically derived conceptual categories, before we can determine whether current childhood behaviors are truly unhealthy, merely innocuous, or even benign.

Is Age the "New" Gender?

Age compression in the form of upward striving toward maturity that had so dominated notions of personal fulfillment for decades, was eventually overturned during the late 1960s and early 1970s. In its place there arose a contrary valorizing of youth as an ideal to cling to.[51] Maturity was no more "real" because a young person married, had children, and owned a home, than the phase of childhood between the ages of six and twelve is more "real" than other phases of childhood because it is relatively devoid of sexual thoughts, sensations, or activity. If it were, then we might expect that the ideology of family building, with its emphasis on marriage at an early age, home-owning, asymmetrical gender relations, heterosexuality, and child rearing as the well-spring of personal happiness, would have persisted. Instead it was swept away by women's revolt against patriarchy, enlarged opportunities for meaningful labor for women, the sexual revolution, gay rights, and the declining importance of marriage. Both "real" childhood and its adult analogue "maturity" reflect cultural aspirations—ideals that express the values of the dominant culture, to be sure—but aspirations nonetheless.

Whereas the previous wave of age compression that shaped Americans' attitudes about the relationship of childhood to adulthood asked children and young people to "grow up" faster, the current fashion worries that children are growing up too fast, and urges parents to find ways to shield their children from forces that would hasten their exposure to adult things, attitudes, and behaviors. The generation of parents harboring these fears—baby boomers—is the same generation that helped to enshrine youth and youthfulness, and works so hard to be able to afford the kind of leisure that has been so strongly associated with its own childhood and youth.[52]

Concern about youthfulness seems to be at an all-time high. Spend any time watching television programs aimed at middle-aged men and you will be inundated with advertisements for products that compensate for "erectile dysfunction," or medicines that treat the symptoms of an enlarged prostate. Infomercials in the early morning target women who want to return their bodies to shapely prechildbearing years through the latest exercise routine or facial creams that soften wrinkles. Cosmetic surgery, once the preserve of the rich and famous, has become so commonplace that television has produced both fictional dramas and "reality" shows that feature plastic surgeons. The concept of "age appropriate" behaviors, clothing, and experiences, which arose from the spread of the developmental paradigm, is being flipped around as the baby-boom generation ages and reluctantly loosens its grip on youthfulness and sexuality.

In part, we might understand contemporary anxiety about age compression simply as an attempt to reestablish thresholds between stages in the process of growing up—an inevitable revision, perhaps, of the expectations that govern adult-child relations as the current generation of parents struggles to navigate novel and very diverse challenges to its ability to patrol the boundaries between "adult" and "child." These challenges are made all the more difficult by the absence of the kind of consensus that informed parenting when the generation that produced the baby boom unquestioningly trod the short, narrow path to maturity, and at a time when maturity privileged responsibility more than the freedoms of adulthood.

But how are we to understand the desire to isolate one segment of children's maturation as possessing more of the critical elements of childhood than the phases that precede and follow it? We take as self-evident distinctions between age bands, such as childhood, adolescence, adulthood, and even senescence. Enhanced sensitivity to age differentiation during the last half century would seem to make these gross demarcations easier to detect and so, more reassuring. However, this heightened awareness also explains why, I think, age compression raises alarm particularly among middle-class parents, who are so attuned to the implications of subtle, incremental changes occurring in their children. And it makes comprehensible, as well, the desire to believe that there is some part of childhood with boundaries that remain perceptible to all—unspoiled, natural, eternal, and so, "real." That this portion of childhood should reside at its center, or "middle" seems only natural too. For many, middle childhood looms as the only safe haven between the frailty of infancy and early childhood and the tumult of puberty and adolescence, where a parent can breathe easily, if only for a handful of years.

Age compression is not new. The chronological age at which each generation "comes of age" moves up and down with the complex interplay of social, political, economic, and environmental forces.[53] Even the size of successive birth cohorts can alter the "target" age of adulthood for each generation by amplifying or diminishing the odds that the job market for young people will welcome or spurn them.[54] Two phenomena *are* new, however: the inscription of age norms across the spectrum of institutions that socialize children and young adults from birth through the completion of schooling; and the tendency to interpret behaviors associated with the rise and fall of birth rates. As infant mortality declined, the life span increased, and the developmental paradigm came to dominate the way parents imagined the unfolding of their children's lives, they worry more and conceive of themselves, potentially, as *having more control over* their children's progress toward autonomy.

As a consequence, the increasing prominence of age as a way of understanding human experience during the latter half of the twentieth century, of childhood in particular, is rife with contradiction. On the one hand, a widely held view of every child as deviating from, or conforming to, a "healthy" sequence of developmental changes reifies the normative aspects of scientific discourse about aging. On the other hand, the more we know about children's development, the more we are struck by the enormous diversity of children's experiences of growing up—a diversity that would seem to defy any possibility of generalization. Similarly, whereas the tendency to psychologize all aspects of the life course from birth to death arises from a cultural context, which is variable and changing, the aim of psychology is to universalize. So a central paradox nourishes contemporary ideas about growing up in the United States: the developmental paradigm offers a pathway to autonomy for children, a guide for parents in promoting their children's independence and self-reliance, but its effect is the opposite; in the words of Mintz, it "juvenilizes" the young. It "protects and insulates them, organizes their activities, and renders them increasingly dependent on adults."[55] As several of the essays in this volume conclude, children are growing up both faster, and slower, than was true even at the mid-point of the twentieth century.

One of the fundamental distinctions between humans and other species is our lengthy period of dependency on adult caretakers. Indeed, the concept of childhood itself derives from the functionality of institutionalizing this protracted phase of dependency and protection.[56] As economic productivity has become increasingly free of physical human strength and more reliant on technology and organization, however, relationships—like gender and race—that govern concepts of age have come into question. As Joan W. Scott concluded about the salience of gender to the way power is "conceived, legitimized, and criticized" throughout history, we might think of categories of age, such as "child," "adult," "minor," "senior," "puerile," and "senile," as having differing relationships to the individual's perceived competence, autonomy, and power in society. If we think about age analogously, then these relationships, in Scott's words, become "problematic rather than known," "something contextually defined, repeatedly constructed."[57]

A long cycle of economic depression and war deferred parenting for large numbers of people during the two decades that preceded the baby boom and was rewarded by a cycle—of roughly equal duration—in which parenting was given pride of place among the achievements of adulthood. The parents of the baby boom underwrote popular familiarity with child development, "age appropriate" behaviors, and the minutiae of "healthy" and "unhealthy" practices associated with growing up at every stage. The two decades after World War II in the United States thus stand today as a moment in the recent past in which age became "problematic," "contextually defined," and consciously constructed. Our own time constitutes another such epoch in which age has been problematized, constructed and defined contextually. "Adult" experiences push down into childhood for ill, for nil, for good, or with misguided good intentions, depending on your perspective. But the developmental paradigm is concerned with every aspect of the life span, and Americans will, predictably, turn increasing attention to the "golden years" as the baby boom enters fully into retirement, and confronts its own physical and mental decline.[58] This problematic awaits us.

5

Whose Child? Parenting and Custody in the Postwar Period

Mary Ann Mason

Mark and Crispina Calvert were a married couple who desired to have a child in the last decade of the twentieth century. Crispina had undergone a hysterectomy but her ovaries remained capable of producing eggs, and the couple eventually considered a surrogate to bear the child for Crispina. Anna Johnson heard about Crispina's plight from a coworker and offered to serve as a surrogate for the Calverts.

They signed a contract and Anna agreed to give up all parental rights. The Calverts paid her $10,000 and promised to provide $100,000 in life insurance. Almost as soon as the embryo was implanted, the parties began to fight. The Calverts claimed Anna had not disclosed her history of several stillbirths and miscarriages, and Anna claimed they had not purchased the life insurance. Anna demanded full payment or she would not give up the child. The Calverts sued and Anna countered. The baby was born amid this contention and was assigned to the Calverts.

By the time the case had worked its way through three legal stages to the California Supreme Court, the baby was three years old. The Supreme Court weighed the claims of the women in a modern day Solomon-like choice and decided that a baby under these circumstances could not have two mothers. In choosing between them the court did not dwell on the significance of pregnancy and childbirth or even biology, but instead, borrowing from intellectual property law, developed a new doctrine of "intentional motherhood":

"when the two means (genetic tie and giving birth) do not coincide in one woman, she who intended to procreate the child—that is she who intended to bring about the birth of a child that she intended to raise as her own—is the natural mother under California law."[1]

With this reasoning the court awarded the child to Crispina and her husband, the child's genetic father. No mention was made of the "best interests of the child" in the majority opinion nor was the gender or name of the child ever revealed. None of the judges sought to determine the developmental needs of a three-year-old child.

The sole dissenting California Supreme Court justice strongly objected to the majority's reasoning based on intellectual property law and argued forcefully for considering the "best interests" of the child: "The problem with this [the court's] argument, of course is that children are not property. Unlike songs or inventions, rights in children cannot be sold for consideration or made freely available to the general public."

Welcome to the postmodern family, a landscape of various family configurations, not always united by marriage or related by biology, where no clear rules prevail and the child is rarely given a voice when adults vie for custody.

Child custody determinations have had a roller coaster of a history, reflecting the jagged evolution of the American family. The largest chunk of American history, roughly two hundred years, found its authority regarding parents and children in divine law. This era corresponded with the period of colonial settlement and the birth of the new republic.

Not surprisingly, the divine order of the family closely reflected the political economy of the family and political balance between men and women during this period. Fathers were the masters and held complete rights over everyone in the household. The children in the household might include young indentured servants, and in some regions slave children, in addition to the master's natural children and those of orphaned relatives. Family survival depended on the labor of all the members of the family, including the children and the father as the boss of the household labor team.[2]

The second major historical era, which introduced the doctrine of the best interests of the child and maternal preference, roughly held sway from the last half of the nineteenth century through the first half of the twentieth century. After the founding of the American republic the concept of a divine plan was steadily replaced by the Enlightenment concept of natural law. Here also there were clear rules that human beings need only apply to a specific fact situation, but God was no longer actively involved in presenting the rules and could not be called upon as authority.[3] As New York's highest court noted in an 1842 decision awarded to the mother of a sickly daughter, "The law of nature has given to her an attachment for her infant offspring which no other relative will be likely to possess in equal degree."[4]

This drastic swing in the status of mothers and children was precipitated by a shift in the household economic structure during the nineteenth century. America gradually changed from a self-sufficient farm economy into a new industrial nation. The "modern" family evolved as fathers moved out of the house to work in factories and offices and mothers took their place as heads of the domestic scene. Some children who 100 years earlier would have been put to work as soon as possible now, for the first time, experienced a childhood as we have come to know it, focused on school and play. Even children who lost their parents were now placed in what was considered a great leap forward, the orphanage, where they were schooled and treated as children rather than placed in a poor house with adult vagrants, or recycled back into the labor force as apprentices. Some children were sent to work in factories and many still worked on the farm, but for growing numbers of them childhood became a way of life.

Children and childhood were not actually invented in this era, but they were thought of quite differently than before. Children were now seen as tender creatures that required nurturing, rather than creatures whose innate evil tendencies must be curbed with a strong hand or a stick. And it was mother, at home alone now with the children, who was seen as the nurturing parent, the one who most determined the child's development.

In consideration of the new emphasis on children and childhood the term "the best interests of the child" has been used continuously from the mid-nineteenth century to the present to justify where and with whom the child shall reside when a family breaks down. Its interpretation, however, has reflected frequently shifting public values. During the last third of the twentieth century alone, this term has taken several distinct turns in how Americans perceive the child's interest in the event of a family breakdown.

In the 1950s and early 1960s, it was still common wisdom that children were almost always better off in an intact family. Parents, it was believed, must sacrifice their own happiness and avoid divorce in "the best interests of the children." Then in the 1970s it became accepted dogma that children were happy only if their parents were happy and that divorce was preferable to an unhappy marriage. Divine and natural law explanations were abandoned and social scientists were increasingly called upon as authorities to justify the claim that a family in conflict was more damaging to children than divorce. Divorce became far easier but at first the maternal preference was still largely followed. Beginning in the 1980s joint physical custody began to be promoted as a way of giving children access to both parents while allowing the parents freedom of divorce. More social scientists were called upon to validate the shift. Joint custody became the new standard of what was considered "in the best interests" of the child. Custody guidelines and public attitudes turned rapidly in this direction.

By the advent of the twenty-first century other family configurations were challenging the "best interests" rule. As the percent of children born out of wedlock edged toward 40 percent, the rights and obligations of the unwed father drew great attention. Gay and lesbian couples, now politically active, vied for recognition of their family status, promoting new psychological investigations into what "healthy families" looked like, and what rights a nonbiological parent could claim. Nonbiological parents also fought for recognition as stepfamilies, while relatives and other caretakers staked their claims as well.

Egalitarian Marriage

The first great modern shift in considering the best interests of children began during the 1970s, precipitated by a change in the political and economic balance of the household as women began to work outside the home. Whether they were spurred by necessity, by choice, or by the third wave of feminist ideology, the balance shifted. Women demanded and received a larger share of gender equality in the workplace and to some extent in the home. But in the gender struggles that ensued they also lost their special status in custody decisions, the maternal preference, which had prevailed since the mid-nineteenth century. California, which led the nation in these domestic relations matters, passed no fault divorce in 1970, forbade gender consideration in custody decisions in 1975, and enacted a preference for joint custody in 1980. All of these shifts were advertised as in the best interests of the child, although the actual child was rarely represented or heard from in custody disputes.

By the last third of the twentieth century legal terms such as "in the best interests of the child" and "joint custody" had permeated the casual discourse of everyday life: indeed, few families were untouched by a custody matter. A child born in 1980 had a good chance of falling under court jurisdiction in a case involving where and with whom the child would live.[5] Unlike previous eras, where child custody issues usually involved orphans or children of parents who could not care for them, the great majority of child custody matters in the last third of the twentieth century were the product of an exploding divorce rate.[6]

The advent of easy and acceptable divorce rearranged the tentative symmetry between mother, father, and the state with regard to children's custody ideas that had prevailed since the nineteenth century. State legislatures and courts weakened mothers' legal claims to the custody of their children following divorce actions, systematically wiping out the maternal preference of the tender years doctrine and leaving only the vague "best interests of the child" standard. Some lawmakers replaced the maternal preference with new gender-neutral preferences, such as joint custody and primary caretaker, hoping to provide consistency in decision making where there was no longer an easy choice.

Some of the legal rhetoric for treating mothers and fathers equally derived from the feminist movement for equal rights. The movement, beginning in the late 1960s, held at times incompatible groups and ideologies together for more than a decade by an ultimately unsuccessful campaign for an equal rights amendment. The long, hard-fought but failed campaign that ensued represented not only a bid for equal treatment before the law but for equal participation with men in all spheres of life, especially the marketplace, but also the family.

The National Organization for Women founding statement in 1967 decried the "half equality in the marriage relationship" and called for a reexamination of laws governing marriage.

> We reject . . . that home and family are primarily woman's world and responsibility—hers, to dominate—his to support. We believe that a true partnership between the sexes demands a different concept of marriage, an equitable sharing of the responsibilities of home and children.[7]

Yet, in spite of the forceful language of the NOW platform, feminists were rarely prominent actors in the legal revolution that transformed divorce and custody law over the next twenty years; it was more often fathers who used their language. The California no-fault divorce law was passed in 1969 by a nearly all male legislature before the Equal Rights Amendment crusade was launched. And when California, the pioneer no-fault state, once again led the nation in 1980 by legislating a preference for joint custody, a newly formed fathers' rights group pushed the bill over legislative hurdles.[8]

It was not only feminist rhetoric promoting equal treatment that persuaded legislators and judges to abandon the maternal presumption; equal treatment arguments were combined with the reality that great numbers of women had abandoned full-time housekeeping for the workplace. Moreover, most of these new workers were mothers. In the 1970s only 27 percent of women with children under age three were in the workforce; by 1985 this figure was more than 50 percent and by 2004, 64 percent of mothers with children under age six and 56 percent of mothers of infants (under one year old) were employed.[9]

The shift in the law away from a maternal preference toward joint custody was impelled by political forces, but often justified in the courtrooms by an increased reliance on social science. Social science evidence was employed in custody decisions to support several at times contradictory positions. Fathers argued that social scientists tell us that men and women are equally suited as parents. Mothers argued that early maternal nurture matters. As an example of this new thinking, a New York court, in *Watts v. Watts*, rejected the notion that mothers and children share a special bond by invoking the authority of anthropologist Margaret Mead, who charged, "This is a mere and subtle form of anti-feminism by which men—under the guise of exalting the importance of maternity—are tying women more tightly to their children than has been thought necessary since the invention of bottle feeding and baby carriages."[10]

Dependence on the social sciences accelerated late in the twentieth century. The gradual abolition of fault-based divorce and, more gradually, the maternal presumption in almost all states promoted this dependence. The use of social sciences expanded in three ways. First, social science scholarship, usually in the form of psychological theories supporting the primacy of mother, father, or both parents, influenced both legislators in draft laws and judges in custody disputes following divorce. Second, expert witnesses, most often mental health professionals trained in the social and behavioral sciences, were called upon to testify as to the capabilities of particular parents. Third, the courts moved toward the use of the therapeutic model of mediation in place of the adversarial mode of litigation in all matters of family law.

Social science studies were sometimes used to provide authority for widely differing results. The concept "psychological parent," for instance, which grew out of attachment theory, was used in various courts first in the 1970s to justify the maternal preference, then in the 1980s and 1990s to justify father custody, then primary caretaking and sometimes joint custody.

The psychological parent theory is most closely associated with the 1973 book, *Beyond the Best Interests of the Child*, by Joseph Goldstein, Anna Freud, and Albert Solnit.[11] They deemed that the "psychological parent" was the one individual, not necessarily the biological parent, with whom the child most closely associated. In their opinion this person should have total and, if necessary, exclusive custodial rights, including refusing visitation to noncustodial parents.

In the early years the theory was mostly used to justify awarding mothers sole custody (with father visitation), but as a gender-neutral standard was promoted by both feminists and fathers' rights groups, father-child interactions, an area previously ignored by social scientists, took off and fathers increasingly became designated as the "psychological parent." Most father researchers studied father-infant relationships in a laboratory setting where fathers were assigned tasks usually performed by mothers. The findings from the many studies were ambiguous, and produced heated debate among legal scholars regarding their appropriate application to custody standards.[12] Nonetheless, the message heard by lawmakers was that fathers were, on balance, interchangeable with mothers.

While father studies first promoted a gender-neutral preference that supported the model of a single custodial parent, who could be the father rather than the mother, these same studies quickly became the ammunition for advocates of shared or joint parenting. The argument posed that if parents were equally good at parenting, a child could have two "psychological parents." Depriving the child of one of them was not in the child's best interest.

Some courts enthusiastically imposed joint custody arrangements, even over the disagreement of the parents. The practical consequences for the children were rarely considered. In a Maryland case on appeal, the judge described the joint custody arrangement for Christina, age four and Neil, age three, decreed at the time of the trial.

> Both parents teach school. The father's workday is from 8:30 AM to 4:15 PM and the mother's 12:30 PM to 4:15 PM. . . . Their base is in the father's home, but their mother probably sees them more of their waking hours. The mother is in the home with the children Monday to Friday from 7:30 AM to 12:30 PM. The mother has the children in

her home from 4:15 PM to 8:00 PM Tuesday and on alternate weekends from 10:00 AM Saturday until 8:00 PM Sunday. The paternal
grandmother babysits Monday to Friday from the time the mother
leaves until the father gets home. The father pays his mother $29.50
weekly. The mother pays no child support.[13]

The subsequent research on shared or joint parenting, like the father
studies, ultimately yielded ambiguous findings. One of the most respected of
these researchers, Frank Furstenberg, conducted a five-year study of children
with a variety of parental arrangements, including joint custody families. Re-
viewing his own study and the longitudinal research of others, he concluded:

> The policy implications of findings reported here are unsettling be-
> cause they clash with the prevailing practice that attempts to invent
> policies which increase parental involvement. On the basis of our
> study we see little strong evidence that children will benefit psycho-
> logically from the judicial or legislative interventions that have been
> designed to promote parental participation.[14]

Yet inconclusive findings did not dampen the ardor of those convinced
that shared parenting was the best custodial arrangement. By the late 1980s
courts could choose from a number of studies that supported shared parenting. In *Zummo v. Zummo*, where there was a conflict of religion between the
parents, the court nonetheless decided on shared parenting. The demise of
gender stereotypes and a wide and growing body of research indicating the
importance of both parents to healthy child development have caused courts
to reconsider the efficacy of the sole custody/visitation concept of postdivorce
allocation of parental authority.[15]

Determinations regarding the best interests of the child took yet another
turn as decision making moved out of the court and into the mediator's office.
The trend toward mediation was rooted in the escalation of no-fault divorce.
Judges were overwhelmed by the swelling number of divorces, which in turn
produced an unprecedented volume of custody disputes; they pushed the
parents toward mediation. Mediators, usually (but not always) mental health
professionals, sought to achieve agreement between parents. This agreement
was based, theoretically, on the parents' own concept of fairness, not that invoked by state law. Children were not welcome in mediation, which was considered to be a process of negotiation between the parents, not a democratic

family council. Exact figures are not available, but a high percentage of mediated custody disputes resulted in joint custody; in one California county, 54 percent chose this option.[16]

Critics of the process claimed that it didn't work and that it penalized mothers. Very few parents could sustain an arrangement in which the child actually resided with each parent about half of the time. Inevitably the child soon drifted into spending most of the time with one parent, usually the mother. Child support, however, was usually configured differently for joint custody. A mother could find herself with effective sole custody but less support than a sole custodian might receive. [17]

The Postmodern Family—Nonbiological Parent, Stepparents, Gay Parents, and Other Cohabitors

By the advent of the twenty-first century, the traditional family configuration of a married mother and father had broken down radically. With 40 percent of children born out of wedlock by 2007 in the U.S.[18] marriage no longer defined parental relationships, and increasingly neither did biology as large numbers of non-biological parents, such as stepparents and gay partners vied for recognition. Other relatives, such as grandparents, also demanded parental rights.

Unwed Fathers

The percentage of children born out of wedlock, more than any other fact in recent history, changed the nature of the family and provoked a serious national debate. The vigorous crusade for fathers' rights following divorce in the 1980s had been taken up by few unwed fathers, but the rights of unwed fathers to their children was pursued far more forcefully by the federal government in its relentless campaign to wrest child support from them, most of whom did not pay child support. It was found that almost 70 percent of women on welfare were unmarried when they had their first child. In a conscious effort to tie the obligation of support to the right to custody of the child, courts and legislatures increasingly promoted the rights of unwed fathers. This very political shift was grounded not in psychological theory regarding the best interests of the child, but in the political need to impose financial responsibility.

The results of this initiative were mixed. While more child support was collected, some bizarre results occurred. The concept of "best interests of the child" is thrown out in cases of a biological parent versus a nonbiological contender, even when the biological parent is an unwed father who has never laid eyes on the child. This most often occurs in cases when the child is put up for adoption by the mother. In one such California case, *Michael U. v. Jamie B.*, the parents were underage. When their son Eric was conceived, Jamie was twelve years old and Michael was sixteen. Jamie placed their son up for adoption at birth and Eric lived for five months with the Whites, the family who had agreed to adopt him when Michael sought temporary custody. In California a grant of temporary custody would have allowed Michael to prevent the adoption of his child and to sue for permanent custody.

The trial court found in favor of Michael and awarded him temporary custody. A divided California Supreme Court agreed that the law was on his side, but that in his case, with a poor academic and attendance record and the dean's description of Michael as "very defiant," they found that he would be detrimental to the child. Except for one judge, there was no consideration of the "best interests of the child" standard.[19]

The public's drive for child support has caused even wrongly attributed nonbiological fathers to be held responsible. With the greater accuracy and simplicity of determining paternity with DNA tests in the twenty-first century, a large number of men who believed they were fathers and acted as such found that they were not in fact the fathers. Nevertheless the courts have mostly held them to continue with their child support payments. L was eleven years old when Mike, who had assumed he was her father learned from a DNA test that in fact her father was Rob. Mike and L's mother divorced and Rob married L's mother.

Mike asserted that Rob, the biological father and now man of the house, should pay to support the child. The trial court tried to split the responsibility since Mike still wanted visitation rights and had not immediately brought an action for fraud after the DNA discovery. The Pennsylvania Appeals Court, however, declared that a child could not have two fathers and pushed back all financial responsibility to Mike. The Pennsylvania Supreme Court refused to hear the appeal and allowed the judgment against Mike to stand. [20]A concern for "the best interests of the child" was never voiced.

Stepparents

In the wake of the divorce revolution, remarriage occurred almost as frequently as divorce. About 70 percent of mothers remarried within six years. Sometimes there was more than one remarriage. In addition, the 40 percent of unwed mothers often eventually married someone who was not the father of their child. Children were shifted around with the new marriages and remarriages and a large new class of parents developed—stepparents. It was estimated that about a third of the children born in the early 1980s would live with a stepparent before reaching adulthood.[21]

Other large classes of long-term cohabiting adults acted as parents, but were not married to the biological parent. The reasons these couples did not marry were numerous, including the fact that some couples were legally forbidden to marry because they were of the same sex. No matter what their reason for not marrying, they were all treated like stepparents, as legal strangers.

Stepparenting was not a new phenomenon; it was negatively invoked in most cultures long before Cinderella's wicked stepmother became the diva of fairy tales. The difference was that modern stepfamilies were a result of divorce, not death, leaving the child two biological parents. American law was not prepared to deal with nonbiological parents, much less the existence of three parents. State legislatures adopted the legal form of adoption reluctantly, beginning with Massachusetts in 1857, and the law that evolved clearly cut off rights of at least one biological parent before allowing adoption.

Not all stepparents wanted legal rights to custody or visitation in the event that the stepfamily disbanded due to divorce or death, but those who wanted these rights did not fare well. The rights of the biological parent were always considered foremost.

Such was the case in *Howell v. Gossett*. The Howells had divorced when their daughter was an infant, and Billy Howell agreed to forego custodial or visitation rights in exchange for having no child support obligations. For the mother this was a clean break and she married Grant Gossett a year or two later. For seven years Grant acted as a father toward the little girl until the day her mother was killed instantly in an automobile crash. Billy Howell then returned from a seven-year absence to claim his daughter. The trial court first awarded the little girl to her stepfather, saying the biological father had abandoned his child. On appeal the higher court disagreed, stating

On the death of the parent who holds custody of a child under a divorce the prima facie right to custody automatically inures to the surviving parent. In refusing to award the child to her father in this case the trial judge must of necessity have found that the father was not a fit and proper person to have custody of his daughter.[22]

Gay Parents

Gay parents who were not biological parents faced even more barriers than stepparents. First, they could not marry in all but a few states and were still considered "unfit" by many people and by the laws of a few states. "Moral fitness," particularly concerning mothers, had been a cornerstone of custody law since the maternal preference was adopted in the nineteenth century. It was assumed that it was harmful for children to be raised by mothers who deviated from the sexual mores of the time. For most of history "fitness" focused on heterosexual adultery, but the focus in the late twentieth century shifted to homosexuality.

In some states, following a divorce, even a biological mother could lose custody to a biological father or relative if she engaged in homosexual activity. As the court stated in a Virginia case that shifted custody from the lesbian mother to the grandmother in spite of the fact that a custody evaluator's opinion that the mother child relationship was healthy,

We have previously stated that living daily under conditions stemming from active lesbianism practiced in the home may impose a burden upon a child by reason of "social condemnation" attached to such an arrangement, which will inevitably afflict the child's relationships with its peers and with the community at large.[23]

A few states banned adoption by homosexual couples entirely; many more did not allow "second parent" adoptions where the nonbiological parent in a gay family adopted the child.[24]

Homosexual nonbiological parents were actively discouraged in many ways. Even in California, a notably progressive state in family law matters, Michele G. was denied even visitation rights in 1991 to the two children she had parented since birth—with her name on their birth certificates as father—when her cohabitation relationship with Nancy S. of more than a decade ended.

The court claimed they did not want to expand the definition of parent to include "child care providers of long standing, relatives, successive sets of stepparents or other close friends of the family."[25]

Grandparents

There was, however, a growing recognition of the fact that a large proportion of children were being raised by parent figures or relatives who were not their biological parents, and different courts in different states crafted rules or exceptions to include those acting as a parent, but who had no legal claim, creating an inconsistent and arbitrary set of rules regarding the best interests of the child.

Grandparents produced a large class of those asking for recognition in the postmodern family, as they increasingly stepped in to fill parental roles. Prior to 1965, their role was not well recognized: they had no legal right to seek visiting privileges, and were blocked from seeing their grandchildren, usually by the parents. As divorce rates, out-of-wedlock births, and drug use increased, states began passing laws bolstering grandparent rights when parents died, divorced, separated, or were jobless or disabled. Grandparents had more appeal than stepparents or gay parents and all states developed guidelines or laws that allowed them visitation, or sometimes custody.

The pendulum swung back, however, in 2000 when the Supreme Court, which did not normally enter the troubled waters of family law, sided with Washington state's high court in a grandparent visitation suit, *Troxel v. Granville*,[26]and struck down a state law that had allowed anyone—even a nonrelative—to seek the right to visit if it served the best interests of the child. More than a third of the states with nonparent visitation rights pulled back.

Political pressure by gay rights organizations, and even the American Association of Retired Persons (AARP) forced lawmakers in every state to seriously reconsider the confused issue of who had claims to a child in the event of divorce, desertion, or death.

De Facto Parent

In 2000, the turn of the millennium, the prestigious American Law Institute (ALI), founded in 1923 by a group of prominent American judges, lawyers, and teachers, including future Supreme Court Justice Benjamin Cardoza and famed federal jurist Learned Hand, who sought to address the uncertain and complex nature of early twentieth-century American law, now turned attention to the uncertainty and complexity of early twenty-first-century law. They attempted to craft a uniform rule that could apply to all nonparents in child custody or visitation disputes. In the rule they chose, a "de facto" parent was defined as a person who shared (at least) equally in primary childcare responsibilities while residing with a child for reasons other than money for at least two years.[27] The concept owes much to the social science contribution of "psychological parent" first introduced in the 1970s.

The high bar of parental involvement time would leave many contenders, such as most grandparents who were not residing with the child, out of the race. It would also leave out nannies and other employees who were paid. But it would probably serve well the stepfather Grant Gossett, who had parented the child as a father, and Michele G., the lesbian partner, who has also fully shared in parental responsibility.

Families of Assisted Reproduction

The beginning of yet another wave of family change, which seriously challenges our ability to define the "best interests of the child" in the future, has begun to appear in disputes involving "reproductively assisted" families, like the Calvert surrogate mother case described in the beginning of this chapter. Reproductive techniques now permit adults to circumvent each stage of the normal procedure of insemination, conception, pregnancy, and childbirth. These technological interventions, often involving a test tube at some juncture, raise basic questions regarding the essence of motherhood and fatherhood; they also raise new issues regarding the custody rights over the products of each discrete stage in the cycle of reproduction from ova to baby. The cast of competing characters goes beyond traditional custody battles. The competitors in a surrogate parent suit may include, but are not limited to, the biological (sperm-supplying) father; the biological father's wife; the biological mother's husband; the biological (ovum-supplying) mother; and the surrogate mother who carries either another woman's ovum (the sperm donor's wife's or another ovum donor) or her own ovum-fetus-child to term under an agreement (possibly for hire) calling for the relinquishment of the child upon birth to one or both biological parent(s) or adoptive parent(s).[28]

The cases thus far are few in number and conflicting in their decisions. One of the earliest, a frozen embryo dispute, has provoked even more political and religious issues than have the surrogacy cases. In March 1989 a Tennessee resident, Junior Lewis Davis, sued his wife in a divorce action to restrain her from having any of their seven fertilized eggs implanted. During their ten years of marriage Mrs. Davis had experienced five tubal pregnancies that led to infertility. At an in vitro fertility clinic the doctors harvested her ova and twice attempted, unsuccessfully, to implant the eggs fertilized with her husband's sperm in her uterus. When the couple divorced, five frozen pre-embyros were still awaiting implantation.[29]

The ensuing court actions reveal a painful confusion about the respective legal rights of mother, father, and the frozen embryos. Mary Sue Davis originally asked for control of the "frozen embryos" with the intent of having them transferred to her own uterus in a post-divorce effort to become pregnant. The trial court awarded them to her, but the appellate court disagreed, claiming that Junior Davis has a "constitutionally protected right not to beget a child where no pregnancy has taken place."[30] The appellate court granted them "joint control," effectively granting each former spouse veto power.

While the case dragged through the legal system, working its way up to the Tennessee Supreme Court, the facts changed. Each of the parties remarried, and Mary Sue decided she did not want to use the embryos for herself; rather she would donate them to another needy couple. The court chose its words carefully. It decided that pre-embryos as frozen matter have no rights, and the test is not a "best interests of the child" test, but rather a contest between the rights of adults. They chose Junior Davis, deciding that "he would spend a lifetime of either wondering about his parental status or knowing about his parental status but having no control over it."[31]

This carefully restricted wording was not convincing to all states nor to all ethicists. While avoiding the word property, the Tennessee Supreme Court did not give the pre-embryos any legal status. Louisiana, however, the only state to pass a law, declared that disputes between parties should be resolved in the "best interests of the embryo," and that interest should be "adoptive implementation."[32]

In the early part of the twenty-first century it is no longer simply a question of who is considered a parent; the more fundamental issue of who or what is considered a child or a pre-human must be addressed. In this arena, custody judgments are backing into the turbulent waters of the abortion wars.

The language of law and the findings of scientists may give way to ethicists and philosophers, and of course, politicians.

The Future of the Best Interests Standard

In the dizzying shifts and changes of law regarding who had rights to the child over the past fifty years, all supposedly based on the "best interests of the child," one voice was almost never heard or acknowledged, that of the child. During this same time period the law determined that a child who steals a candy bar is entitled to a lawyer, and a girl may have an abortion in most states without even notifying her parents. Yet a child subject to a brutal tug of war between adults remained powerless. The wishes and feelings of the child, even teenagers, were rarely considered or even sought.

Increasingly the United States has grown out of step with the rest of the world in not focusing on the child's interests and developmental needs. We are the only nation that has not signed the 1989 UN Convention on the Rights of the Child, which asserts that children have the right to a nurturing environment in accordance with their developmental needs; the right to legal representation; and the right to economic and emotional support from their parents and the state (Arts. 3.1, 12.1, 6.2). Several other countries, including England and Scotland, have issued explicit legislation regarding the rights of children that guarantee representation in all administrative and legal proceedings that pertain to them.

In some states a small movement has begun in the new millennium that considers the wishes and feelings of children themselves, not just those of the parents. Colorado and several other states have rethought their custody laws and moved away from parental rights to parental responsibilities; children are provided with special advocates in all disputes. Washington state issued developmentally sensitive custody guidelines that consider custody not a one-size-fits-all matter, and that growing children have changing needs. Many courts across the country are combining juvenile and family courts so that all issues affecting children can be heard in a court prepared for children's issues, where children are listened to and can receive support from social services. Still, without adopting the principles of the UN Convention on the Rights of the Child there will be no clear progress in attaining a national consensus on the "best interests of the child."

6

Children, the State, and the American Dream

Kriste Lindenmeyer

Just two days before the 2009 United States presidential inauguration, *Parade Magazine* published an article by president-elect Barack Obama. Entitled, "What I want for You—And Every Child in America," the essay was an optimistic message written in the form of a letter to Obama's daughters, ten-year-old Malia and seven-year-old Sasha. Obama recalled childhood memories of his Kansas-born grandmother reciting lines from the Declaration of Independence in order to teach him about the nation's core values and their relationship to the American Dream. He also acknowledged, however, that his grandmother's teachings included stories of struggle by brave individuals fighting to secure equality of opportunity as the key to accessing that dream. Obama cautioned, the United States "is not great because it is perfect, but because it can always be made better." Continually striving to provide "greater equality of opportunity for all . . . is a responsibility we pass on to our children, coming closer with each generation to what we know America should be." The American Dream, Obama explained, is what "I want for you—to grow up in a world with no limits on your dreams and no achievements beyond your reach. And I want every child to have the same chances to learn and dream and grow and thrive you girls have."[1]

Barack Obama's words echo the hopes for America's children expressed by U.S. presidents and politicians for more than one hundred years. Beginning with Theodore Roosevelt's 1909 White House Conference on the Care of Dependent Children, measuring the welfare of America's youngest citizens served as a litmus test for assessing the nation's progress in meeting its highest ideals. Talking about the anticipated effects of new policies on children is a popular tool for arguing both for and against proposed reforms. In a broad context, throughout U.S. history various groups of adults asked the federal government to protect an individual's right to independence, self-determination, and autonomy as the best means for ensuring access to the American Dream.[2] For the nation's youngest citizens in the twentieth century, however, instead of arguing for greater independence and expanded individual rights, child welfare advocates asked the federal government in cooperation with the states to provide a protected dependency as every child's right. In other words, modern child welfare policy in the United States is built on the idea that it is a federal/state responsibility to enforce every child's right to a protected dependency as the key to securing equality of opportunity and thereby access to the American Dream. But in practical reality, the result is a U.S. child welfare system that is more pluralistic than uniform. In addition, policymakers, politicians, and the American public continue to struggle with balancing protections for children, and the perceived rights and values that are part of the nation's history.

The United States became an early leader in shaping children's relationship to the modern nation state when President William Howard Taft signed legislation establishing the U.S. Children's Bureau (Stat. L., 79) on April 9, 1912. This federal agency was the first in the world to focus solely on a nation's youngest citizens. The legislation mandated that the bureau "investigate and report . . . upon all matters pertaining to the welfare of children and child life among all classes of our people." The agency's creation acknowledged children as a distinct age cohort in need of special attention from the federal government. Its first two decades of work focused on defining cooperation between the federal and state governments with help from private philanthropies. Early initiatives were designed to help reduce the nation's high infant mortality rate, improve child health, end most forms of exploitive child labor, and promote the use of birth certificates. Birth certificates were important because they certified an individual's age as the determining factor for accessing the right to government-protected childhood dependency. In the early twentieth century, states and local governments held the responsibility for implementing and controlling child welfare policies, while the federal government's U.S. Children's Bureau lobbied for uniform standards and promoted a universal definition of a protected childhood as a civil right.[3]

By the 1930s, the New Deal opened the door for expansion of direct federal intervention in child welfare. Most important, passage of the 1935 Social Security Act (SSA) codified a universal dependent and protected status from birth through age seventeen in federal law for the first time.[4] The SSA also included the most important federal programs for children that continued to be the core of U.S. child welfare policies throughout the twentieth century.

At the turn of the twenty-first century, the modern ideal of childhood dependency is a fundamental part of the relationship between American children and the state. However, as President Obama's words suggest, that embrace did not secure universal access to the American Dream. In 2009, the U.S. Census Bureau counted 15.5 million American children living in poverty, one out of every five individuals under eighteen years of age. This is an improvement over the 1960 rate of just under 25 percent, but is clear evidence of weaknesses in the U.S. child welfare system.[5] Furthermore, a 2009 study showed that economic mobility in the United States ranks behind Canada, Norway, Sweden, Denmark, France, Spain, and Australia: 42 percent of children living in households in the bottom fifth of U.S. income levels are likely to remain in poverty as adults.[6] It is also revealing that a 2006 public opinion poll found, "for the first time in the nation's history, a majority of Americans believe that the next generation will fare worse than their parents." An unemployment rate since 2008 of just under 10 percent further adds to the public's anxiety about the viability of the American Dream.[7]

A variety of social and economic factors in the United States contribute to the mixed results of the more than century-long effort to establish a nation where every child has equality of opportunity. Part of the explanation for this situation is also ideological. Americans have not fully reconciled the idea of a government-protected childhood dependency from birth through adolescence in the context of traditional American values celebrating independence, individual responsibility, and individual achievement. On the flip side, American ideals may subconsciously equate dependency with incompetence and diminished value. Since 1945, the federal government's role as the ultimate protector of children's dependency expanded, but, as Obama's 2009 pledge to his daughters and all American children suggests, the ideal of providing greater equality of opportunity for every child to achieve the American Dream is still a work in progress.

Defining the American Dream for Children
in a Modern America

In the midst of the Great Depression, the historian James Truslow Adams explained that the American Dream was not simply about becoming rich. Instead, like the stories of Horatio Alger, Jr.'s popular nineteenth-century adolescent heroes, Adams argued that the American Dream rested on the idea of opportunities for self-betterment through education, hard work, personal integrity, and a little luck. The United States was "a land in which life should be better and richer and fuller for everyone, with opportunity for each according to ability or achievement." The American Dream was "not a dream of motor cars and high wages." Instead, the vision involved "a social order where everyone shall be able to attain to the fullest stature of which they are innately capable, and be recognized . . . for what they are, regardless of the fortuitous circumstances of birth or position."[8]

The idea that securing this level playing field for all children was a federal responsibility paralleled the rise of a broader role for the federal government in the daily lives of all Americans. The transition to a modern economy heightened this trend over the twentieth century. In 1900, federal and state spending made up about 7 percent of the Gross Domestic Product (GDP); it rose to 11 percent by 1950 and was more than 33 percent by 2010. The rise in federal spending was partly spurred by arguments that government should play a role in providing the level playing field needed to access the American Dream. Nonetheless, as suggested earlier, children were not necessarily benefited as much as other groups in this expansion in federal spending. Some critics argue that government funding for child welfare is inadequate because children are not voters. Other policy analysts conclude that the limitations of the American semi-welfare state highlight structural weaknesses that cannot be fixed by mere tweaks in government programs originally framed to meet the needs of adults. Judith Sealander maintains in *The Failed Century of the Child* that despite "an unprecedented American effort" in the twentieth century, the United States "did not meet its own goals . . . to use state regulation to guarantee health, opportunity, and security to the country's children." Ultimately, good intentions were thwarted by "inconsistent expectations of government." While Americans "lauded democracy . . . they also embraced prejudices that divided society by race, ethnic origins, class, and gender."[9]

The argument that only a single federal agency could effectively advocate on behalf of "the whole child" was a philosophy promoted by the U.S. Children's Bureau's leadership as key to successful child welfare policy. However, from the beginning the idea was not a reality. For example, responsibility for promoting public policy in schools remained with the Bureau of Education even as the U.S. Children's Bureau first opened its doors. Most important, after only a few years of bureau operation, the Public Health Service (PHS) relentlessly criticized the agency's child health work as inappropriate. Interestingly, the Children's Bureau's successes at expanding federal responsibility for child welfare in the New Deal ended up undermining the agency's "whole child" philosophy. In 1946, President Harry Truman's administration reorganized the federal government. The new structure prioritized function over constituency. The Children's Bureau was moved to a lower rung in the federal hierarchy within the new Federal Security Agency and its administrative authority for children's programs was transferred to other agencies. The reorganization also removed "U.S." from the bureau's name, which seemed to symbolize its diminished influence and the federal government's rejection of the "whole child" philosophy. Children no longer had a single agency to lobby on their behalf at the federal level. Programs for children competed for the attention of bureaucrats and politicians primarily responsible for the concerns of adults. Despite a growth in federal spending on child welfare, state governments retained significant power, which contributed to inequality in the implementation of social welfare programs directed at children. This structure also led to dramatic clashes between federal and state authorities over important issues affecting children after 1945: desegregation, expanding economic social welfare, debates over criminal justice policies, immigration, and health care.[10]

Despite the dismemberment of the "whole child" philosophy in 1946, expanding the power of the federal government to build a more level playing field for securing children's access to the American Dream was a laudable goal that achieved some success. In the decades after the Second World War, the U.S. population more than doubled (from 150 to 308 million). Americans under age eighteen became a smaller proportion of the total, but a more visible group in terms of public policy. A 2007 Urban Institute study reported federal spending on Americans under eighteen rose from $55 billion in 1960 to $354 billion in 2007 (adjusted for inflation). This is an increase from 1.9 to 2.6 percent of GDP.[11]

With the onset of the Cold War, politicians and the public became hyperfocused on promoting the ideals of the American Dream in the world's largest democracy, and children were an essential part of rhetoric surrounding hyperpatriotism. The Allied victory bolstered Americans' confidence. Democracy was intensely equated with justice, individual freedom, and opportunity for all, in contrast to negative perceptions about communism's lack of opportunity for young people. The ability to sustain a more stable economy after the initial traumas of conversion from a wartime to peacetime economy also lifted the national spirit and suggested that children's lives were more secure than that of earlier generations. By 1950 unemployment averaged only 4 percent, an 84 percent decrease from historic heights in the Great Depression. Unemployment rose again by the late 1950s, but never reached the levels of the Great Depression decade. Family stability also looked strong: 87 percent of American households included married couples and 58 percent included children. On average, families had more money than in the 1930s and spent only 68 percent of household income for food, clothing, and housing. This was a 16 percent decrease from the mid-1930s. Perhaps most important as a visible part of the postwar American Dream, home ownership rose from 20 to 48 percent.

These data hid the reality that in 1960 more than a quarter of all Americans lived in poverty, with children the most likely of all age cohorts to be poor. The New Deal's programs and expansion in the postwar years helped lift many from the ranks of the poor, but benefits were not equally distributed across age groups. Federal spending increasingly favored the old over the young. Programs directed at Americans sixty-five years and older quadrupled from 2.0 to 7.0 percent of GDP from 1960 to 2007, three times more than funding spent on the nation's youngest citizens in the same period.[12] In addition, the child welfare system relied on the states to partially match and fully implement federal programs directed at children. This, as Judith Sealander argues, resulted in systematic pluralism rather than uniformity. In contrast, federal programs for Americans over sixty-five, such as Social Security's old age pension and the 1965 Medicare program, do not require matching funding or bureaucratic oversight by the states.[13]

Roots of the Modern Ideal of Childhood
Dependency in Public Policy

At its core, the history of U.S. public policy reveals a complicated relationship between citizens and their government, especially for children. For most of the nation's history, agriculture dominated the economy and families lived in rural settings or small towns. Children were legal dependents of their parents (specifically fathers), but also important contributors to their families' economic survival.[14] At the extremes, many young people were responsible for their own support if orphaned or neglected and adolescents fit a fluid category based on physical capacity rather than age. In the early nineteenth century the spread of public schools and limited public support for orphans and abandoned children led to the idea that local and state governments had a role in children's lives. However, the federal constitution said nothing about the government's responsibility for establishing discrete rights, privileges, or responsibilities for the nation's youngest citizens.[15] There was no federally protected right to childhood dependency.

The modern definition of a protected American childhood from birth through age seventeen was a new ideology that entered popular culture in the mid-nineteenth century. This ideal of a modern protected childhood was rooted in the expanding urban middle class, and took many decades before it was accepted as the normative experience for all American children. In the same period, a national trend toward smaller families met advances in medical knowledge and public sanitation to lower child mortality rates and lengthen life expectancy. These shifts made children a shrinking segment of the population, but more visible. Advanced education became more important and a symbol of a family's middle-class status. Consequently, many parents extended their children's dependent status for longer periods of time—through high school and college. Rather than spending their days in one-room schoolhouses, laboring on the family farm, or working for wages, the children of the urban middle class spent much of their time sitting in age-graded classrooms supported by public funds. By the late nineteenth and early twentieth centuries, social workers, psychologists, and educators promoted this middle-class ideal as the model for *all* children. Advocates maintained that government intervention was the best way to guarantee a universal protected childhood as a civil right in the world's largest democracy. Therefore, guaranteeing children's security and equality of opportunity through government-protected dependency was equated with fostering the American Dream for each new generation.[16] Within this ideological construct, state and local governments established and expanded institutions providing services for children. Rural communities, especially in the Jim Crow South, lagged behind. But rhetoric about protecting children's interests as a moral and civil right became fully engrained in discussions about the future of public policy by the early twentieth century.

In 1909 President Theodore Roosevelt recognized a federal responsibility for protecting childhood by calling for the first White House Conference on the Care of Dependent Children. Roosevelt's initial meeting was the first of seven decennial White House meetings on children's issues that took place once each decade from 1909 to 1970. Roosevelt justified this unprecedented federal outreach by arguing, "The interests of the nation are involved in the welfare of this army of children no less than in our great material affairs." The 1909 conference's final report formalized government rhetoric promoting a protected and dependent childhood as the right of every young American and called for the establishment of a federal children's bureau.[17] Shifts in public policies at the state level also signaled changes highlighting policymakers' acceptance of the idea that it was at least partly government's responsibility to protect an extended dependency of childhood through adolescence.[18] New laws restricting the minimum age of marriage were evidence of this change in popular culture. By the mid-1930s, every state in the nation restricted the right of individuals under sixteen, and under eighteen for males in some jurisdictions, to marry without parental consent. Marriage was clearly viewed as a privilege of adult independence and denied to individuals considered to still be in a dependent status. By the 1930s it was clear that age, not physical capacity or individual circumstance, marked the shift from childhood dependency to adult independence.[19]

The U.S. Children's Bureau led the drive to incorporate the new ideology about government responsibility and public policies throughout the country. The agency conducted, published, and distributed social science research about the diversity of experience in the lives of young Americans, advocated best practices for protecting children's welfare, lobbied to curtail exploitive child labor, and educated mothers and professionals about modern health care practices. Initially, the agency also collaborated with other federal offices such as the Bureau of Education and the PHS. But soon turf battles strained relations with the PHS, especially after passage of the 1921 Sheppard-Towner Maternity and Infancy Act. The PHS recognized the need for improving child and maternal preventive health care, but charged that such efforts should be under the control of male doctors in the PHS rather than the female-dominated Children's Bureau.[20]

The PHS continued to be a formidable opponent to the Children's Bureau's philosophy that a single agency should control all aspects of child welfare policy. In the early 1930s, Children's Bureau research showed that young Americans were hit hard at the onset of the Great Depression. By the winter of 1932, many states and municipalities simply ran out of funds for the minimalist child welfare programs that developed in the late nineteenth and early twentieth centuries. School districts reduced their terms or closed. Malnutrition and homelessness was most common among children, as charities and the American Red Cross were overwhelmed with requests for help. After the 1932 presidential election, the Children's Bureau and its supporters urged Franklin Roosevelt to respond. The New Deal generally targeted adults, but children benefited when fathers and mothers earned paychecks from the Works Progress Administration (WPA) and other federal work-relief programs. The WPA and similar initiatives also built thousands of modern age-graded schools, playgrounds, and other recreational facilities that reinforced the modern childhood ideal as something that should be accessible to all young Americans. [21]

The New Deal Civilian Conservation Corps (CCC) offered two million sixteen-, seventeen-, and eighteen-year-old boys, and young men the opportunity to learn middle-class standards of behavior and values while they earned money to help their parents and siblings. Many also joined the middle class while in the CCC, at least in status, by earning a high school diploma (General Educational Development Alternative). The National Youth Administration (NYA), another popular New Deal program, carried the idea of advanced education as a universal value even further by including girls as well as boys. The NYA is a good example of the growing acceptance of the idea of extending childhood dependency through adolescence and beyond. The program required participants to remain in school and live with their parents or a guardian through high school and even college. The popular embrace of this shift in thinking is visible in the fact that for the first time in American history, half of all seventeen year olds graduated from high school in 1937. The trend for remaining in school for longer and longer periods continued through the postwar years, even though the CCC and NYA ended in 1943.[22]

Besides defining childhood dependency in federal law, passage of the 1935 Social Security Act (SSA) created an economic social welfare safety net that included specific federally funded programs for children. The act's Title IV Aid to Dependent Children (ADC) section spelled out the federal-state partnership on a model similar to the state-based mothers' pension systems established in the early twentieth century. The original ADC limited benefits to children born to "worthy" mothers, judged by community values of morality that also allowed states to exclude families based on negative racial, ethnic, and class stereotypes. Children living with single fathers were not eligible, nor were those born outside marriage, or children whose parents divorced.

Title V was another part of the SSA that was also informed by an earlier child welfare program, in this case, the 1921 Sheppard-Towner Act. In some ways Title V was broader than its predecessor, but also contained aspects that were more limited. It provided federal funds for actual health care for mothers and babies living in poverty, but was not available to all children. Title V also neglected the broad educational effort that was key to the effectiveness and popularity of the Sheppard-Towner Act.

Title VII expanded federal outreach by creating funding for "crippled" children, but again it only went so far. The definition of "crippled" did not include all disabilities (notably, deafness was not considered a handicap). Furthermore, the implementation of all SSA programs depended on state cooperation, matching funds from state legislatures, and opened the door for unevenness as programs were applied. Despite these obvious weaknesses, the children's sections of the SSA's most important contribution was the formalization of federal responsibility for protecting children's right to dependency from birth through seventeen.[23]

The 1938 Fair Labor Standards Act (FLSA) also recognized children's special dependent status in federal law. The legislation prohibited the employment of children under fourteen and regulated wage-based employment of sixteen- and seventeen-year-olds. While this suggests a universal application of children's right to dependency, children laboring in agriculture or domestic service were not covered.[24]

The shifts in child welfare policy in the New Deal reveal a general acceptance of a significant federal role in children's lives. Children should be treated differently from adults, but as President Roosevelt explained in 1935, all programs were limited by the idea that most Americans did not want "a paternalistic system which tries to provide security for everyone from above . . . [this] calls for an impossible task and a regimentation utterly uncongenial to the spirit of our people."[25] The idea of government dependency, even for children, made many Americans uncomfortable.

Although tempered by American values celebrating independence and personal responsibility, by the mid-twentieth century Americans understood that the answer to the question "How Old Are You?" was a major indicator of an individual's relationship to the state. The American childhood ideal also influenced international policies directed at children. The end of the Second World War drew international attention to the exceptional vulnerability of the world's children. On November 20, 1959, the UN General Assembly adopted the Declaration of the Rights of the Child. The document pointed to many of the same concepts outlined in American child welfare policy. The document was also built on ideas spelled out in the 1948 Universal Declaration of Human Rights, but noted, "the child by reason of his physical and mental immaturity, needs special safeguards and care, including appropriate legal protection, before as well as after birth." Furthermore, the 1959 declaration explicitly acknowledged that governments had a special responsibility to guarantee children a status of dependency not given to adults. "The child shall enjoy special protection, and shall be given opportunities and facilities, by law and other means, to enable him to develop physically, mentally, morally, spiritually and socially in a healthy and normal manner and in conditions of freedom and dignity." Only "in enactment of laws for this purpose, the best interests of the child shall be the paramount consideration" (Principle 2). The Declaration did not guarantee opportunity and freedom from exploitation for all children, but it brought the language of children's dependency as defined in the United States to an international platform. Americans were not the only nation adopting the model of an extended and protected childhood dependency. Some countries, such as Sweden as explained by Bengt Sandin in this volume, developed even more extensive child welfare systems. In 1989 the UN revised the 1959 charter as the Convention on the Rights of the Child. Somewhat ironically, the U.S. refused to sign the treaty, but mainly for reasons more related to international politics than directly connected to the ideology of childhood.[26]

Cold War Kids, Housing, Schools, and the American Dream

For its first hundred years of existence, the United States was a young nation with about half its population seventeen or younger. As the twentieth century approached, birth rates fell, life expectancy rose, and immigration increased, resulting in a continuous rise in the nation's median age. By 1940, children and teens made up only 24 percent of the total population. As the war helped lift the economy out of the Great Depression, young adults had more children, and by the end of World War II birth rates rose. In 1964, at the end of the period known as the baby boom era, children and teens comprised 36 percent of the U.S. population. At the height of this significant demographic change, a Population Clock installed in the lobby of the Department of Commerce in Washington, D.C., noted the birth of a new American citizen approximately every 7.5 seconds. Even with limited immigration, the overall U.S. population climbed from approximately 140 million in 1945 to just under 192 million in 1964, including more than 76 million children and teens.[27]

The Servicemen's Readjustment Act, signed by Franklin Roosevelt on June 22, 1944, was an important platform for spreading the modern childhood ideal in the postwar era. This significant legislation, popularly known as the GI Bill of Rights, changed the American economy by making middle-class security more likely for a larger share of children and their families than ever before. Benefits paid to male military veterans included health care, housing assistance, unemployment compensation, loans for small businesses, funding for college tuition or vocational training, and a stipend of up to $90 a month for married military veterans. Women and children benefited as dependents. Enrollments at the nation's colleges and universities exploded with the wave of returning GIs and the growing pool of new high school graduates.[28] Most students were the first in their families to spend any time in college, much less earn a degree. In the postwar years, well-paid union jobs in factories and the skilled trades increasingly demanded at least high school education. By the end of the twentieth century, Americans constituted the best-educated workforce in the world and a college degree served as the major marker of membership in the middle class.[29]

The GI Bill and other federal programs eased the transition from a wartime to a peace-time economy. Rising economic security encouraged young adults to marry and have children. The GI Bill's housing benefits, along with similar programs offered by the Federal Housing Administration (FHA), expanded the pool of first-time home buyers. A lack of residential construction during the Great Depression and war years created a short supply of affordable housing. New developments like Levittown on Long Island, New York, Levittown, Pennsylvania, and in New Jersey were models of a postwar suburban lifestyle focused on young families with children. Critics derided such suburbs for their dull conformity and discriminatory "redlining" practices barring blacks, Hispanics, and low-income whites. Redlining kept all but a few of the new neighborhoods—and therefore, local schools—racially, culturally, and socially segregated.[30] Still, despite this ugly history, the new suburbs shaped the lives of millions of young baby boomers in an image of middle-class prosperity that served as the framework of the American Dream. Such communities acted as magnets for families and their Cold War kids. As one

Levittown resident remembered growing up in the 1950s and 1960s, "Seems like every family in the early days of Levittown had a bunch of young kids. There were hundreds of kids in my neighborhood. It was not unusual for many of the families you know to have 4, 5 or 6 kids."[31]

Entrepreneurs like Abraham Levitt and his two sons William and Alfred used mass building techniques in their communities that sped up construction and kept costs low. They also took advantage of the government mortgage programs encouraging home ownership for young families. Of course children did not sign home loans, but they directly benefited from this public and private partnership. Houses in the Levittowns sold for only $7,990 at a time when the national average annual household income rose to over $4,200. In addition, buyers needed $90 or less to close a deal. Most developments included Cape Cod, colonial, and ranch style houses. The designs encouraged families to sit together in the living room while watching a seven-inch television that came standard with each house. Living rooms also had a large picture window overlooking a ubiquitous suburban front lawn. Houses included a modern kitchen equipped with a refrigerator, electric stove, and washing machine. Young mothers were attracted to such domestic conveniences as well as a kitchen sink under a window with a view of the children's backyard play space. Most units had only one bathroom and two bedrooms, but many also had a sloped ceiling attic that could be converted into additional bedrooms for a total living space of just under 1,000 square feet. Families needed the extra room because they were generally larger than those of their parents' generation. Popular advertising and network television provided images of the ideal with lots of children playing a big part in the postwar suburban lifestyle. On television, children lived in picture-perfect suburbs or comfortable small towns where they spent days in school and playing with peers. Dads were part of their children's lives on weekends. Gender roles were clearly defined. Women were housewives and men used gasoline-powered lawnmowers and barbequed on outdoor grills, or spent time working on hobbies in each household's one-car garage.[32]

Postwar marriage rates peaked in 1950 at 11.1 per 1,000 population and only dropped below 10.0 in the 1980s, where the rate has remained into the twenty-first century. But marriage stability was growing more elusive. The divorce rate doubled from 2.6 per 1,000 population in 1950 to 5.2 in 1980. Divorce rates declined after 1980, but the percentage of adults who chose to never marry rose.[33] Housing was important to the lives of all American families, especially as school-based education through high school continued to gain value in the Cold War years.

Schools were the primary institution linking the state and the child after 1945. Residents in the nation's new communities expected local officials to build new, modern, age-graded schools to accommodate the wave of baby boomer children and teens. Building on the trend that expanded in the 1930s, graduating from high school was the norm for the age cohort called "teenagers" in the Cold War era. The negative descriptive "dropout" also entered the American lexicon.[34]

Despite the "happy days" image of the postwar years perpetuated on television, the expansion of age-graded schools also highlighted the inequities in American public education. The poor quality of most public schools serving black children and teens as well as other minorities contradicted the rhetoric about democracy creating universal access to the American Dream. A long history of challenges to the separate but equal doctrine was spelled out in the Supreme Court 1896 decision in *Plessy v. Ferguson*. President Truman's decision in 1947 to desegregate the U.S. military through an executive order raised questions about continued racial segregation in all government facilities, including the nation's schools. Change did not come, however, until the court's 1954 reversal of *Plessy* in the seminal *Brown v. Board of Education, Topeka, Kansas* case.[35] For a growing number of Americans, eliminating racial segregation in schools was the next major step toward ending racism as an obstacle in the pathway to the American Dream. As the Supreme Court explained in the *Brown* decision, public education "is a right that must be provided to all on equal terms." The *Brown* case reinvigorated civil rights activists and served as a model for calls from other minorities hindered by poor quality educational facilities. For example, in 1974, congressional hearings and student protests drew attention to the limited education available to American Indian children living on reservations. This resulted in a change in federal Indian policy that had endured for more than forty years.[36]

Children, teens, and youth played important roles in fostering the dramatic social and political change in postwar America rooted in the Black Civil Rights movement and calls for expanded civil rights by other minority groups. The 1955 murder of fourteen-year-old Emmett Till by two white men in Money, Mississippi, grabbed the attention of young Americans throughout the United States. Racial violence against black males was nothing new, but as Rebecca de Schweinitz argues, the murder of young Till "marked a decided shift from earlier lynching cases in which whites murdered blacks who supposedly transgressed racial boundaries or otherwise posed a threat to the white community." Till grew up in Chicago, attended a desegregated school, and was geographically separated from the South's Jim Crow codes of behavior. Till's mother, Mamie Till Bradley, decided to display her murdered child's battered body in an open casket funeral. The media covered the funeral and *Jet Magazine* featured a photo of Till's grotesquely disfigured body. The mainstream white media also emphasized the crime's brutality perpetuated on a child. Roy Wilkins, head of the National Association for the Advancement of Colored People (NAACP), announced, "It would appear from this lynching that the state of Mississippi has decided to maintain white supremacy by murdering children." Even if Till had breached accepted social norms by "whistling after looking at a white woman," Money's white deputy sheriff, John Cothran, reported that even "the white people around here feel pretty mad about the way that poor little boy was treated."[37]

Rhetoric emphasizing the vulnerability of children, even black children, in a nation that believed it had defeated the worst ethnic and racial prejudice perpetrated by the Nazis, became a major tool of the modern civil rights movement. It is significant that at age fourteen Till was viewed as a child, not a man-boy, not because he was black, but because his age placed him in the category of childhood dependency. In comparison, the media described all the black adolescent defendants in the 1930s Scottsboro case as "boys," referring to their race and not their childhood dependency as teens.[38] As Till's case shows, by the 1950s the term "children" referred to anyone who fell within the federal definition of childhood dependency. The struggles of the Black Civil Rights movement became the most visible evidence of the need for greater intervention by the state, meaning the federal government, to protect the universal right to a protected and dependent childhood for all young Americans.

Schools, of course, were the most visible arm of the government in children's lives. Nevertheless, schools were under local and state control, not federal authority. The Supreme Court altered that situation through the *Brown* decision. It is not surprising that schools were and continue to be the major battleground involving debates over the proper relationship between the child and the state. This was especially true in the fight to desegregate America's schools.[39] Violent protests by pro-segregationists followed a decision in Anderson County, Tennessee, to obey a 1956 federal desegregation order that followed the *Brown* decision. As a gesture of compliance with the ruling, county school officials allowed twelve black students to attend the formerly all-white Clinton High School. It appeared that racial tensions had quieted by May, 1957, when Clinton's Bobby Cain became the first black student in the South to graduate from a formerly all-white high school. The next October, however, several sticks of dynamite were exploded in the school, which severely damaged the building. White and black students supported by their parents responded by attending classes in nearby Oak Ridge. CBS television's Edward R. Murrow featured the story on his network program, *See It Now*. The students at Clinton and their parents were seen as examples of how some southerners supported the Supreme Court's efforts to level America's educational playing field as part of the Cold War era American Dream.[40]

The following fall semester, President Dwight Eisenhower committed the federal government to enforcing the *Brown* decision. He ordered the 101st Airborne Division to protect nine black teenagers trying to attend the formerly all-white Central High School in Little Rock, Arkansas. Media attention centered on the courageous "Little Rock Nine" rather than the shouting crowds of whites protesting outside the desegregated school. Julian Bond was seventeen at the time: "I was a happy-go-lucky teenager," he later recalled, whose "role models . . . were white teenagers . . . [that] danced five afternoons a week on ABC's *American Bandstand* . . . suddenly the nine brave young people of Little Rock's Central High School . . . replaced my former idols." Bond said he especially identified with high school senior Ernest Green, a member of the Little Rock Nine, "who seemed to me to represent everything a college-bound young man should be."[41]

Over the next few years, tensions dissipated in some communities, but rose in others. For example, in 1959 in Prince Edward County, Virginia, the school district closed its doors rather than desegregate. White school officials handed out tuition vouchers to white students that were accepted at newly organized private schools. Community leaders prevented any such educational opportunities for blacks until The Free School was finally organized in 1964. That same year, the Supreme Court ordered the reopening of all Prince Edward County schools. Discrimination and intimidation continued even after federal orders like the one directed at Prince Edward County. In 1965 only 12,000 of the more than 230,000 black students in Virginia attended desegregated schools.[42]

As these stories suggest, the focus on public schools placed children and teens across the South at the front lines of the fight to end racial segregation. On September 15, 1963, a bomb at Birmingham's Sixteenth Street Baptist Church forced Americans again to look at the brutality of discrimination and its toll on children. The bomb took the lives of four black girls: Denise Mc-Nair, Carole Robertson, Cynthia Wesley, and Addie Mae Collins. Birmingham police killed sixteen-year-old Johnny Robinson. Police shot Robinson as he was throwing rocks at white passengers in a car. Friends said Robinson was angry about the deaths of his peers, at the Baptist Church. In another incident following the bombing, two white teenage boys shot and killed Virgil Wade, a thirteen-year-old black boy living in Birmingham.

These violent attacks highlighted the hypocrisy of Cold War rhetoric touting the equality of opportunity for children in the world's most powerful democracy. The stories of abused and murdered children from Birmingham and elsewhere fueled sympathy for the civil rights movement. Diane Nash, a young black activist in Nashville, Tennessee, in the early 1960s explained it this way. "The media and history seem to record it as Martin Luther King's movement . . . young people should realize that it was people just like them, their age, that formulated goals and strategies and actually developed the movement."[43] Children, teens, and youths were not simply the targets of civil rights rhetoric and violence. They were activists and self-appointed symbols of resistance demanding a protected status for all American children as fundamental to making the American Dream a reality for everyone.

By the late 1970s, major resistance to desegregation of schools in former Jim Crow states calmed down, but court-ordered busing in northern cities led to passionate and violent protests. Some parents, both black and white, as well as students, fought forced busing plans and voiced concerns about government-imposed diversity. Meanwhile, demands for higher quality educational opportunities spread among various minorities. In 1968, Latino/a students in Los Angeles staged massive walkouts protesting inferior schools and ethnic discrimination. School officials prohibited students from speaking Spanish on school grounds and tracked the vast majority of Mexican Americans into vocational programs rather than college preparatory classes. The Young Citizens for Community Action and members of the Chicano Youth Leadership Conferences organized protests and led 20,000 students in a strike against the school district.[44]

The tide of protests by students died down by the 1980s, but controversies over education continued. By the last decades of the century, America's schools were both more diverse and at the same time more segregated by socioeconomic class. School shootings in places like San Diego, California's Cleveland School in 1970, and Colorado's Columbine High School in 1999 suggested that schools were also more dangerous than in the past. Simultaneously, private schools and home schooling gained popularity while adult perceptions of failing public schools and growing school violence rose. At the same time, high school and college degrees were more important for securing middle-class status than ever before. By the last decades of the century, debates about public schools focused less on desegregation and more on how the federal government could best shape school curriculums and measure outcomes as the best means for equalizing educational opportunities. Funding for schools largely remained the responsibility of state and local governments, but there was a growing call for more federal regulation.

The federal government played a limited role in the history of public schools in the United States until the Cold War. Unlike countries like Sweden, schools in the United States are considered the responsibility of state and local governments. The federal government contributes only 3 percent of general funding for schools. Local school districts benefited from federal spending during the Great Depression and World War II, but that money generally disappeared immediately after the war. The onset of the Cold War, however, became the impetus for some new federal intervention in K-12 curriculums.[45] The expanded number of students in the baby-boom years meant that by the 1960s most suburban districts were overcrowded and underfunded. Interestingly, rural and urban school districts faced the opposite problem: declining student populations and diminishing revenue. A combination of white flight from the cities to the suburbs, deindustrialization, decline in family farms, and an increasing concentration of students from poor and disadvantaged families in urban and rural schools made the wide disparities in school quality a hot issue.[46]

In the 1960s sociologists and liberal activists focused new attention on poverty as a major hurdle hindering children's academic success, and their access to equality of opportunity. The Head Start Program, established in 1964 as part of Lyndon Johnson's War on Poverty programs, helped prepare preschoolers from low-income families to successfully compete in elementary school with peers from more privileged backgrounds. Debates over the federal government's role in children's education continued, but Head Start is generally seen as a success story. Concern that American students were falling behind their Soviet peers included criticism of unfit young bodies as well as minds. In response, Eisenhower established the President's Council on Physical Fitness Program in the late 1950s and President John F. Kennedy expanded the effort. Elementary and junior high school–aged children across America participated in games that measured their ability to perform to a prescription of established physical standards. Those that met the challenges earned a President's Council on Physical Fitness Badge. The attention to physical fitness and civil rights merged in 1972 when the Education Act included Title IX, mandating greater gender equality in public school and university sports as well as academic curriculums. Eighteen years later the 1990 Americans with Disabilities Act required equal opportunity for children with mental and physical handicaps in accessing public schools. By the 1990s, public schools were simultaneously chastised and praised as central components in a protected American childhood dependency. Debates over curriculum, teacher quality, and safety intensified. The heated controversies led a growing number of parents to opt out and instead choose to home school, or send their children to expensive private schools.[47]

The 1950s and 1960s cemented the central role of grade- and age-based education in the lives of American children and teens. Compulsory school attendance laws established in most states by the late nineteenth century took on greater importance after the Second World War as access to quality education was embraced as essential for achieving equality of opportunity. Schools were the portal for addressing what the U.S. Children's Bureau identified, as early as 1912, as the needs of "the whole child." Federal law mandated greater attention to standardized curriculums and learning outcomes. The legacy of the Cold War's effects on education is evidenced in passage of the 2001 No Child Left Behind Act (NCLB). Critics warned that the legislation forced schools to "teach to the test," narrowed the curriculum to reading and math, and ignored the diverse needs of individual students. Supporters said the law helped to improve the quality of teachers and raised standards for all students, not just those lucky enough to live in the more privileged and well-funded districts. The debate over NCLB continues, but the Obama administration has shifted the program's funding mandates. A brief search of an online bookstore for the phrase "No Child Left Behind" revealed more than 6,000 books published since 2001.[48]

The story of public schools in children's lives since 1945 is mixed. Many American schools are more racially and ethnically diverse than they were sixty years ago. But today's classrooms are more highly segregated by socioeconomic class. Others are racially and ethnically segregated at levels comparable to the days prior to the *Brown* decision. Overall, American student achievement levels rank behind those of many other wealthy nations. A 2008 United Nations study found that "one-quarter of fifteen-year-old students in the United States scored at or below the lowest proficiency level on an international test of mathematics literacy." Expenditures per pupil range from $14,000 per student in New York and New Jersey to $6,000 in Utah. Students attending schools with a high proportion of children from families living

below or near the federal poverty line are more likely to be taught by uncer-
tified teachers than young people in schools with a higher proportion from
more privileged families. Poor children in urban and rural communities are
more likely than students attending suburban schools to drop out of high
school before earning a diploma. Public schools are the foundation of the
relationship between the child and the state since 1945, but debates over the
best means for heightening the benefits of that relationship for the nation's
young people continues as another generation moves quickly to adulthood.[49]
Times have changed, with 89 percent of eighteen- to twenty-four-year-olds in
the United States earning at least a high school diploma in the first decade of
the twenty-first century, and 67 percent immediately enrolling in college after
completing high school.[50]

The importance and rising cost of a college education is a major factor
in the lives of young Americans coming of age today. In 1940 less than 6
percent of adults earned at least a four-year college degree. In 2005, college-
educated Americans made up 28 percent of the population. An individual
young person's access to a college education is closely linked to his or her
family's socioeconomic status. Only 10 percent of students from the poorest quarter of American families earn a B.A. by the time they reach twenty-
four. Among the wealthiest quarter, the rate is 81 percent.[51] The increased
use of computer technology may widen or shrink such gaps in the future depending on whose crystal ball is correct. In 1984 only 8 percent of American
households had a computer; in 1997 the proportion was 37 percent. Ten years
later, the Census Bureau reported that 78 percent had at least one computer.
Among children aged three through seventeen, one study estimated the computer ownership rate was three of every four. Access to information is clearly
readily available to most children and teens, but questions remain about how
young seekers process the information they access and the guidance they receive about how best to apply it.[52]

Youth Violence, Juvenile Delinquency, and Antisocial Behavior

U.S. entrance into the Second World War intensified public demands for policymakers and politicians to do something to curb crime and antisocial behavior among adolescents and youth. Studies show that antisocial perceptions
about young people were increasingly higher than what the facts showed.

Nevertheless, the war years drew teens and youth into areas near military bases and war production facilities. The theaters, dance venues, and other public spaces that catered to young people's entertainment interests made their activities more visible to adults. In addition, many of these young people came from families hit hard by the Great Depression. The more prosperous wartime economy offered jobs, spending money, and greater autonomy. Concern about youthful "Khaki-Wacky Girls" and "Good Time Charlies" during the war was transformed into the images of motorcycle-riding and/or marijuana-smoking teens and youth in the postwar years. In the Cold War era, rising public anxiety about juvenile delinquency was showcased in the hearing of the 1950-1951 Senate Special Committee to Investigate Crime in Interstate Commerce. Chaired by Estes Kefauver (D-Tenn.), the committee concluded that movies and comic books were major contributors to antisocial behavior among young Americans.[53] Some adults called for censorship of the media, but over the long term, as other essays in this volume discuss, commercial interests, traditions concerning free speech in a democracy, and continuing new technologies made controlling young people's media exposure as public policy almost impossible.[54]

This public attention to juvenile antisocial behavior ran into an interesting constitutional twist by the 1960s. Some child advocates equated children's individual constitutional rights with that of other minority groups seeking access to the American Dream in the 1960s and 1970s. For the most part it made sense that children were a part of the trend broadening the rights of access to equality of opportunity through constitutional protections as civil rights. However, for the nation's youngest citizens, the growing emphasis on federal responsibility for protecting civil rights sometimes conflicted with the federally protected childhood dependency that had been the core of child welfare policy in the twentieth century. For example, in 1967 the Supreme Court reversed practices that had been in place in the nation's juvenile courts since 1899. The court declared that individuals under eighteen had the same procedural rights guaranteed to adults (*In re Gault*). This reversed the notion of protected dependency so dear to earlier child welfare advocates, who believed children's interests were best protected by establishing separate, but paternalistic, court proceedings that often ignored individual children's constitutional rights. This change, however, was consistent with the universal individual rights' rhetoric of the 1960s and 1970s. Six years later, in 1973, the Supreme Court went even further by ruling that the constitution also guaranteed juveniles the right to trial by jury (*McKeiver v. Pennsylvania*).[55]

An unforeseen negative backlash to these decisions manifested in calls to suspend all special rules for juveniles charged with violent offenses. The legal system's back and forth debates on this issue mirrored the nation's history of ambivalence about the definition of childhood dependency, especially for older adolescents. In 1973 the federal government reinstated the death penalty for convicted violent offenders. Initially, children convicted of such crimes seemed to be protected from the death penalty because their trials took place in juvenile courts. However, in 1989 the U.S. Supreme Court ruled that the death penalty was also an appropriate sentence for juveniles at least sixteen years of age, convicted of murder, and tried as adults. On its surface the 1989 decision seemed to suggest a return to a pre-1935 definition of childhood, at least for older adolescents, which recognized competency, independence, and its associated adult responsibilities and privileges. In 2005, the Supreme Court reversed itself on this issue, stating that a death sentence was cruel and unusual punishment for anyone under eighteen.

In November 2009, the issue was extended to questions about the justice of life sentences without parole for juvenile offenders. Only thirteen when he raped a seventy-two-year-old woman, Joe Sullivan was sentenced by a Florida court to life in prison without parole. Terrance Graham was sixteen when he was convicted of armed robbery; he served twelve months in juvenile detention, and then committed another violent robbery after his release. A Florida court also sentenced Graham to life without parole. Sullivan's attorney argued before the Supreme Court that "to say to any child of 13 that you are only fit to die in prison is cruel. . . . It cannot be reconciled with what we know about the nature of children. It cannot be reconciled with our standards of decency." In May 2010, the Court agreed in a 6-3 decision.[56]

The State of Children's Dependency
in the Twenty-First Century

The federal government has played an increasingly larger role in the lives of American children since 1945. Politicians made changes and adjustments to federal policies that broadened access to equal opportunity for many young people. For example, children of divorced parents, those living with single fathers, or youngsters living with a mother who never married gained eligibility for benefits through the SSA in the mid-1950s. However, morality tests for mothers remained through the 1960s. Controversies about foster care continue to make national headlines. Poverty rates among children began to decline after the enactment of the War on Poverty programs in the 1960s, but rose again after 1980. Decades of debate about the federal government's proper role in providing economic security for children culminated at the end of the century in President Bill Clinton's call "to end welfare as we know it." Passage of the Temporary Assistance to Needy Families Act (TANF) in 1996 revised the SSA's child welfare provisions, but did not alter the definition of childhood dependency from birth through age seventeen. TANF did, however, make some important changes in federal social welfare policies. It limited lifetime eligibility for federal aid to five years for adults, required that parents living below the poverty line work or attend job training in order to receive assistance for children, and expanded funding for day care. Perhaps the most interesting of these changes was a recognition that most American children lived in households with parent(s) who worked outside the home. The original SSA Aid to Dependent Children program was designed to keep mothers in poor families at home with their children. By the close of the twentieth century, the majority of all mothers worked outside the home.[57]

Since the 1970s the gap between rich and poor has expanded, and the American middle class has contracted. The shift to a global, and more technology- and service-driven economy further emphasizes the importance of a quality education as a means to greater equality of opportunity. At the end of the twenty-first century's first decade, the nation's poorest counties also had the lowest percentage of population over age twenty-five with bachelor's degrees (less than 10 percent); the wealthiest counties were among those with the highest percentage of college graduates (with the highest in Falls Church, Virginia, at 69.5 percent).[58] In contrast, the Netherlands' Bernard van Leer Foundation—charged with granting "foreign aid" to children and families in "oppressed societies"—funds an education project in remote Quitman County, Mississippi. The fact that a rural Mississippi community qualifies for aid from a Dutch foundation working to end child poverty is a clear irony for the wealthiest nation in the world.[59]

The rise in racial and ethnic diversity in the United States that strengthened in the postwar years continues to grow in the twenty-first century. Recent census data counts 56 percent white non-Hispanic; 22 percent Hispanic; 15 percent black; 4 percent Asian; and 5 percent "other races." Nearly 40 million immigrants entered the country since passage of the 1965 Immigration and Naturalization Act eliminated the racist and ethnically biased quota system in place since 1924 (National Origins Act). U.S. immigration policy since

1965 places priority on family reunification rather than nation of origin. Like immigrants throughout America's history, recent arrivals cite educational and economic opportunities for their children as the major reasons for coming to the country. However, the pattern of immigration has changed, since newcomers are flocking to the suburbs for jobs and better schools rather than following the late nineteenth- and early twentieth-century concentration in cities.[60] The resulting greater diversity across the U.S. population seems to be fostering tolerance as an American value. Although examples of intolerance persist, the election of the nation's first multiracial president in 2008, and passage of the December 22, 2010, legislation repealing the military's "Don't Ask Don't Tell" policy on homosexuality, suggests that there is a growing acceptance of diversity.[61]

Entering the twenty-first century, Hispanics are the fastest growing ethnic group in the country, rising from 9 percent in 1980 to an estimated 22 percent in 2010. A 2009 Pew Research Center report shows that one in four newborns and one in five school-aged children is Hispanic. The report also shows a significant complexity in the varied experiences among American Hispanic youth. Children in this group born in America to at least one immigrant parent are more likely to do better in the key economic, social, and acculturation indicators than foreign-born peers of the same age. On other measures of cultural assimilation, however, the reverse is true. The report notes, "native-born Latino youths are about twice as likely as foreign born to have ties to a gang or to have gotten into a fight or carried a weapon in the past year. They are also more likely to be in prison."[62]

In the area of children's health, young Americans are healthier overall. The results stem from government policies, more affordable and easily accessible food, as well as medical advances. For example, polio was the scourge of the early postwar years, but federal support for development of a vaccine made the disease a rarity for later generations. In recent decades there is great concern about rising obesity rates among American children, but new evidence suggests this trend may be stabilizing and that solving the problem among adults will directly benefit children.[63] The establishment of Medicaid in 1966 provided diagnostic and medical care for children living in poor families. By the 1990s, however, it was obvious that many parents above the poverty line needed help providing health care for their children. In 1997, President Bill Clinton and Congress expanded health care for children in needy families through the State Children's Health Insurance Program (SCHIP). In 2008, however, President George W. Bush vetoed plans to further expand the initia-

tive to families in the contracting middle class. Congress reversed that decision in 2009. Most significant, the Obama administration passed the nation's
first major health insurance reform in 2010. The Patient Protection and Affordable Care Act requires all Americans to carry health insurance, extends
coverage under parents' insurance plans for children into their twenties, and
prohibits insurance companies from denying coverage for preexisting conditions for children and adults. In the light of the growing national debt and
lagging economy, the 2010 election included calls by some politicians to repeal the new health care law. On January 5, 2011, incoming House majority
leader John Boehner (R-Oh.) announced that repealing "Obama care" was
his highest priority. While it is likely that the Republicans will not be able to
completely repeal the Obama health care reforms, the legislation will probably be revised and adjusted, similar to the Social Security Act. These changes
will directly affect children and their families. Illness and its associated costs
are the most common reason for families to fall into economic difficulty. And
as the child welfare advocates in the early twentieth century understood, the
right to a healthy childhood is a necessity in protecting children's access to
the American Dream.[64]

As Steven Mintz argues in his sweeping history of childhood in the
United States, "There has never been a time when the overwhelming majority of American children were well cared for and their experiences idyl-
lic." In the latter half of the twentieth century, protecting childhood through
government intervention became an ideal accepted as a key facet in shaping
a nation where greater equality of opportunity for accessing the American
Dream was a high priority. According to a 2008 *New York Times* poll, most
Americans like to believe that the United States is a place with "a level playing field, for anyone willing to dream big, work hard, and 'just do it.'" Yet,
a 2008 UN report found that, although "Americans are well aware that all
children do not share the same starting line," 80 percent believe that disad-
vantages of birth can be "overcome by hard work and perseverance." The UN
report concludes, "These somewhat contradictory findings highlight the gap
between the promise and practice of the American dream" in the modern
United States.[65] The African American civil rights movement and the federal
government's attention to the needs of groups previously left out of public
social policy initiatives, are evidence that the state can make a difference in
children's lives. Linda Perlstein's sensitive study of the NCLB program in an
Annapolis, Maryland, school reveals the complexities and consequences of
public policies shaped with the best intentions. Student scores improved, but

Perlstein shows that young people are not absorbing the skills for success in adulthood that education reformers intended by enacting NCLB.[66]

Many of today's problems among the nation's children mirror the same concerns thought to be on the way out in 1945. Despite the fact that U.S. per capita income ranks second in the world, its infant mortality rate is thirty-fourth and the country ranks only forty-second in overall life expectancy. The lack of a strong social and economic safety net for children and their families helps to explain why in human development measures counted by the UN America fell from second in 1980 to twelfth in 2005.[67] For students of U.S. public policy it is somewhat ironic that the nation that created some of the first federal social welfare legislation on behalf of children has not been the most successful in protecting the interests of its youngest citizens over time. The inability to reconcile traditional values of independence, self-sufficiency, and family autonomy with the modern definition of a protected childhood dependency continues to hinder access to the American Dream for all children. The break-up of the U.S. Children's Bureau in 1946 also left children without a strong voice in the federal government to advocate solely in their interest. History suggests that in order to achieve President Obama's wish for his daughters and all American children "to grow up in a world with no limits on [their] dreams and no achievements beyond [their] reach," demands a stronger bond between the state and children's interests independent of those prioritized for adults.[68]

7

Children and the Swedish Welfare State: From Different to Similar

Bengt Sandin

The twentieth century, it was once thought, would become "the century of the child." This was certainly how it was described by Swedish writer Ellen Key, who had clear ideas on how it was to be accomplished.[1] Regardless of later views on "the century of the child," it is clear that children were at the center of the Swedish welfare state's efforts to change society directly *and* indirectly. The welfare state was formed in the period immediately before and following the Second World War, which raises questions about contemporary views on children's roles and the meaning of childhood shifted, but also about who, or what, social and political interests opted for new definitions of childhood. The meaning of childhood, and the relationship between children, parents, society, and state, have been affected by the construction of the welfare state and the changes to it over a relatively long period.[2] In this chapter I analyze childhood within the welfare state in the light of a series of political issues that were crucial to the construction of the Swedish welfare system,[3] and how these issues interacted with professional and institutional interests. The roles of women and men were fundamentally reshaped by the emergence of the welfare state. Some scholars argue that Sweden has become a very individualistic society, governed by the relationship between the individual and the state; the phrase much used in this context is "state individualism." Studies of cultural systems around the world show that Sweden holds an extreme position as a individualistic and modernistic society that sets it apart from societies in which traditional values—religion, family, and so on—play a larger role, as for example in the United States.[4]

Clearly Sweden can be understood as a counter point to the U.S. in terms of attitudes to and provisions for children. The discussions about children and childhood are today largely international but are given different national interpretations. The UN Convention on the Rights of the Child has established a common framework, subject to interpretations and adoption at a national level, which creates unique meanings to the changes of childhood at national and regional levels as is very evident in Sweden since 1945.

The Swedish Welfare State—Formation and Change

The post-1945 period is distinctive in the history of Sweden for both the realization of the welfare system and its adaptation to changing political and economic conditions.

After the Second World War, Sweden became renowned as a welfare society. This idea originated with some important measures put in place earlier by the Social Democrats and their government coalition partners, but it was primarily after 1945 that the principles of a welfare system began to leave their mark on the everyday life of families and children. Welfare programs were initiated to combat the effects of the Depression of the 1930s, much in the same way the Keynesian approach characterized the Roosevelt administration. The war put the reform efforts on hold, subsuming them under the need to mobilize people and the economy. The war greatly affected Sweden even though the country was not directly a theatre of war. After the peace settlement Social Democrats proclaimed that it was time to reap the harvest sown before the war. The principles of the welfare society underwent a slow transformation into political programs, which were compromised and adjusted to create broad electoral bases that in turn became the basis for political decisions that were only implemented after much delay. Social Democrats dominated Swedish politics thanks to their strong electoral base and talent for creating political alliances; negotiations with their coalition partners in the political center were oriented toward broad consensus solutions.[5]

The welfare state was founded politically in Western-style democracy, with capitalism as its economic base. A growing economy, fueled by both tax and fiscal revenues, enabled the construction of welfare institutions. Welfare programs adopted from other countries were often applied more consistently in Sweden than in their nations of origin. Ideologically, the political mainstream, including the Social Democrats, had strong Western leanings with a particular bias toward things Anglo-American. The United States became a cultural model. The welfare system had sources of inspiration from progressive experiments in the U.S. and other Western countries, and it took a period of time—and an internal debate among the Social Democrats—to sort out the route to modernization. Sweden's education system was modelled on the American one, but the health system was based on a strong government commitment to provide care to all citizens. In the end welfare schemes intending to redress the needs of those on low incomes were framed to include everyone; they were defined as a response to social issues of a general nature so as not to stigmatize those in need. Beneficiaries of welfare support were, in reality, largely those with moderate incomes, who in due course became the broadened political base for the Social Democrats. Desperate to appeal to these voters, other political parties also embraced far-reaching welfare schemes at the same time as the Social Democrats embraced the middle classes and a position toward the political center.[6]

Swedes reaped the benefits of the new welfare state. Health improved significantly, schools attained similar levels for children of all social classes, and day care made it possible for women to participate more easily in the labor market. But it was only in the 1970s that some of the important, internationally symbolic facets of the celebrated system became a reality: generous maternal leave and sick benefits; a day care system that catered to all children; very generous housing subsidies that allowed a middle-class lifestyle; and an expanding university system based on student loans.

It was also during this period that the cost of the welfare system began to have economic consequences. Ironically, the celebrations of the welfare system's successes came on the eve of an economic crisis in the early 1990s that shook the foundations of the system, and forced the government to tighten spending and question some of the system's ambitions. Attempts to control the economy became the chief government objective in the 1990s, irrespective of political background; all claimed success, and in due course credit for the stabilization and improvement of Sweden's finances. The consequence was a modification of the levels of welfare support and, starting in the 1990s, a fundamental change in the character of state intervention and support with consequences into the new millennium.[7]

Children and Childhood Redefined—Trends

The difference between childhood and adolescence was of great interest in the early twentieth century, the period that saw a redefinition of the meaning of childhood based on the development of the educational system. Parenthood was also redefined for men and women alike. This transformation can of course be explained in terms of changes in the ideological climate, but more important were the social and political changes that set their stamp on the century and resulted in Sweden's so-called "child laws" on foster care, adoption, delinquency, and so forth. The legislation paralleled the development in most other Western nations during the epoch of child saving. The child laws laid down the framework for the protection, punishment, and regulation of children. Protection involved protection of society, and thus also created a fine line between protection and punishment. Childhood and youth became a time for schooling, and schooling the foundation for the definition of citizenship and its limits. Schooling made it possible to define the normal child and adolescent and thus establish what the educational system required of both parents and children. Childhood was characterized by important distinctions between children from different social classes and genders. The system of schools included different schools for different classes, and from the age of thirteen or fourteen also for the majority of boys and girls. This system created separated avenues to adulthood and was far from uncontroversial, as it was repeatedly questioned by the political left and center, that is, Communists, Social Democrats and Liberals.[8]

Some common traits characterized childhood as it was formed by the educational provisions and social policy. Childhood was seen as a period of limited capacities, and growth and adulthood the very norm to be attained in due time according to the system of socialization. Childhood was also, during the early twentieth century, shaped as a special part of life, and children were described as having distinctive features and special rights. In the realization of childhood, the parents also had specific roles: the female role of motherhood and the male role of breadwinner. These roles were seen as particularly important to transfer to families and children of the working classes by middle-class activists and ruling elites such as reformer Ellen Key. Knowledge of children was based on advances in the "child study movement" (national and international), and in behavioral science. Interest in children led to a huge number of new publications and journals, professional societies, and so on. The educational system would prove to be of great importance to the changes in the definition of childhood and to social programs dependent on the educational system.[9]

These developments also brought a need to specify the social commitments of the emerging welfare state at a central and local level, and to clarify the role of professionals in child care, particularly in relationship to children of the working classes. The concept of child saving was clearly directed toward urban and rural poor families and children. Philanthropic welfare organizations traditionally had their social base in upper-class philanthropy, but this shifted to professional groups during the first decades of the century, looking to financial support from local taxpaying communities, not just to political support in national politics. Steps were taken in civil society to tie organizations' ambitions to the creation of a welfare state and to national cooperation between local organisations.[10]

For a long period many initiatives and social services for children were implemented by nongovernmental organizations in a manner relatively free of conflict, but their ambitions, combined with those of the child care professionals and politicians, led them to seek full-scale state support during the 1930s, as did child and maternity clinics and school lunch programs. General welfare schemes replaced more selective measures. The state also aspired to act in loco parentis in protecting the best interests of the child; in a sense, the institutions' ambition to defend the social rights of children thus questioned the ability of the family to care for its children.[11] Thus the meaning of childhood was intimately associated with the welfare organization being created in Sweden during the twentieth century. The welfare state and its agencies would guarantee a good childhood through schools, social services, and family, with an ambition to be less selective and normative than the philanthropic organizations. It was to be a social right, the same for all, and in large measure irrespective of income and social standing.[12]

With the conclusion of the Second World War the coalition government was terminated and the Social Democrats looked to reap the benefits of prewar efforts. School reforms were extended and the state became active in family policy and support programs of a different kind, along with social and health programs aimed directly at supporting children. General welfare provisions for children were developed during the 1950s, but strong critical voices about conditions for children in state and private institutions also emerged in that decade. During the 1960s and 1970s children became the focal point of social reforms to sustain the population, counter the falling birth rate, and make the programmatic intentions of the welfare system a reality for a majority of children. Advocates of social engineering celebrated triumphs and could point to areas of the Swedish model's superiority: a minimal child death rate; decreasing class differences in health; expansion of health and care services for children; maternal and child leave allowances after childbirth; cheap, quality housing through housing subsidies—along with a relatively stable birth rate and increasing gender equality. The late 1970s through the 1990s were characterized by, in contrast to the U.S., a strong emphasis on the rights of children as individuals, state protection from abuse by parents and institutions, and the right to physical, mental, and emotional integrity.[13]

During the latter part of this period, however, the state began to deemphasize its role as a guarantor of rights. Children were still a central commitment, but the system of governance changed, with transferral of authority to community and civil society organizations. The changes in the relationship between government, families, and children formed the basis for the characterization of Swedish childhood in the years after 1945. I will trace that by discussing a number of thematic issues: the role of the state; the family as private or public sphere; the individualization and autonomy of children; children's physical and mental integrity and cultural and political agency; and the changing role of professionals and their effect on how childhood was defined. I will trace the consequent transformation of the definition of children from one that was different from that of adults to one that became the same. In the last section the changing role of the Swedish state will be discussed in relationship to globalization and the redefinitions of childhood and the children's rights in Sweden during the late twentieth- and early twenty-first centuries.

The Importance of the State

Childhood in Sweden evolved into a state venture. Even if we look upon the state as a combination of many actors and faces and at different political levels, the result was still that the state tended to address the needs of children through institutions and professionals that drew their legitimacy from the fact that they represented local or central government.[14] This new society was to be built on active and responsible children, little citizens in the making. Such emphasis on responsibility and growing was also an important aspect of the League of Nations charter of children's rights from the 1920s. However, in Sweden no coherent formulation of children's civil rights was expressed similar to, for example, President Herbert Hoover's charter of children's rights from 1930. This is evidenced by a 1944 government-issued pamphlet, *Svenska Barn i Bild* (*Images of Swedish Children*), that gives us an understanding of how children's rights were conceptualised. The pamphlet illustrates the social rights of children as protected and embraced by the state in its attempt to meet the goals of the population and health policies of the government.

Svenska Barn i Bild depicts the whole world of the Swedish child. The pamphlet, officially sanctioned, was produced by a committee of high-ranking civil servants, administrators, and politicians, of whom the most important was chairman of the Swedish Population Commission, Tage Erlander, who became leader of the Social Democratic Party and prime minister at the zenith of the postwar welfare state. The pamphlet makes claims about the history of children that sound very familiar. Unsurprisingly, it begins with a reference to Ellen Key and her vision of the century of the child, and later to her statement that marriage will be a private matter while children will be a public one. The proposed reforms drew on child psychology, concentrating on the first formative years of a child's life. This emphasis had created a new understanding of childhood, it was claimed. An older understanding of the child as a little adult gave way to one of the child as an independent being with particular qualities, and childhood as a period of life with its own characteristics. The organization of welfare at state and local levels is described in some detail; the contribution made by foundations and philanthropic organizations is also recognized. However, the authors declare, it is time for better, more coherent cooperation to ensure the long-term quality of child care under the motto "more children of better quality." Pictures show institutions and welfare provisions, child care professionals rather than parents, examples of order, control, supervision, inspection, good health and care, and children under the gaze of the professionals, but also children playing and interacting with each other. This is not the place to analyze the images, but they still serve to illustrate that the welfare institutions brought an increased will to display and visualize not only children but also childhood in the making—and for that matter, professionals in the making.

Svenska Barn i Bild amounted to an official version of Swedish childhood. It laid out the way it should be imagined and contextualized relative to population, housing, equality, and so on. Yet although it was clearly aimed at protecting children's social rights and access to their share of welfare, nowhere were these described in terms of the rights of the child. Nevertheless, it was a rather impressive list of reforms that directly benefited children and enabled postwar developments: among them, child guidance, maternity clinics, child welfare boards, and child representatives (*barnavårdsman*).[15]

Thus the history of the first half of the twentieth century was characterized in Sweden by increased professionalization of child care in its broadest sense. Professionalization made itself felt in child rearing within the family, and in the identified need of supporting institutions for children. In many respects, it also involved questioning the family's ability to meet society's demands regarding children and child rearing. Such questioning of the competence of the families was the upshot of social planning and views on childhood formed by the society's child experts. The larger social undertakings of school, family counseling, and parental education were expressions of this process, as were maternity and child care centers, with their clear intention to intervene in family life. Child rearing transcended the boundary between public and private. Child care and child welfare were definitely matters of public interest, a crucial arena just as worthy of state intervention and regulation as other sectors of society: the labor market, agriculture, and the like.[16] This intervention was conceptualized as an expression of the care and responsibility of the state for the youngest members of society. From a more theoretical perspective we can identify the development of an individualizing gaze invoked by the professions who earned their legitimacy by association with the state.[17]

Thus, in the early and mid-twentieth century the government was shaping a system of intervention to protect and care for children and grant them special treatment that emphasized the differences between child and adult. To be a child was to be partial and incomplete; childhood could be a dangerous period in the care of incompetent adults. In government inquiries into parental education and the need for kindergartens, nursery schools, and the like, some views on children and childhood held the family to be a problematic unit of socialization. State activities, with central agencies established to take care of such matters as children's environment, play, and so on, also give a clear idea of the way the state perceived its role as the children's safeguard in the face of parental neglect and abuse. This also involved mobilizing philanthropic organizations in support of family child care, and questioning parental competence. We will see that this process had unforeseen consequences; it changed the very meaning of childhood by redefining the way it was understood.

Welfare and Changes to Childhood

Vulnerable Childhoods and the Public and Private Divide

The notion of childhood as a vulnerable period underpinned educational thinking and reform during the latter part of the twentieth century. Swedish educator Torsten Husén argued in the 1950s that children had little contact with adults either inside or outside the family. The nuclear family was a fragile construction. The failings of the family's social network necessitated an expansion of public institutions. Since more mothers now worked, latchkey children were not met by adults when they came home from school.

> The childrearing task of the family has decreased and the public sector (schools) has had to take on greater responsibility . . . the educational system has to take an essential part of the social and moral care of the children . . . which the schools in certain ways are better equipped to handle than the homes (one- and two-parent families) and their limited social network.[18]

The helplessness of children was much emphasized, as evident in the following statement from a government inquiry on child care during the 1970s. The developing child was said to need the support of an institution:

> Psychology and child psychiatry have taught us how early disturbances can continue over many years with changed symptoms. Damage of a serious nature during the first years of life can continue as contact difficulties and aggression among preschool children, as discipline and learning problems among schoolchildren, and as asocial behaviour and criminality among adolescents; it can also lead to disease of a psycho-physical nature among adults. This is one of our most powerful and noticeable chain reactions. Behavioural science has shown that many personality disorders, character disturbances, and illnesses are due to unsatisfactory emotional conditions during our long, helpless childhood, when personality and character are established.[19]

The dependence on professionally run institutions was a logical consequence of such ideas and in many political contexts was used to motivate the expansion of institutions. It is interesting to note that British psychologist John Bowlby had a very limited influence, unlike in the UK and the U.S. Swedish psychologists and psychiatrists resisted his emphasis on the attachment between mother and children, arguing for more modern, institutional solutions to family problems.[20] Before the war, institutional solutions were often motivated by the poverty of working families, but in spite of improved economic standards such solutions became even more frequent after the war. The pattern of change indicates that families also saw such help as preferable to placing children in foster care. Institutions created to help working and "worn-out" mothers expanded during the 1950s, as did child guidance clinics, which before the war had been closely associated with disciplining school children, but now gained acceptance among parents. Child psychiatry disassociated itself from the criminal justice system and social services and established a professional identity with a focus on individual therapeutic treatment.[21]

The expansion of the welfare system in this way gained legitimacy because it also offered tangible support: free school lunches (1947), family allowances (from 1949), and cheap hospital care. Support was sometimes tied to measures of disciplining the population to certain modes of behavior, and educational efforts aimed at forming particular attitudes to child rearing and adult behavior, easily identifiable in the maternity and child welfare centers. The most extreme of these was the government's acceptance that the "feeble-minded" could form families (to marry), conditioned on the sterilization of the women.[22]

After 1945 the increasing significance of schooling as a tool to fashion a democratic society established that the compulsory educational system was the bulwark of democracy and the link between children, school, parents, and the state. Mistrust of parents' capacities took a variety of forms, yet it was a tendency that was reinforced, keeping pace with the changing role of professionals. Parents had to be educated to become the professionals' allies. The role of parents and their responsibilities relative to developments in school were discussed, for example, in connection with the school reforms of the 1950s and with government inquiries on child mental health. Parent education became a central feature of a number of political issues, and also involved educational curricula. Parents were to be included in the national school policy with a view to "easing the work of principals and teachers," as it would be put much later in 1969.[23] The relationship between the private and public spheres is less clear as a result, because public policy depends on cooperation with, and also governing of, the private sphere. This position became increasingly clear in the debates around child care and parenting starting in the 1970s, when the government demanded that families organize themselves around principles of gender equality among children. The normative basis for such positions was not always very explicit or publicly discussed but, with a system of public support of family reproduction, it seemed clear that child care, parental support systems, and the like followed the expectation that families should adhere to the norms of behavior reflecting the new policies.[24]

Another important cultural undercurrent in the era is the understanding of the relationship between state and the market in Sweden. Commercialization and the market are commonly understood as restricting individuals and families, due to class or gender, from expressing or realizing life projects, whereas the state guarantees freedom from such economic and social limitations. The state thus represents freedom as much as regulation in Swedish popular and political understandings, though various political interpretations exist. This situation also has a linguistic expression. The English word "state" can be translated as both "samhälle" and "stat," which collapses the words for "civil society," "society," and "state" and blurs the distinction between government and civil society organizations. Such definitions of state and society are closely related to the relatively high level of trust in Swedish society and the proximity between the electorate and the political leadership, and as well as a homogeneous structure of values that celebrates political and social participation, democracy, and modernization.[25] Only starting in the 1990s have distinctions between civil society and state been made clearer in political discourses by the introduction of the term "civil society" along with the redefinition of the role of the state, clarifying the domain of state apparatus.[26] These developments had direct effects on children's policies.

Children's Physical Integrity—Individualizing Childhood

During the 1950s Sweden was at last ready to create a school system for all social classes—a comprehensive school (*bottenskola*)—very much influenced by American educational ideas. Until then, education had been based on a very traditional system of schools that operated with different curricula issued according to social class and gender. The school system was created around a number of different schools that severely hampered girls and working-class children of both sexes. The vision of a school for all mobilized the political left and the center. It included curricular change and new pedagogical ideas as well a merging of the main educational systems. The high school and the elementary school (*folkskola*) permitted different ways to discipline children, which also reflected the social makeup of the school. Corporal punishment had been allowed in the elementary schools but banned in the high schools. The merging of the schools led to a reevaluation of which system of discipline should be used, ending with a blanket ban on corporal punishment as early as in 1957. Henceforth discipline in the educational system would use methods adopted from psychology, not physical punishment.[27]

The important issue was that in the process children were given the same right as adults regarding the integrity of their bodies, thus transcending, in a manner of speaking, the traditional limits of childhood. In fact, they received special protection and access to social rights but not bodily (or mental) integrity. But the ban marked the beginning of a discussion about children's integrity in such terms that was taken farther in the late 1960s. A ban on parents' rights to physically discipline children, implemented in 1979, was included in the family law code.[28] In doing so, the state displayed its intent to protect the individual child and also to educate the parents.

Individualization as such can be observed in many other contexts and follows the pattern already established in other aspects of social policy and was related to a strong welfare state, and an egalitarian, comprehensive educational system.

Family Benefit or Child Benefit—Familial Independence

In the long view, education had multiple meanings for understanding childhood. We can see how the start of working life was postponed, and participation in work was regarded as unsuitable for children. This expresses the basic understanding of childhood as synonymous with a period of education and dependence that is seen in many countries. In Sweden the first ban on child labor was passed in the 1850s; the first effective legislation was passed in 1883, with notable exceptions for labor in agriculture and certain industries. The legislation was much like school legislation in that it was designed to ensure the moral upbringing and character of working-class children. But the school system remained a parallel system up to the time of the reforms discussed above. Enrollment in the new democratic school system evolved dramatically from the 1950s to 2000 in a manner easily comparable to the development in the United States.

When the education system was reformed the government also decided in 1947 that families needed compensation for lost incomes and the increasing costs of bringing up the young, since children would spend a longer period in schools. This was compounded by the decision to finance free school meals for all children, to be introduced over a period of ten years. All families were given a family allowance, "child support," without individual evaluation of need.[29] Over the years this benefit has grown, but only slowly; today it amounts to some 1,000 kronor (approximately $160) per child per month. There is also a bonus for a third child.

The symbolic meaning of child support, however, has changed significantly over the years. At first children's wages earned outside the family were replaced, where families could afford it, by pocket money distributed by the family head, again a symbol of dependence within the family. But some forty years later the child benefit is looked on as the children's own money. It has become a symbol of adulthood—albeit within the family—and of trust in the children as independent consumers, capable of planning their own consumption of clothing, cinema visits, mobile phones, and the like. The support is also an expression of the direct relationship between children and the state—state individualism. Children typically get access to these money transferrals at age fifteen. At the same time, families and parents value work experiences by children at home and also outside the home during the summer. A good upbringing includes children working to earn money and contribute to the family economy—to take responsibility and foster economic and social independence.[30]

This system also has a bearing on the financial independence produced by the Swedish system for financing higher education. From age eighteen, young people finance university attendance with a state loan, independent of the income or inclination of their parents. This system was created in the mid-1960s, replacing a system of bank loans based on various guarantees from institutions and parents. Since the 1960s young people have been individually responsible for their loans without the legal backing of their parents or institutions. Repayment is spread over a long period and is related to an income-based mortgage plan. The relationship formed is between the young person individually (as an adult) and the state, not mediated by the family nor defined by a filial identity. This decision was made by the government to counteract the limitations of wage-earning families, to create an individual-state relationship that would promote educational expansion and accessibility for broad layers of the population. Equal access to education promoted the idea

of economic independence and an individual relation to the state.[31] A fundamental cultural consequence is that Swedish parenting does not involve saving for children's education, since university education is financed through a
different form of income-generation—taxes and government administered
student loans. This stands in sharp contrast to the U.S. role of education in
relation to family as described in Paula Fass's article, and reveals the difference Kriste Lindenmeyer discusses between dependence and independence.

Active Children, Cultural Integration

Schools in the late 1970s were designed to compensate for differences in educational background and to develop children's productive use of spare time
as well as to make parents share in their children's education. A number of
reforms deemphasized special education and stressed integration in a joint
curriculum and the democratic value of a shared educational experience
transcending class, gender, ethnicity, and region. On the local level and in the
curriculum, the school system placed great emphasis on cooperation with
parents to help with homework and facilitate school teaching by supporting educational development of their children at home in a variety of ways.[32]
The family was defined as an educational entity to meet the demands of the
educational system, but parents were not to participate in instruction on a
voluntary basis in the schools as in the United States.

In the early twentieth century, children's spare time activities became
objects of local and some central government intervention. Social welfare
boards organized educational and moral boosting activities in leisure clubs
for the young. During the 1940s and 1960s the local community supported
building swimming pools; an important goal for voluntary associations and
local governments was to make the whole population able to swim 200 me-
ters, which set a national standard for swimming proficiency in a nation of
many lakes and long coastlines.[33]

During the 1960s many spare-time activities became gradually associated with organized sports and leisure associations outside schools, with a
clear demarcation from the educational system. School sports were never
major social phenomena in Sweden. However, addressing acceptable spare-
time activities became an issue for the educational system rather than the
social welfare board. This was particularly notable during the late 1970s,
when one of the tasks of the national educational system was to channel

children into suitable leisure activities. . . . This is in part an extension of
the school role as an institution for social policy, where medical considerations and preventive health care have also been crucial for how children
are defined. The state and local educational system thus also assumed responsibility for overall cultural integration of children in their spare time
according to the reforms of the late 1970s. This responsibility has since then
been undermined by economic constraints, but it is still the legacy that the
government uses at election time.[34]

Leisure centers and associations now seem to organize more and more of
Swedish children's time, much as elsewhere in the Western world. Leisure in
the sense of truly free time has shrunk; organized leisure is mostly planned
and defined by adults. Steven Mintz's chapter bears witness to a similar process in the U.S. Municipal authorities in Sweden encourage leisure pursuits
with an educational content. Parents use similar reasons to justify activities
seen as preparing children for the future. As a result, leisure has not just been
organized, it has been educationalized. Parents see an educational value in
organized sports. Children must not be idle, and parents have a key role in
facilitating this educational venture.

Similarly, day care is also evaluated for its educational value. A 1980s
study of parental attitudes to forms of child day care indicated a preference
for school-like professional institutions rather than private, home-based
care.[35] The institutions, it was argued, increased children's competence and
better prepared them for life as schoolchildren. During the 1990s child care
became increasingly educationalized, with an emphasis on learning processes
and preparation for educational advancement. The process was supported by
the political establishment: the state was interested in the international com-
petitiveness of Swedish education, and trade organizations (teachers/care
personnel) focused on the advantages of being seen as a teaching rather than
a caring profession. In the late 1990s the last year of child-care eligibility was
redefined as a preparatory school year.[36]

Culture as a separate sphere of public policy made children's cultural
expressions a key political arena during the 1970s. Government supported
art centers, theaters, and schools of music and the arts as part of its social
responsibility for children and youth, along with leisure-time activities
organized through schools. Legislation to curb commercial advertising,
aimed at children in the printed news media, was an important aspect of
the support for independent culture and the efforts to control the growing
influence of the market. Television advertising was not an issue until 1992,

as the Swedish market up to that time was dominated by publicly funded channels without advertisements. Regulation thereafter focused more on limiting the commercialization of children's culture than on the moral content of the television media.[37] Much of this process and public focus on children's culture was also marked by worries over the deterioration of children's traditional culture, the consequences of modernization, and the influence of modern media technology in ways very similar to the processes described by Mintz. The intervention by the state, through economic and organizational support, both at local and central level, in supporting children's culture and the culture of children, reflected a critical attitude to market solutions and conversely a trust that only through the state could diversity and quality of culture be upheld. It also represents an egalitarian distribution of resources and access to culture for children in culturally deprived environments. However this was also an early arena where the state and local community relied on civil society and parent organizations to create the spare-time activities of children sponsored by state subsidies.[38] These attitudes were associated with public support for the culture of children as an arena for the state and local community in Sweden. They have had a profound effect on notions of childhood, play, and learning.

Childhood, Family, Professionals—The Importance of Children

Children's living conditions were enormously improved as a result of the general postwar development of welfare and special supportive measures, among which day care was one of the most important.[39] Female participation in the work force outside the home in Sweden is among the highest in the world, and was actively encouraged by the government and industrial interests in the 1960 and 1970s. It was also closely linked to the discussion of gender roles and feminist claims for equality.[40] The idea that women could work and men could participate in child rearing gave extra urgency to demands for parental education and an expansion of day care. The new, equality-minded men were to be produced by means of information and education and women almost forced out into the labor market. Women's participation in the work force was made possible by new forms of child care, but men's share in child care expanded less rapidly.[41] The corollary was the increased cultural significance of care outside the family in children's experience of growing up. The irony here is that such institutions follow traditional gender lines. The Swedish labor market is strongly gendered, and children spend their time in a largely female environment as child care facilities and the lower levels of schools recruit predominantly female personnel.[42]

For children, institutionalization means that behavior modifications—emotional control, punctuality, adapting to large groups, and so on—that were previously learned before starting school is now encountered at an earlier age. As we have seen, child care was in part motivated by children's need for protection and to compensate for an inferior upbringing in the home. The Swedish child-care system addressed a number of the issues at the fore of the Head Start program in the United States, but managed to base it in a coherent educational and care context. There were also other consequences. At the start of the twentieth century absentee fathers were discussed solely as a problem of poor relief—how could they be made to pay maintenance to mothers and children so that they did not become a burden on society? The children's need for their father, and for that matter the men's need for their children, received no attention. It was only relatively late in the twentieth century that a child's need for its father came to the fore in political discussions on absentee fathers, marking a transition from an issue of economic support to one of emotions and identity and attachment between children and fathers.[43] The transformation of male roles is naturally one result of women's greater participation in work outside the home. The changing role of women has necessitated a new male identity defined in relationship to children. Swedish males' share of responsibility in child care is not on the level with that of women during the first year after birth, but it has increased significantly. Clearly, the shared responsibility for children is attached to general discussions about equality in the labor market, sharing of household work, and child care.

One can also note the role of the government in this change. The fact that absentee fatherhood could be defined as an emotional dilemma must partly be understood in relation to the fact that single parents do not depend on contributions (family support) from a father or mother. If child support is not paid by the parent the local government social services will forward the money and charge the failing parent.[44] The state creates the material bases for defining fatherhood primarily in relational terms.

Even more important, given the extent of child poverty in the earlier part of the twentieth century, many children were placed in foster care or other institutions to combat the consequences of neglect and often caused by poor living conditions. The number of children in institutions such as orphanages and reform schools peaked in the 1930s with almost 10,000 children, and then dropped significantly first during the 1940s and then during the 1970s to around 2,000 in 1980 (while Sweden's population doubled). The changes clearly mark different phases in the development of the welfare system. The drop in numbers corresponds to changes in the ideology of social care of children as expressed in a negative view of such institutions as orphanages and foster care, but it is also a result of the expansion of day care as a system of family support. The number of children placed in orphanages and foster care decreased as a publicly accessible and inexpensive day care system made it possible for more single women and men to be not only carers but also better parents. This was important because more women and men were given the opportunity to be carers; indeed, given a broad definition of family, more had the opportunity to be a family.[45] In this sense the expansion of public care—welfare—made stronger family ties possible, and allowed for a multifaceted definition of family.

Thus strong family ties, state regulation of, for example, gender relations and public institutions go hand in hand in the Swedish model. Social welfare institutions and public day care made it possible for single and poor parents to maintain their families. The importance of biological family ties was emphasized from the 1950s on, parallel to the importance of state responsibility to fend for children.[46]

The increasing importance of public institutions does not mean that children have diminished in importance to their parents. Far from it. Today nearly all Swedish women have children, unlike in the early nineteenth century, when many women remained unmarried and never had children. Having children has become a required part of a woman's lifecycle in a way never seen before. The family focus is exemplified by the strong determination to maintain family networks over Christmas, weekends, and national holidays.

Having children is thus a normal expectation for women and men alike.[47] Deviation from this pattern is regarded as abnormal, underlining social criteria for normalcy. This also influences adoption practices and the volume of foreign adoptees to Sweden. Financing a "child of emotion" is an expensive endeavor. For same-sex couples the struggle for the right to adopt children, and for female couples to have access to IVF, have become important symbols of social acceptance and indeed of normal family life.[48]

The institutions for children I have discussed allow adults of both genders to work and be parents at the same time, but also rely on the symbolic imagery of nature and play associated with children as well as positive growth and maturity associated with the institution.[49] Ironically, as childhood became more and more organized, the most popular figures in children's literature were small children who revolt against the adult world and refuse to follow its rules and conventions. Astrid Lindgren's "Pippi Longstocking" is the one that first springs to mind. *Pippi Longstocking* was written at the end of the 1940s and depicted a motherless child living in a house all by herself with a monkey, a horse, and a sack of money. In her interaction with the neighboring families and their children she came to represent the antithesis of middle-class norms and values. She was a child who spoke out against narrow-mindedness, educational constraints, and small town middle class value systems; she spent money on whatever came to mind, slept upside down in bed, was stronger than any adult, and lived a life without normal borders and limitations.

Thus the establishment of the welfare system was parallel to the establishment of images of children as independent agents, strong and oppositional moral epigones to the adult world, fighters for rights and justice for themselves but also for animals and the downtrodden. Astrid Lindgren's is only one, though no doubt the most renown, of a series of children's rights champions in the vast children's literature in Swedish. It is a unique tradition that in many ways can be expected to have fed into and expressed the moral basis of the centrality of children's rights to welfare and care in the Nordic countries.[50] Institutionalization of childhood was not associated with notions of children as passive objects of welfare distributions, but rather the contrary, as claim makers and moral norm setters. In this context it is interesting to note that some sociologists have argued that the growth of institutions also enabled children in real life to develop skills in finding loopholes in the system and thus to create free space of their own. Institutionalized care does not necessarily produce children as passive and obedient subjects; it can do the very opposite.[51]

Treating Children the Same as Adults—Negotiating Childhood and Children's Rights in the Welfare State

The politics of childhood in the post-1945 period were clearly not just a matter of national debate and the implementation of various measures; they were negotiated in people's everyday interaction with authorities, professionals, and families. The involvement of the state in family life means not just control but also assistance. There are obvious examples of how society sets out to steer childhood, but also of how professional experts and mothers have interacted to a common end, and how welfare institutions can be used by one parent against the other.[52] In many respects, the social services have sought to act in the interests of children, sometimes against the parents. The state—through the social services—has acted in loco parentis, and thus in one sense has constructed the child as an individual rather than merely an underage family member. Childhood has a new guarantee of quality backed by the various state agencies, vouching for the right to such a childhood for each child, especially in terms of social benefits and care. Ideas about what constituted a normal child—and an atypical child—were also affected by these changes of institutional arrangements.

In the period when the welfare state was under construction, up to the 1960s, the strong position of the state relative to families was justified by referring to children's needs for protection and parents' incompetence. The state and the professionals associated with it were thereby identified as competent to give the children protection, and in the process children were singled out as a special social category in relationship to the state; they became objects created by state individualism. The concept of childhood would change, however, becoming increasingly described as an autonomous, adult-like period. The competent child was discovered, constructed, and romanticized, as a partner in collaboration with the professionals.[53] Once children became described as moral and ethical paragons, the distinctive nature of children also came in for a reappraisal, and legislation increasingly emphasized their competence and parity with the rights of adults: similarity rather than difference began to dominate understandings of childhood in Sweden. Yet this also highlights the question of a child's simultaneous needs for protection and care, underlining the need to re-evaluate parental competence as well. The competent child needs parental roles that correspond to an image of a competent child, and this of course also necessitates a changed relationship with the representatives of the state. The child is increasingly seen as a competent co-actor alongside the state and civil society, with the duties and responsibilities of the citizen, but also with a citizen's rights. The changed civic role of the child is also expressed in changed judicial rules for children.

In the 1970s the focus on the development of gender equality and public day care for all children was based on the requirements of the labor market.

Women were encouraged to work, while the reforms necessitated a redefinition of gender roles, but none of this was initially defined or propelled by the needs of children or their civil rights. Gender balance in child care was important as a symbol of a new social order; it did not include a focus on children's individual rights. At the same time, childhood expressed a national culture that centered on child welfare.

As noted above, corporal punishment in schools was forbidden during the late 1950s. It was not possible to retain corporal punishment in the compulsory educational system when it merged with the upper secondary schools into a system similar to the U.S. high schools. The decision questioned the notion of children as different from adults with separate rights. It proved to be a stepping stone toward the formation of a new ideology of childhood and a new children's rights regime that emphasized autonomy and competence. During the 1960s children's rights were discussed in relationship to a new legal family code, but this was not deemed necessary as beating children was already prohibited under criminal law. But in the late 1970s a provision established a ban on physical disciplining and mental abuse of children in families. As part of the family code it remained inconsequential, as it was not tied to a specific penalty and only introduced as a pedagogical tool. The criminal code, however, regulated the consequence of crimes against children, putting them explicitly on equal footing with abused adults.

The new law on child abuse made it necessary that all families were to be informed about the correct way of bringing up children and the need to abstain from punishing children in a way that did not respect their physical and mental integrity. That is how it was interpreted, at least, and the need for parent education in these respects became a central political issue. But not only parents were informed. Children are also carefully informed by the government and nongovernmental organizations about their rights to physical integrity. Respect for children's physical integrity paved the way toward a discussion in the 1970s and 1980s about the obligation to respect children's opinions and their independent creativity.[54] It was occasionally suggested that the voting age should be lowered to fourteen; that children should be paid a proper wage for their work at school, thus making them independent; and that children should have the right to divorce themselves from their parents.

Thus this new concept of childhood is based on similarities with adults, not differences, and in a manner of speaking it voids the differences between children and the older generation.[55] Children's rights are thus understood to be equivalent to those of adults, making them autonomous within the family—or at least not simply subsumed into it—with the right to be respected as individuals with opinions, knowledge, and skills, and in possession of civil rights as Swedish citizens. Being a child is no longer just a matter of being, of existing as a half-adult, but is transformed into life's great project, "becoming," for children and parents alike.[56] Becoming, is a potential bound up with active parenting in helping children realize their true potential and observing their rights and thus respecting them as full individual beings.

By the 1980s and 1990s we detect the outlines of a childhood presented with new characteristics: early maturity; shared experience of the adult world through the media; quick learning of adult behavior and the codes that apply in the adult world by participating in institutions outside the home; and a life of play and spare time, yet no longer unstructured but consciously planned as a preparation for adulthood. It is a childhood full of expectations of achievement—the interactive, competent child. If children are to succeed, they must begin their education early by participating in sports, the arts, and so on. Just as the innocent, romantic view of childhood in the nineteenth and early twentieth centuries presupposed a new kind of motherhood, so this new, equally romantic view presupposes a new kind of parenting—educationally aware, responsible, and a keen social secretary—shared equally between the parents. State individualism created in Sweden a thrust toward upholding children's identity as competent and independent rights holders that is in many ways very different from the changes in the U.S. during the same period of time, as Michael Grossberg's and Kriste Lindenmeyer's chapters demonstrate.

This new competent Swedish child has a role in the commercial world, since children are increasingly important as consumers. The imagery of child consumers carries an important message that plays on children's own abilities to make decisions. The institutional changes, combined with the new role of the family and shifts in political governance, seem to have created a visible position for children as competent actors and individuals in their own right, similar to adults and consequently also independent co-actors with professionals. It is also quite clear that age compression in aspects where the markets influence notions of childhood as consumers and sexual objects mark the lives of Swedish children much in the same way as Stephen Lassonde shows in his chapter.

The Deregulated State and the Best Interests of the Child

What happened to this powerful model of thought—this autonomous and competent child—when the state redefined its role and system of governance late in the twentieth century in response to the need to control budget deficits and cut welfare costs? A distinct change of course is evident in the formulation of a new system of governance in the 1990s. It was based on a larger degree of local self rule and less emphasis on national standards and homogeneous systems of support and social provisions. Local and regional service providers were given a larger amount of autonomy in defining their roles vis-à-vis children and the family. The state limited its role in evaluation and measuring to generally defined political aims.[57] It consequently took less detailed responsibility for shaping children's living conditions, and instead "the best interests of the child" was held up as a goal for social policy, referencing the UN Convention on the Rights of the Child. In essential respects the terms of interaction between state, professionals, and children had to be negotiated in new political and social arenas, at a time when many other actors—the market, self-appointed experts, the media, and the like—all started to interact in new ways.

The best interests of the child is a flexible, ambivalent, and at the same time increasingly significant political concept in Sweden. Sweden's ratification of the Convention and the establishment of the official children's ombudsman, together with a bill concerning the implementation of the Convention at the local level, have resulted in a formal role for what has come to be called the children's perspective in political debate and in steering documents of various kinds regulating educational and social service provisions. The importance of this concept can only be understood by recognizing the fact that it fills a void left by the state when it was no longer visible locally through directives defining childhood standards. Thus, a novel aspect in Sweden was also a consequence. Because of the new reliance on children's perspective the courts became important in determining definitions of children's rights—particularly in relationship to services rendered by public institutions like educational facilities and in negotiations about the meaning of childhood.

The concept of the child's best interests has functioned in the courts more as a principle than as a rule, which has broadened the scope of the concept and simultaneously rendered it yet more ambiguous. Its flexibility seems necessary for reconciling conflicting perspectives, making it possible for different actors to adapt it to their own ends. But it is significant that in the last decades of the twentieth century, child law was established as an independent sphere of jurisprudence. The distinctive features of these laws are that it is the child and the child's own legal relationships to society and its members that are central to any judicial assessment. In this respect, child law distances itself from earlier legal practice concerning children, whereby the child was treated as dependent on adults' legal relationships.[58]

Swedish child law thus also introduces a link to international conventions by invoking the transnational concept of the best interests of the child, which in turn is linked to the issue of whether it is reasonable to assert universal best interests that are subordinate to the culture in which they are applied. Johanna Schiratzki has shown that the "best interests of the child" serves as a unifying principle rather than a concept with a specific meaning, opening the way for interpretations that vary according to the context and for very different meanings. The issue of children's rights is thus raised as a part of a general discussion of rights.[59]

With the new emphasis on the best interests of the child, a link was also instituted between everyday life in Sweden and the global convention on children's rights. The altered system of state control gives local bodies the task of implementing political decisions, while the state evaluates and supervises. The Swedish children's ombudsman that was created in the late 1980s thus has the function of ensuring that the UN Convention on the Rights of the Child informs all the various activities that are of significance for children's lives, and the National Agency for Education has the task of ensuring that the School Act is followed in respect to the rights of children. If the Convention itself is no longer problematic in Sweden, the meaning of the child's best interests is the more disputed. It is constantly renegotiated on many levels and with more actors involved, and often mobilized to reconcile conflicting professional perspectives between organizations and agencies acting in as advocates of children. At the same time there is another point to be made. This emphasis on the rights of children is not unique but parallel to the introduction and political importance of other rights claims regarding women and the handicapped, as well as a number of important government commissions about the necessity of strengthening democratic structures and institutions. The important point is that children and young people are not excluded but rather included in the insistence on democratic institutions and processes for marginalized groups.[60] Interestingly however, and ironically, such insistence on rights runs parallel to cut-backs in economic support to families and children in day care and social services during the 1990s that was partly a consequence of the shift in central state regulation and spending to more local control over the economy. Social rights were emphasized less as the focus shifted to civic rights. This ironic twist stood in stark contrast to how little focus was placed earlier on children's civic rights during the construction of the welfare system. The welfare of children was stressed in Swedish government inquiries and in social work at the beginning of the twentieth century, and was sometimes expressed as an interest in protecting the child's best interests.

The emergence of child welfare committees, child health care, educational policy, legislation on adoption, fostering, delinquency and family policy can all be understood as examples of the way that children were viewed as politically important objects of welfare.[61] Exactly what that interest has entailed has varied enormously, and was obviously interpreted in different ways by the various agents involved, who subordinated it to other priorities, such as the need to solve poor relief problems, the rights of adults to parenthood, and the rights of the family over the rights of the child. Children's rights were primarily an issue of social rights rather than civic rights. Throughout the twentieth century, the child's best interests in cases of adoption has, for example, clearly been overwhelmed by the sheer number of children in need of adoption and definitions of the nature of a family as a legal, psychological, social, or biological unit.[62] Clearly the best interests of the child was evoked in situations when children were subject to problematic social situations, and the "normal' living conditions afforded by the protection of a biological family were wanting.

By the late twentieth century children's rights became the primary means of addressing children's issues in Sweden. The phrase "the child's best interests" had been critical to legislation in 1970s and 1980s that classified children as autonomous and competent individuals. In the media the phrase first appeared in conjunction with children's rights and at a time when state's role as the guarantor of childhood was redefined.[63] The emphasis shifted to the judicial system's responsibility to define children's rights in relationship to the UNCRC. The emphasis on children's autonomy, competence and independent agency also opened a chance for civil society and professional organizations to offer children support, protection, or legal advice in lieu of the guarantees previously afforded by the state. The child's best interests became a unifying concept that is enlisted by partially rival agents—government authorities, voluntary organizations, lawyers, professional organizations and scholars—who view themselves as mediators of children's rights and thus children's best interests and are prepared to listen to the voices of children, while at the same time representing and voicing their professional interests.

Competence, Citizenship, and the Right to be Heard

By the late twentieth century children were expected to step forward as agents of their own interests, even when such interests are administered or supervised by others.[64] One way to do this is to let the child speak as a citizen. Unsatisfactory conditions in school or in other child environments are examined in court and are the object of public opinion, beyond the spatial and social frameworks of the institutions themselves undermining their autonomy as cultural and political entitites.[65] But the role of the state in defining what is good for children is left to various actors to interpret within the framework of the welfare system and legal system, with the support of the international norms of children's rights, which formulate the premises for defining appropriate living conditions. Children, like other citizens, are thus subjects of politics, and various systems of social and state regulation allow them to speak freely.

A recent article in a Swedish newspaper bears this out. The chairwoman of the largest Swedish teachers' union announced that it was about time to close down all religious schools. Her argument was that children had the right not to be influenced by religion until they could make their own independent, individual decisions based on nondenominational information. This right belonged to the children themselves. In other words, the child's best interests and rights should be protected by the state in the form of providing them professional and therefore nondenominational teachers. Children's rights to form their own decisions and be spared religious indoctrination override parents' wishes for a religion-based education.[66]

The best interests of the child are rhetorically linked to the concept of the *child's perspective*, implying that children are an important source of information about what actually is *in their best interests*.[67] The child's perspective can also be viewed narrowly as children's voices that can be recorded and surveyed. As a (child) citizen, one is given a voice in matters of importance. If it is accepted that children are competent, then they are also the ones who know what is best for them—transforming the child's perspective into an issue of information and dialogue with children as citizens. This extends democracy to young people, but at the same time it is an invitation to the competent child to be governed, which comes with having rights and a voice and responsibilities. Equally, it is an invitation to professional groups, nongovernmental organizations, and some government agencies to interpret and represent the voices of children, and to the social services and government agencies to rely on families to take care of children.

When children are approached directly for information, these processes also alter the sense of the social differences that exist between citizens—in this context, children—who live in a vast variety of social circumstances. Children's living conditions in Sweden are relatively good, as has been shown in the inquiry by the Committee for Local Welfare Management Systems (Välfärdsbokslut), but for certain groups the situation is liable to create future inequality.[68] It is the children of single mothers or first-generation immigrants who do not receive their equal share of the welfare pie. These figures show that children's living conditions are closely related to their parents' position in the labor market, which means in turn that the political measures for redistributing income are unable to create equality among children from different social classes.

Children's voices have added qualitatively to such analyses by introducing information about physical and psychological health, framed in ways similar to how adults describe their living conditions. These voices have created a novel understanding of a whole new spectrum of social and health problems among young people that are very similar to the problems affecting adults, including stress, anxiety, and work-related worries, underpinning the similarities between young and adult in modern Swedish society.[69] But the realization that children, in spite of general welfare, good education standards, and the like, do not necessarily feel content with their lot in school and at home has shifted the focus from poverty and material needs to political attention on children's mental health and emotional well being and the relationships between parents and young.

The consequences are serious in several ways. Despite the current trend of emphasizing children's competence, the voices of children in need and expressions of distress about them have encouraged renewed discussions of children as dependent. Will the focus on children's competence leave the child in need clearly without both the aid of the justice system, social services, and schools? The contraction of some forms of social support and government regulations has cast doubt on the ability of the state to protect children.

Sweden's social services remain dependent on the family to deliver care and protection, and the increased emphasis on biological family bonds has begun to undermine the cultural and political autonomy of children.[70]

Another outcome of this trend is to put the focus on the need to reevaluate and support parental competence. Competent children also need parents with matching skills. Media images are dominated by so-called nanny programs designed to strengthen disciplinary regimes and reestablish parental authority in the family. In many ways these programs question the notions inherent in the understanding of children as competent. More significant is the concerted effort by the current Swedish government to create and support parental educational programs run by local communities. The government would like to see evaluation systems that reach parents with tuition arranged by schools, social services, or parent organizations. The establishment of these programs is based on a close interaction with Sweden's academic community. In many ways it resembles the child-saving movement of the beginning of the twentieth century—with the participation of nongovernmental organizations, local communities, and central government organizations, as well as an assortment of different academic disciplines. The result is a range of different efforts to reach parents and children. Contrary to the previous attempts, the emphasis is on educating the older generation in order to strengthen the family with professional and formal educational support rather than building welfare institutions and eliminating poverty. As a result, the role of education, preschool, and social services is portrayed in a different light that challenges the understanding of existing professional roles as defined, for example, by the Ministry of Education for which the emphases has been on educational standards.[71]

Summing Up

We can see, then, that childhood in the late welfare state of the twenty-first century in Sweden has made the child's competence increasingly visible, matched by the changing role of the state, which now assumes a less normative and regulatory role, relying instead on children's rights defined on the basis of international conventions. Such concepts as the child's best interests and the children's perspective serve to mobilize children as citizens and competent legal subjects, emphasizing the child's autonomy relative to the family, while children's rights are instead negotiated in terms of the norms established in the Convention on the Rights of the Child. The child is constructed as a citizen, while the role of the state as a guarantee of childhood is on the wane. Meanwhile the decline of systems of social support makes the government dependent on families. The understanding of children's living conditions that is now determined to some extent by children's own voices, which depict lives marked by stress and anguish, have of late been the bases for renewed attempts by the liberal and conservative government to reach parents and children through parental educational programs. The concept of the child's best interests becomes a link between the individual and the state, between children's everyday life and international norms, and between norm formation and politics. It also creates a basis for nongovernmental organizations to launch themselves as children's advocates, and thus continue the transformation of the Swedish welfare state and childhood.

Notes

Chapter 1

1. Benjamin Spock, *Baby and Child Care*, new, enlarged ed. (New York: Pocket Books, 1973), 11.

2. See Arlene Skolnick, *Embattled Paradise: The American Family in an Age of Uncertainty* (New York: Basic Books, 1991), and especially Natasha Zaretsky, *No Direction Home: The American Family and the Fear of National Decline, 1968–1980* (Chapel Hill: University of North Carolina Press, 2007). Christopher Lasch was the best known of the critics of the time and is discussed by both Skolnick and Zaretsky. See Lasch, *The Culture of Narcissism: American Life in an Age of Diminishing Expectations* (New York: Norton, 1978).

3. Ulysses S. Grant, *Personal Memoirs*, reprinted in *American Childhoods: An Anthology*, ed. David Willis McCullough (Boston: Little, Brown, 1987), 74.

4. Count Adam C. de Gurowski, *America and Europe* (New York: Appleton, 1857), 380.

5. Ibid., 381.

6. John Dewey, "The Child and the Curriculum," in John Dewey, *The Child and the Curriculum and The School and Society* (Chicago: University of Chicago Press, 1971), 22, 8, 31 (my emphasis).

7. For the debates, see Ann Hulbert, *Raising America: Experts, Parents, and a Century of Advice About Children* (New York: Knopf, 2003).

8. Harriet Martineau and Reinhard S. Speck, *Society in America*, Cambridge Library Collection (Cambridge: Cambridge University Press, 2009).

9. Spock, *Baby and Child Care*, 247 (my emphasis).

10. For these various changes, see Lizabeth Cohen, *A Consumer's Republic: The Politics of Mass Consumption in Postwar America* (New York: Knopf, 2003); Kenneth Jackson, *Crabgrass Frontier: The Suburbanization of the United States* (New York: Oxford University Press, 1985); Dolores Hayden, *Building Suburbia: Green Fields and Urban Growth, 1820–2000* (New York: Vintage, 2004); Elaine Tyler May, *Homeward Bound: American Families in the Cold War Era* (New York: Basic Books, 1988); Skolnick, *Embattled Paradise*.

11. Cohen, *A Consumer's Republic*.

12. Peter Stearns, *Childhood in World History* (London: Routledge, 2006), 55-59.

13. See Paula S. Fass, *Outside In: Minorities and the Transformation of American Education* (New York: Oxford University Press, 1989).

14. *120 Years of American Education: A Statistical Portrait*, ed. Thomas D. Snyder, National Center for Educational Statistics, U.S. Department of Education, Office of Educational Research and Improvement (January 1993), http://nces.ed.gov/pubsearch/pubsinfo.asp?pubid=93442, 37.

15. John Modell, *Into One's Own: From Youth to Adulthood in the United States, 1920–1975* (Berkeley: University of California Press, 1989), 226. See also Kelly Schrum, *Some Wore Bobby Sox: The Emergence of Teenage Girls' Culture, 1920–1945* (New York: Palgrave Macmillan, 2004), 12–13.

16. Skolnick, *Embattled Paradise*, 13; statistics 16.

17. Paul Goodman, *Growing Up Absurd* (New York: Knopf, 1956); Edgar Z. Friedenberg, *The Vanishing Adolescent* (Boston: Beacon Press, 1959); Kenneth Keniston, *The Uncommitted: Alienated Youth in American Society* (New York: Harcourt Brace, 1965).

18. David Riesman with Nathan Glazer and Reuel Denney, *The Lonely Crowd: A Study of the Changing American Character* (New Haven, Conn.: Yale University Press, 1950).

19. Thomas Sugrue, *The Origins of the Urban Crisis* (Princeton, N.J.: Princeton University Press, 1996).

20. Skolnick, *Embattled Paradise*, xx.

21. Modell, *Into One's Own*, 228–53, 294–99.

22. For an early discussion of these changes, see Kenneth Keniston and the Carnegie Council on Children, *All Our Children: The American Family Under Pressure* (New York: Harcourt Brace, 1977), chap. 1.

23. For the significance of rock 'n' roll music, see Glenn C. Altschuler, *All Shook Up: How Rock 'N' Roll Changed America* (New York: Oxford University Press), 2003.

24. Ibid., 105, 108; Freidenberg, *The Vanishing Adolescent*.

25. Erik H. Erikson, *Childhood and Society* (New York: Norton, 1964); Erikson, *Identity: Youth and Crisis* (New York: Norton, 1968).

26. Daniel P. Moynihan, *Family and Nation* (San Diego: Harcourt Brace, 1986), xi, citing the president of the Population Association of America.

27. Keniston, *All Our Children*, chap. 1.

28. Beth Bailey, *Sex in the Heartland* (Cambridge, Mass.: Harvard University Press, 1999).

29. See some of the findings of psychologist Thomas Weisner, with Greg Duncan and Aletha Huston, *Higher Ground: New Hope for Working Families and Their Children* (New York: Russell Sage, 2007).

30. For divorce and its relationship to the other changes, see Modell, *Into One's Own*, 286–90.

31. "'07 U.S. Births Break Baby Boom Record," *New York Times*, March 19, 2009, A13.

32. For the Great Depression, see Glenn Elder, *Children of the Great Depression: So-*

cial Change and Life Experience (Chicago: University of Chicago Press, 1974). For World War II, see William M. Tuttle, Jr., *Daddy's Gone to War: The Second World War in the Lives of America's Children* (New York: Oxford University Press, 1993).

33. Kay S. Hymowitz, *Liberation's Children: Parents and Kids in a Postmodern Era* (Chicago: Ivan Dee, 2003).

34. Annette Lareau, *Unequal Childhoods: Class, Race, and Family Life* (Berkeley: University of California Press, 2003).

35. Paula S. Fass, *Kidnapped: Child Abduction in America* (New York: Oxford University Press, 1997).

36. LynNell Hancock, Pat Wingert, Mary Hager, Claudia Kalb, Karen Sringen, and Dante Chinni, "Mother's Little Helper," *Newsweek*, March 18, 1996, 51–53.

37. For camping as it developed in a very different perspective on childhood as a period of freedom and play, see Leslie Paris, *Children's Nature: The Rise of the American Summer Camp* (New York: New York University Press, 2008).

38. William H. Whyte, Jr., *The Organization Man* (New York: Simon and Schuster, 1956; reprint Philadelphia: University of Pennsylvania Press, 2002).

39. Howard P. Chudacoff, *Children at Play: An American History* (New York: NYU Press, 2007).

40. Jerome Kagan, *The Nature of the Child* (New York: Basic Books, 1984).

41. Robert D. Putnam, *Bowling Alone: The Collapse and Revival of American Community* (New York: Touchstone, 2000).

42. Kaitlin Flanagan, "Driving Miss Chloe," *New York Times*, Sunday Opinion, March 16, 2008, 14.

Chapter 2

1. *Tinker v. Des Moines Independent Community School District*, 393 U.S. 503, 506 (1969).

2. Peter David, "The Sex Offender Next Door," *New York Times Magazine*, July 28, 1996, 20–27.

3. David Archard, *Children, Rights and Childhood*, 2nd ed. (New York: Routledge, 2004), chap. 5.

4. For a full analysis of the case, including interviews with Mary Beth, see John W. Johnson, *The Struggle for Student Rights: Tinker v. Des Moines and the 1960s* (Lawrence: University Press of Kansas, 1997); and see Gael Graham, *Young Activists: American High School Students in the Age of Protest* (DeKalb: Northern Illinois University Press, 2006), 104–6. For a more critical view of the case and its subsequent history, see Anne Proffitt Dupre, *Speaking Up: The Unintended Costs of Free Speech in the Public Schools* (Cambridge, Mass.: Harvard University Press, 2009).

5. For a fuller development of these points see Michael Grossberg, "A Protected Childhood: The Emergence of Child Protection in America," in Wendy Gamber, Michael Grossberg, and Hendrik Hartog, eds., *American Public Life and the Historical Imagination* (South Bend, Ind.: University of Notre Dame Press, 2003), 213–39. And for

a similar assertion of a long tradition of children's activism see Rebecca de Schweinitz, *If We Could Change the World: Young People and America's Long Struggle for Racial Equality* (Chapel Hill: University of North Carolina Press, 2009), chap. 4.

6. Child mine leader quoted in Robert Bremner with John Barnard, Tamara K. Hareven, Robert M. Menne, eds., *Children and Youth in America: A Documentary History* (Cambridge, Mass.: Harvard University Press, 1971), 2: 631.

7. N. Ray Hiner and Joseph M. Hawes, "Introduction," in N. Ray Hiner and Joseph M. Hawes, eds., *Growing up in America, Children in Historical Perspective* (Urbana: University of Illinois Press, 1985), xiv.

8. De Schweinitz, *If We Could Change the World*, 192.

9. Holt quoted in Beatrice S. Gross and Ronald Gross, eds., *The Children's Rights Movement: Overcoming the Oppression of Young People* (Garden City, N.Y.: Anchor, 1977), 321.

10. Kenneth Keniston, *All Our Children: The American Family Under Pressure* (New York: Harcourt Brace, 1977), 184.

11. *In re Gault*, 387 U.S., 1, 3 (1967); Frank Zimring, *The Changing Legal World of Adolescence* (New York: Free Press, 1982), 14.

12. *Brown v. Board of Education of Topeka*, 347 U.S. 483 (1954); Peter Irons, *Jim Crow's Children: The Broken Promise of the Brown Decision* (New York: Penguin, 2002); Mildred Wigfall Robinson and Richard J. Bonnie, eds., *Law Touched Our Hearts: A Generation Remembers Brown Versus Board of Education* (Nashville, Tenn.: Vanderbilt University Press, 2009); de Schweinitz, *If We Could Change the World*, chap. 5.

13. *Goss v. Lopez*, 419 U.S. 565 (1975); and see Graham, *Young Activists*, 40–41.

14. *Pendley v. Mingus Union High School District No. 4 of Yavapai County*, 504 P.2d 919 (1972); 460 F.2d 609 (5th Cir. 1972); *Tinker v. Des Moines*, 508–9. For sources of the hair rights discussion see Gael Graham, "Flaunting the Freak Flag: *Karr v. Schmidt* and the Great Hair Debate in American High Schools, 1965–1975," *Journal of American History* 91(2004): 522–43; and see Graham, *Young Activists*, chap. 4.

15. Graham, "Flaunting the Freak Flag," 533, 534, 535, 536; National Association of Secondary School Principals report cited in Graham, *Young Activists*, 5.

16. *Bellotti v. Baird*, 443 U.S. 622 (1979); and see Robert Mnoonkin, "*Bellotti v. Baird*: A Hard Case," in Robert Mnookin et al., *In the Interest of Children: Advocacy, Law Reform, and Public Policy* (New York: Freeman, 1985), 149-264; Elizabeth Scott, "The Legal Construction of Childhood," in Bernadine Dohrn, Margaret Rosenheim, David Tannehaus, and Frank Zimring, eds., *A Century of the Juvenile Court* (Chicago: University of Chicago Press, 2002), 124–29.

17. For general assessments of censorship changes in the era, see James C. Paul and Murray L. Schwartz, *Federal Censorship, Obscenity in the Mail* (New York: Free Press, 1961), chaps. 3–5; Paul S. Boyer, *Purity in Print: Book Censorship in America from the Gilded Age to the Computer Age*, 2nd ed. (Madison: University of Wisconsin Press, 2002), chaps. 10–11.

18. American Library Association, http://www.ala.org/ala/issuesadvocacy/banned/index.cfm.

19. *Board of Educ., Island Trees Union Free School Dist. No. 26 v. Pico*, 457 U.S. 853 (1982); *Ginsburg v. New York*, 390 U.S. 629 (1968); and see generally Marjorie Heins, *Not in Front of the Children: "Indecency," Censorship, and the Innocence of Youth* (New York: Hill & Wang, 2001), 76–88.

20. http://www.unhchr.ch/html/menu3/b/k2crc.htm; and see Roger J. R. Levesque, "Child Advocacy in the United States and the Power of International Human Rights Law," in Kathleen Alaimo and Brian Klug, eds., *Children as Equals: Exploring the Rights of the Child* (Lanham, Md.: University Press of America, 2002), 183–96; Mary Ann Mason, "The U.S. and the International Children's Rights Crusade: Leader or Laggard," *Journal of Social History* 38 (2005): 955–63. For a recent assessment of the implications of ratifying the convention in one country, see Lisa Payne, "Twenty Years On: The Implementation of the UN Convention on the Rights of the Child in the United Kingdom," *Children & Society* 23 (2009): 149–55. See in particular the extensive use of the Convention in Sweden explained by Bengt Sandin in his essay in this volume.

21. Kate Douglas Wiggin, "Children's Rights," *Scribner's Magazine*, August, 1892, 242, 244-7; Fuller cited in N. Ray Hiner, "Children's Rights, Corporal Punishment, and Child Abuse, Changing American Attitudes, 1870–1920," *Bulletin of the Menninger Clinic* 43 (1979), 239–40.

22. Grossberg, "A Protected Childhood"; *Pierce v. Society of Sisters*, 268 U.S 510, 535 (1925); Lee Teitelbaum, "The Meanings of Children's Rights," *New Mexico Law Review* 10 (1980): 238.

23. For a general discussion of adult fears of the era, see Philip Jenkins, *Moral Panic: Changing Concepts of the Child Molester in Modern America* (New Haven, Conn.: Yale University Press, 1998); Peter N. Stearns, *Anxious Parents: A History of Modern Child-rearing in America* (New York: New York University Press, 2003); Paula Fass, *Kidnapped: Child Abduction in America* (New York: Oxford University Press, 1997), chap. 6.

24. Bruce Hafen, "Children's Liberation and the New Egalitarianism: Some Reservations About Abandoning Children to Their Rights," *Brigham Young University Law Review* (1976): 607, 656.

25. Edward Wynne, "What Are We Doing to Our Children?" *Public Interest* (1981): 13–14, 18.

26. Martin Guggenheim, *What's Wrong with Children's Rights* (Cambridge, Mass.: Harvard University Press, 2005); and see Laura Martha Purdy, *In Their Best Interest? The Case Against Equal Rights for Children* (Ithaca, N.Y.: Cornell University Press, 1992); Sigal R. Benporath, "Autonomy and Vulnerability: On Just Relations Between Adults and Children," *Journal of Philosophy of Education* 37 (2003): 127–45.

27. For an assessment of juvenile justice changes in the 1990s, see David S. Tannenhaus and Steven A. Drizin, "'Owing to the Extreme Youth of the Accused': The Changing Legal Response to Juvenile Homicide," *Journal of Criminal Law & Criminology* 92

(2002): 641–706; Frank Zimring, *American Youth Violence* (New York: Oxford University Press, 1998).

28. Zimring, *The Changing Legal World of Adolescence*, 3–4; http://www.madd.org/about-us/mission/, accessed April 11, 2011.

29. *Bethel School District v. Fraser*, 478 U.S. 675 (1986); *Hazelwood School District et al. v. Kuhlmeier* et al., 484 U.S. 260 (1988); *Morse v. Frederick*, 551 U.S. 393 (2007); Heins, *Not in Front of the Children*, 131–36.

30. Bruce Hafen, "Developing Student Expression Through Institutional Authority: Public Schools as Mediating Structures," *Ohio Law Journal* 48 (1987): 663.

31. "Gun Free School Act of 1994," 20 U.S.C. Chapter 70.

32. *Bivens v. Albuquerque Public Schools*, 899 F. Supp. 556 (D.N.M. 1995); and see *Board of Education v. Lindsay Earls* (2002); *The Nation*, December 15, 2003, 17–19.

33. *HL v. Mathewson*, 450 U.S. 398 (1981)

34. *Planned Parenthood v. Ashcroft*, 462 U.S. 476 (1983).

35. "Parental Involvement Laws for Abortion Out of Step with Other Laws Ensuring Minors' Right to Consent to Health Care," Alan Guttmacher Institute (2000), http://www.guttmacher.org/pubs/.

36. Sex education anecdote quoted in Judith Levine, *Harmful to Minors: The Perils of Prohibiting Children from Sex* (Minneapolis: University of Minnesota Press, 2002), 105; see also *Carey v. Population Services International*, 431 U.S. 678 (1977).

37. Kevin Saunders, *Saving Our Children from the First Amendment* (New York: New York University Press, 2003), 257.

38. Communications Decency Act of 1996; *Reno v. American Civil Liberties Union*, 521 U.S. 844 (1997); *U.S. v. American Library Association*, 539 U.S. 194 (2003); Heins, *Not in Front of the Children*, chaps. 7–9.

Chapter 3

1. Sue Samuelson, "The Cooties Complex," *Western Folklore* 39 (July 1980): 198–210.

2. The earliest reference in the *Oxford English Dictionary* is from 1967.

3. While an expanding number of works focus on facets of the history of children's culture, such as toys or play, relatively few have sought to treat children's expressive and meaning-making activities as a culture; examples include William A. Corsaro, *The Sociology of Childhood* (Thousand Oaks, Calif.: Pine Forge Press, 2005); *"We're Friends, Right?": Inside Kids' Cultures* (Washington, D.C.: Joseph Henry Press, 2003); *Friendship and Peer Culture in the Early Years* (Norwood, N.J.: Ablex, 1985); Gary Allan Fine, *With the Boys: Little League Baseball and Preadolescent Culture* (Chicago: University of Chicago Press, 1987); Henry Jenkins, ed., *The Children's Culture Reader* (New York: New York University Press, 1998); Kathleen McDonnell, *Honey, We Lost the Kids: Re-Thinking Childhood in the Multimedia Age*, rev. ed. (Toronto: Second Story Press, 2005); Kathleen McDonnell, *Kid Culture* (Toronto: Second Story Press, 1994); Kathy Merlock Jackson, ed., *Rituals and Patterns in Children's Lives* (Madison: University of Wisconsin

Press/Popular Press, 2005); Barrie Thorne, *Gender Play: Girls and Boys in School* (New Brunswick, N.J.: Rutgers University Press, 1993).

4. Howard Chudacoff, *Children at Play: An American History* (New York: New York University Press, 2008).

5. Anne Haas Dyson, *Writing Superheroes: Contemporary Childhood, Popular Culture, and Classroom Literacy* (New York: Teachers College Press, 1997); Vivian Paley, *Boys and Girls: Superheroes in the Doll Corner* (Chicago: University of Chicago Press, 1984).

6. For examples of declensionist analyses, see David Elkind, *The Hurried Child: Growing Up Too Fast Too Soon*, 3rd ed. (Cambridge, Mass.: Perseus, 2001), and Kay S. Hymowitz, *Ready or Not: What Happens When We Treat Children as Small Adults* (New York: Free Press, 1999). On the place of children in contemporary cultural politics, see Nancy Scheper-Hughes and Carolyn Sargent, eds., *Small Wars: The Cultural Politics of Childhood* (Berkeley: University of California Press, 1999); Sharon Stephens, ed., *Children and the Politics of Culture* (Princeton, N.J.: Princeton University Press, 1995).

7. Lenore Skenazy, *Free-Range Kids: Giving Our Children the Freedom We Had Without Going Nuts with Worry* (Hoboken, N.J.: Jossey-Bass, 2009).

8. Steven Mintz, *Huck's Raft: A History of American Childhood* (Cambridge, Mass.: Harvard University Press, 2004), 275–309.

9. Ron Kovic, *Born on the Fourth of July* (New York: McGraw-Hill, 1976).

10. Homer H. Hickam, Jr., *Rocket Boys: A Memoir* (New York: Delacorte Press, 1998).

11. Susan Allen Toth, *Blooming: A Small-Town Girlhood* (Boston: Little, Brown, 1981); Wini Breines, *Young, White, and Miserable: Growing Up Female in the Fifties* (Chicago: University of Chicago Press, 2001). On Barbie, see M. G. Lord, *Forever Barbie: The Unauthorized Biography of a Real Doll* (New York: Walker, 2004).

12. On the construction of innocence, see Richard Halperin, "Norman Rockwell's Manufactured Innocence," *Chronicle of Higher Education, Chronicle Review* 53, 9 (2006): B14.

13. Laura Wattenberg, *Baby Name Wizard* (New York: Broadway Books, 2005); David Brooks, "Goodbye, George and John," *New York Times*, August 7, 2007, A19.

14. Julia Overturf Johnson, Robert Kominski, Kristin Smith, and Paul Tillman, "Changes in the Lives of U.S. Children: 1990–2000," U.S. Census Bureau, Population Division, Working Paper 78 (2005), http://www.census.gov/population/www/documentation/twps0078/twps0078.html, accessed March 23, 2011.

15. Denise Polit and Toni Falbo, "Only Children and Personality Development: A Quantitative Review," *Journal of Marriage and the Family* 49 (1987): 309–25; Toni Falbo and Denise Polit, "A Quantitative Review of the Only-Child Literature: Research Evidence and Theory Development," *Psychological Bulletin* 100 (1986): 176–89; Toni Falbo, "The One-Child Family in the United States: Research Issues and Results," *Studies in Family Planning* 13 (1982): 212–15; Toni Falbo, "Relationships Between Birth Category, Achievement and Interpersonal Orientations," *Journal of Personality and Social Psychology* 41 (1981): 121–31.

16. Daniele Checchi, *The Economics of Education: Human Capital, Family Background and Inequality* (Cambridge: Cambridge University Press, 2008).

17. "Generation M2: Media in the Lives of 8- to 18-Year-Olds," Kaiser Family Foundation (2010), http://www.kff.org/entmedia/mh012010pkg.cfm, accessed March 23, 2011.

18. Peter Stearns, *Anxious Parents: A History of Modern Childrearing in America* (New York: New York University Press, 2003).

19. Catherine Dressler, "Renting, 'Riting: Teens Use Videos to Do Homework," *St. Petersburg Times*, March 27, 1988, 8F.

20. Thorne, *Gender Play*; Henry Jenkins, "The Innocent Child and Other Modern Myths," http://web.mit.edu/cms/People/henry3/innocentchild.html, accessed March 23, 2011.

21. Elizabeth Segel, "'As the Twig Is Bent . . .': Gender and Childhood Reading," in Elizabeth Flynn and Patrocinio Schweickart, eds., *Gender and Reading* (Baltimore: Johns Hopkins University Press, 1986), 165–86.

22. Stuart C. Aitken, *The Geography of Young People: Morally Contested Spaces* (New York: Routledge, 2001).

23. Sandra L. Hofferth and Sally Curtin, "Changes in Children's Time, 1997 to 2002/3: An Update," NICHD Family and Child Well-Being Research Network, grant # U01-HD37563 (2006); Sandra L. Hofferth and John F. Sandberg, "How American Children Spend Their Time," *Journal of Marriage and the Family* 63, 3 (2001): 295–308; Sandra L. Hofferth and John F. Sandberg, "Changes in American Children's Time, 1981–1997," in Sandra L. Hofferth and T. Owens, eds., *Children at the Millennium: Where Did We Come From, Where Are We Going?* (New York: Elsevier, 2001), 193–229.

24. "Generation M2."

25. See, for example, Juliet B. Schor, *Born to Buy: The Commercialized Child and the New Consumer Culture* (New York: Scribner, 2005).

26. Hofferth and Sandberg, "How American Children Spend Their Time."

27. James U. McNeal, *The Kids' Market: Myths and Realities* (New York: Paramount, 1999); Schor, *Born to Buy*.

28. Lisa Jacobson, *Raising Consumers: Children and the American Mass Market in the Early Twentieth Century* (New York: Columbia University Press, 2005), 3; Lisa Jacobson, *Children and Consumer Culture in American Society: A Historical Handbook and Guide* (Westport, Conn.: Praeger, 2007).

29. Schor, *Born to Buy*.

30. Stephen Kline, *Out of the Garden: Toys, TV and Children's Culture in the Age of Marketing* (London: Verso, 1995).

31. James Paul Gee, *What Video Games Have to Teach Us About Learning and Literacy*, 2nd rev. ed. (New York: Palgrave Macmillan, 2007); Gerard Jones, *Killing Monsters: Why Children Need Fantasy, Super Heroes, and Make-Believe Violence* (New York: Basic Books, 2002); Steven Johnson, *Everything Bad Is Good for You: How Today's Popular Culture Is Actually Making Us Smarter* (New York: Riverhead, 2003).

32. Jenkins, "Children's Culture," http://web.mit.edu/cms/People/henry3/children.htm, and "Complete Freedom of Movement: Video Games as Gendered Play Spaces," http://web.mit.edu/cms/People/henry3/pub/complete.html, accessed March 23, 2011.

Chapter 4

This essay is dedicated to John P. Demos, whose book, *A Little Commonwealth: Family Life in Plymouth County* (Oxford: Oxford University Press, 1970, 2000) first stimulated my thinking about concepts of age and authority many years ago. I would like to thank my fellow authors of this volume for the many thoughtful conversations we shared about our joint enterprise, but Paula Fass in particular for pulling this project together and for her constant support of my work. I would also like to thank Steve Mintz, John Modell, and Michael Zuckerman for their extremely helpful comments on the essay's content, and Howard Chudacoff for introducing me to the phrase "age compression," in his paper "Rethinking Child Development," which he presented at Rethinking Child Development in Interdisciplinary Perspective: A Meeting Among Social Scientists, University of California at Berkeley, October 7–8, 2005. Thanks to Bengt Sandin, Michael Grossberg, and members of the Child Studies Seminar at Linköping University for their astute remarks on a draft of this essay during my visit in November of 2009. Finally, thank you to the two anonymous readers who critiqued the essay for the University of Pennsylvania Press.

1. Personal interview, William H. Sledge, September 12, 2009, New Haven, Connecticut. Sledge is currently a professor of psychiatry at Yale University.

2. If you were to ask anyone today to name the significant markers on the path from birth to adulthood, they could readily compose a list of privileges, rights, obligations, and other changes in status pertaining to specific ages. I asked students in a course I taught on the history of childhood to enumerate significant age markers from birth to "adulthood," which we defined as the point at which an individual possesses all the rights and responsibilities that accrue to adults (the last of which was eligibility to hold the office of President of the United States), and they listed twenty-three such markers. Laws vary by state, so it is difficult to generalize, but a helpful overview by state can be found at the Cornell University Law School Legal Information Institute website, http://topics.law.cornell.edu/wex/category/overview. Still, the discourse about age compression throws into question the very definition of childhood. Since the 1960s adult fashions have mimicked youths' and even children's clothing in a reversal of the reach "downward" to achieve the opposite aim: to extend youthfulness and vitality through adulthood. Indeed, the taste for leisure attire may be inspired by a desire to resist the deadening demands of a society that works longer hours and takes shorter vacations than any other industrialized nation in the world—one in which increasing numbers of people work from home, where clothing reflects these blurred boundaries as well; see Arlie Russell Hochschild, *The Time Bind: When Work Becomes Home and Home Becomes Work* (New York: Metropolitan Books, 1997).

3. Howard P. Chudacoff, *"How Old Are You?": Age Consciousness in American Culture* (Princeton, N.J.: Princeton University Press, 1989).

4. A standard college textbook on children's development enumerates eight stages preceding adulthood: early infancy, late infancy, early childhood, middle childhood, and pre-, early, middle, and late adolescence; Michael Cole, Sheila R. Cole, and Cynthia Lightfoot, *The Development of Children*, 5th ed. (New York: Worth, 2005). In 1948, British biologist, mathematician, and physician James Tanner initiated the Harpenden Growth Study, a twenty-three-year longitudinal study of children in Hertfordshire, England, on which he developed the "first modern growth reference data for height, weight, and skinfolds" by the mid-1960s (455). Tanner is renowned for understanding human growth as a combination of parental height, environment, and social interaction, rather than viewing "growth as a discrete process," and "children as separate from their worlds." The "Tanner Scale," a metric of physiological growth based on the development of secondary sexual characteristics in girls and boys, became the universal standard for measuring maturity by the late 1960s. See Stanley J. Ulijaszek et al., "James M. Tanner (1920–)," in Stanley J. Ulijaszek et al., eds., *The Cambridge Encyclopedia of Human Growth and Development* (Cambridge: Cambridge University Press, 1998), 455; Noel Cameron, "Adult and Developmental Maturity," in ibid., 433–35; and W. A. Marshall and J. M. Tanner, "Variations in Pattern of Pubertal Changes in Girls," *Archives of Disease in Childhood* 44, 235 (June 1969): 291–303.

5. Stephanie Coontz, *The Way We Never Were: American Families and the Nostalgia Trap* (New York: Basic Books, 2000); the most concise expression of the efficacy of the nuclear family is Talcott Parsons and Robert F. Bales with James Olds et al., *Family, Socialization, and Interaction Process* (Glencoe, Ill.: Free Press, 1955); Paula S. Fass, this volume.

6. Steven Mintz and Susan Kellogg, of course, show that the American family moved toward a democratic model by the late eighteenth century, but popular culture in post–World War II America recast fathering within the "American" model in important ways; see Mintz and Kellogg, *Domestic Revolutions: A Social History of American Family Life* (Glencoe, Ill.: Free Press, 1988), chap. 3, and Jane F. Levey's thoughtful essay on gender roles and the democratization of family life in postwar America: "Imagining the Family in Postwar Popular Culture: The Case of The Egg and I and Cheaper by the Dozen," *Journal of Women's History* 13 (Autumn 2001): 125–50; and see the following, cited by Levey: Margaret Park Redfield, "The American Family: Consensus and Freedom," *American Journal of Sociology* 52 (November 1946): 175–83; Ernest R. Mowrer, "War and Family Solidarity and Stability," *Annals of the American Academy for Political and Social Science* 229 (September 1943): 100–106; Norma Bixler, "Democracy at Home," *Parents' Magazine*, September 1944, 289; Margaret Mead, "What's Happening to the American Family?" *Journal of Social Casework* 28 (November 1947): 330; and Alice B. Stone, "One Way to Succeed as a Family," *Parents Magazine*, August 1948, 27.

7. Juliet B. Schor, *Born to Buy: The Commercialized Child and the New Consumer Culture* (New York: Scribner, 2004), 55–58; and CBC Marketplace, "Sex Sells: Market-

ing and 'Age Compression,'" CBC broadcast January 9, 2005. Organizations devoted to reversing this trend, from the Boy Scouts to Commonsensemedia.org, publish online advice in the form of age-graded charts to help parents guide children through "age-appropriate" activities that range from housework to "light sexual humor"; see, e.g., http://www.commonsensemedia.org/reviews/age-grid.php and http://housekeeping. about.com/od/chorechart1/a/ageapprchores.htm, accessed March 21, 2008.

8. Philippe Ariès, of course, was the first historian to write about the "discovery" of childhood and put most starkly the connection between the centrality of the child and the modernization of family life; I invoke Kohli here because his analysis better suits the stress I want to put on age as a new force in interpersonal hierarchies. See Martin Kohli, "Die Institutionalisierung des Lebenslaufes," *Viertejarhesschriftfuer Soziologie und Sozialpsychologie* 1 (1985): 1–29; cited in John R. Gillis, "Life Course and Transitions to Adulthood," in Paula S. Fass, ed., *Encyclopedia of Children and Childhood in History and Society* (New York: Macmillan, 2004), 549.

9. Shulamith Shahar, *Childhood in the Middle Ages* (New York: Routledge, 1990).

10. For a discussion of the many sources of age consciousness see Chudacoff, *"How Old Are You?"*; on age grading in urban public schooling, see Stephen Lassonde, "Learning and Earning: Schooling, Juvenile Employment, and the Early Life Course in Late Nineteenth-Century New Haven," *Journal of Social History* 29 (Summer 1996): 839–70. Jane Hunter describes a well-articulated symbolic system of age-stratified personal adornment among upper-middle-class girls in their mid-teens during the later decades of the nineteenth century; see Jane H. Hunter, *How Young Ladies Became Girls: The Victorian Origins of American Girlhood* (New Haven, Conn.: Yale University Press, 2003), 140–45.

11. Peter N. Stearns, *Anxious Parents: A History of Modern Childrearing in America* (New York: New York University Press, 2003), chap. 2. Stearns has summarized *Anxious Parents* in an essay published in 2009, to which Michael Zuckermann wrote a lively refutation. See Stearns, "Analyzing the Role of Culture in Shaping American Childhood: A Twentieth Century Case," *European Journal of Developmental Psychology* 6, 1 (2009): 34–52; and Michael Zuckermann, "The Octopus and the Child—Another Perspective on American Culture: A Commentary on Stearns," *European Journal of Developmental Psychology* 6, 1 (2009): 53–59. Despite Zuckermann's colorful and penetrating objections, I think Stearns has put his finger on the direction of change during the twentieth century. On the exit of grandparents from twentieth-century households, see Steven Ruggles, "The Transformation of American Family Structure," *American Historical Review* 99, 1 (February 1994): 103–28.

12. Stearns observes that the appearance of *Infant Care*, published by the U.S. Children's Bureau beginning in 1914, followed by the arrival of *Parents Magazine* during the 1920s, reflected a new orientation that addressed both a perceived need by parents for expert, "reach-into-your-home" guidance and the emerging view of children as vulnerable; Stearns, *Anxious Parents*, 18–19.

13. On the general and increasing reliance on expert opinion in the United States

during the twentieth century, see Loren Baritz, *The Servants of Power: A History of the Use of Social Science in American History* (Middletown, Conn.: Wesleyan University Press, 1960); on the "immobilizing" effect of child-rearing advice, see Peter N. Stearns, *Childhood in World History* (New York: Routledge, 2006), 108; and Stearns, *Anxious Parents*; for general treatments of child-rearing expertise during the twentieth century in the U.S., see Julia Grant, *Raising Baby by the Book* (New Haven, Conn.: Yale University Press, 1998), chap. 7; Ann Hulbert, *Raising America: Experts, Parents, and a Century of Advice About Children* (New York: Knopf, 2003).

14. Stearns, *Anxious Parents*, 24.

15. Linda C. Mayes, "Gesell, Arnold (1880–1961)," in Paula S. Fass, ed., *Encyclopedia of Children and Childhood in History and Society* (New York: Macmillan, 2004), 380–81.

16. Still, it was the sensible, more moderate approach of Dr. Spock that in fact straddled the nature/nurture contest that later became the target of cultural conservatives who derided his advice to parents as dangerously "permissive," when baby boomers came of age during the 1960s and 1970s; and see the amusing caricature of Gesell's maturation theory in "Bringing Up Baby on Books . . . Revolution and Counterrevolution in Child Care," *Newsweek* 45 (May 16, 1955): 64–66, 68.

17. Martha Wolfenstein, "Fun Morality," in Margaret Mead and Martha Wolfenstein, eds., *Childhood in Contemporary Cultures* (Chicago: University of Chicago Press, 1955); Joseph Veroff, Elizabeth Douvan and Richard A. Kulka, *The Inner American: A Self Portrait from 1957 to 1976* (New York: Basic Books, 1981).

18. The high school graduation rate passed the 50 percent mark for the first time in U.S. history in 1940, and continued to climb until the 1970s; U.S. Bureau of the Census, *Historical Statistics of the United States: Colonial Times to 1957* (Washington, D.C.: Government Printing Office, 1960), Series H, 233, 207.

19. See, Fass, this volume. Michael Zuckerman attributes a self-serving motive to Spock's approach, which he says *appeared* to bolster parents' trust in their own instincts only to be withdrawn by Spock's inevitable refrain to "call the doctor" in any areas of uncertainty when dealing with children's health and discipline. The result, he concluded, was both a reinforcement of the physician's authority and a further erosion of parents' confidence in relations with their children; see Zuckerman, "Doctor Spock: The Confidence Man," in Charles Rosenberg, ed., *The Family in History* (Philadelphia: University of Pennsylvania Press, 1975), 179–208.

20. Barbara Ehrenreich, *The Hearts of Men: American Dreams and the Flight from Commitment* (Garden City, N.Y.: Anchor Press/Doubleday, 1983); Modell, *Into One's Own*, 227–43.

21. Modell, *Into One's Own*, 253.

22. U.S. Bureau of the Census, *Historical Abstracts of the United States: Colonial Times to 1970* (Washington, D.C.: U.S. Department of Commerce, 1976), Series N, 238–45, 646. This surge owed in large part to the Federal Housing Administration subsidy for new single-family home construction after the war in the form of historically generous loan policies. Between 1948 and 1958, 13 million houses were constructed, 85 percent of

them in America's expanding suburbs, which absorbed almost two-thirds of the nation's prodigious population growth during these years. Kenneth T. Jackson, *Crabgrass Frontier: The Suburbanization of the United States* (New York: Oxford University Press, 1985), chap. 11; Mintz and Kellogg, *Domestic Revolutions*, 183. Modell adds to this observation the pronounced youthfulness of this expansion, citing the fact that 76 percent of metropolitan housing occupied by families in which the husband was under thirty-five was in the suburbs between 1954 and 1956, *Into One's Own*, 221.

23. E. Wight Bakke, *The Unemployed Man and His Family* (New Haven, Conn.: Yale University Press, 1940).

24. Veroff et al., *The Inner American*; Ehrenreich, *The Hearts of Men*; Elaine Tyler May, *Barren in the Promised Land: Childless Americans and the Pursuit of Happiness* (New York: Basic Books, 1995).

25. Veroff et al., *The Inner American*, 141.

26. Modell, *Into One's Own*; Veroff et al., *The Inner American*, 141; Ehrenreich, *The Hearts of Men*.

27. Veroff et al., *The Inner American*, 147–48.

28. May, *Homeward Bound*, chap. 4.

29. Ehrenreich, *Hearts of Men*.

30. See Steven Mintz, this volume.

31. Howard P. Chudacoff, "Rethinking Child Development," paper presented at Rethinking Child Development in Interdisciplinary Perspective: A Meeting Among Social Scientists, University of California at Berkeley, October 7–8, 2005.

32. Linda C. Mayes, Donald J. Cohen, et al., *The Yale Guide to Understanding Your Child: Healthy Development from Birth to Adolescence* (Boston: Little Brown, 2002).

33. American Academy of Pediatrics, http://aap.org/healthtopics/stages.cfm; U.S. Department of Health and Human Services, Centers for Disease Control and Prevention, http://cdc.gov/ncbddd/child/middlechildhood.htm.

34. Cameron, "Adult and Developmental Maturity"; Ulijaszek et al., eds., *Cambridge Encyclopedia of Human Growth*, 433–35.

35. One of Freud's enduring achievements, however false or specious many of his theories are now considered, was the recognition of libidinal impulses in even very young children, in the form of the instinct to suck and derive gratification through oral and anal activity; Sigmund Freud, *Three Essays on the Theory of Sexuality* (1905), trans. J. Strachey, S.E. (London: Hogarth, 1971), 7: 124–244. Also see Anna Freud's commentary on the development of sexuality in children, in "Psychoanalysis of the Child," in C. Murchison, ed., *A Handbook of Child Psychology* (Worcester, Mass.: Clark University Press, 1931), 555–67; in the same volume, see Margaret Mead, "The Primitive Child," 672-73, who cites Malinowski's insight that children's "Oedipal" conflict in families of the modern West did not apply to his Trobriand Islanders, and thus is "not inherent in human nature nor yet in the biological family as such, but are the results of more arbitrary and man-made conditions."

36. W. Andrew Collins, ed., *Development During Middle Childhood: The Years from*

Six to Twelve (Washington, D.C.: National Academy Press, 1984), 3–5. Piaget's contribution was less notable for its novelty than its reorientation of research over the next several decades on this developmental phase as critical to the child's looming intellectual competence.

37. See Mayes et al., *Yale Guide to Understanding Your Child*, 192–93, 91, 310–13.

38. The suspicion directed at the parents of JonBenét Ramsey, after her disappearance and death in December 1996, perfectly illustrates popular alarm over the sexualization of children; see "Justice for JonBenet?" *CNN Interactive*, U.S. News Story Page (1998), http://www.cnn.com/US/9712/26/ramsey.year.later/, accessed April 1, 2009; CBC Marketplace, "Sex Sells: Marketing and 'Age Compression,'" CBC broadcast, January 9, 2005; Lianne George, "Why Are We Dressing Our Daughters like This?" http://www.commericalfreechildhood.org/news, accesssed March 23, 2008. More recently, see the controversy that erupted in Brazil over the selection of a seven-year-old girl as drum corps queen of Carnival: "Seven-Year-Old Rio Carnival Queen Bursts into Tears," *BBC News*, http://news.bbc.co.uk/2/hi/americas/8515791.stm, accessed February 15, 2010. Three of the most prominent international watchdogs of the effects of media on children are Media Awareness Network: Media and Internet Education Resources Age (USA); International Clearinghouse on Children, Youth & Media, The Nordic Information Center for Media and Communication Research, University of Gothenberg (Sweden); and Campaign for a Commercial-Free Childhood: Reclaiming Childhood from Corporate Marketers (Canada).

39. Schor and others call this behavior, "pester power," a phenomenon that began with television marketing on children's programs beginning in the 1950s; Gary Cross, *Kids' Stuff: Toys and the Changing World of American Childhood* (Cambridge, Mass.: Harvard University Press, 1997); Schor, *Born to Buy*, 61–63; Ann Hulbert, "The Way We Live Now: Tweens 'R' Us," *New York Times*, November 28, 2004. Two articles discussing this trend in the last several years both focus on the marketing of Barbie dolls to little girls; see Fern Shen, "Marketing & Advertising: Barbie, Bratz and Age Compression," *Washington Post*, February 17, 2002; Margaret Talbot, "Little Hotties: Barbie's New Rivals," *New Yorker* (December 5, 2006). As Peter Stearns points out, one of the consequences of spreading affluence is that children increasingly have their own discretionary income, and can bypass parents when making purchases; Stearns, *Childhood in World History*, 93–109.

40. See, e.g., Hymowitz, "Tweens: Ten Going on Sixteen"; Hulbert, "The Way We Live Now"; and Douglas A. Kleiber and Gwynn M. Powell, "Historical Change in Leisure Activities During After School Hours," in Joseph L. Mahoney, Reed Larson, and Jacquelynne Eccles, eds., *Organized Activities as Contexts of Development: Extracurricular Activities After-School and Community Programs* (Mahwah, N.J.: Erlbaum, 2004).

41. Two television advertisements for cell phone products employ this scheme. One depicts a circle of sisters discussing the abbreviations they use to send text messages to their friends. Their grandmother, sitting among them, joins in (curiously) but their mother is uninitiated and feels left out. Another involves combinations of classic

mother-daughter and father-son conflict, in which the parent "forces" the teen to accept a cell phone over his or her protestations about the gross "unfairness" of the parent's authoritarian liberality. Schor observes that marketers have developed an acronym to describe the significance of age compression to their demographic targets, which they refer to as "KAGOY" (Kids Are Getting Older Younger); Schor, *Born to Buy*, 56. Marketers are also credited with creating a new subdivision of age, labeling children between ages eight and twelve "Tweens"; see Kay S. Hymowitz, "Tweens: Ten Going on Sixteen," *City Journal* (Autumn 1998); Hulbert, "The Way We Live Now."

42. Two German scholars have argued that more limited monitoring of children's activities corresponds with riskier behaviors; see Laurie L. Meschke and Rainer K. Silbereisen, "The Association of Childhood Play and Adolescent-Parent Interactions with German Adolescent Leisure Participation," *Journal of Adolescent Research* 13 (1998): 458–86.

43. Instances of adult predation on children through the Internet are commonplace; the potential for children and young people to ravage one another psychologically have recently come to light with the "MySpace Suicide Hoax"; see Lauren Collins, "Annals of Crime: Friend Game," *New Yorker* (January 21, 2008): 34–41; Richard Morgan, "Juicy Campus: College Gossip Leaves the Bathroom Wall and Goes Online," *International Herald Tribune*, March 18, 2008.

44. Emily Nussbaum, "Say Everything," *New York Magazine*, February 8, 2007. A survey in 2008 of girls and boys ages thirteen to nineteen revealed that 20 percent of them had sent a nude or seminude picture of themselves by cell phone or posted on the Internet; "Sex and Tech: Results from a Survey of Teens and Young Adults"; Survey conducted by TRU, September 25–October 3, 2008; National Campaign to Prevent Teen and Unwanted Pregnancy and Cosmogirl.com, accessed December 14, 2008; http://www.thenationalcampaign.org/sextech/.

45. David Elkind, *The Hurried Child: Growing Up Too Fast, Too Soon* (Boston: Addison-Wesley, 1981); Sarah Rimer, "For Girls, It's Be Yourself, and Be Perfect, Too," *New York Times*, April 1, 2007; Madeline Levine, *The Price of Privilege* (New York: Harper Collins, 2006). On the surge in children's participation in organized athletics during the last three decades, see M. Landers-Potts and L. Grant, "Competitive Climates, Athletic Skill, and Children's Status in After-School Recreational Sports Programs," *Social Psychology of Education* 2 (1999): 297–313. The Adlers describe the escalation of participation in extracurricular activities in general, but especially in organized athletics as "extracurricular careers," which start informally and spontaneously as recreation and conclude, often times, in high-stakes competition that echoes the "values and social structure of corporate America"; Patricia A. Adler and Peter Adler, "Social Reproduction and the Corporate Other: The Institutionalization of After-School Activities," *Sociological Quarterly* 35 (1994): 309–28, cited in Kleiber and Powell, "Historical Change."

46. See, e.g., Alan Eistenstock, *The Kindergarten Wars: The Battle to Get into America's Best Private Schools* (New York: Warner, 2006); Hara Estroff Marano, *A Nation of Wimps: The High Cost of Invasive Parenting* (New York: Broadway, 2008).

47. http//:www.yourbabycanread.com; I viewed the infomercial for the "Your Baby Can Read" series on CNBC on January 24, 2009. Note that by deploying the verb "delay," the rhetoric here implicates the parent in his or her child's potential "developmental delay," by failing to act.

48. This theme is addressed in many works of Pierre Bourdieu; the most concise is Bourdieu, "Cultural Reproduction and Social Reproduction," in Jerome Karabel and A. H. Halsey, eds., *Power and Ideology in Education* (New York: Oxford University Press, 1977), 287–311.

49. Joan Acocella, "The Child Trap: The Rise of Overparenting," *New Yorker* (November 17, 2008).

50. On the role of childhood "memory" and how it informs contemporary conceptions of childhood and child rearing, see Coontz, *The Way We Never Were*; Stearns, *Anxious Parents*.

51. John D'Emilio and Estelle B. Freedman, *Intimate Matters: A History of Sexuality in America* (New York: Harper & Row, 1988).

52. For an amusing consideration of the reversal of the concept of "age appropriate" fashion, see Kim Johnson Gross, "What's Age Appropriate? What Should You be 'Allowed' to Wear if You're over 40?" *More Magazine*, May 2006; http://www.more.com/style/fashion/age-appropriate-clothing.

53. I'd like to thank Bengt Sandin and Anna Sparrman for their comments during my presentation of this paper at a seminar at the Department of Child Studies, Linköping University, November 24, 2009.

54. See Richard A. Easterlin, *Birth and Fortune: The Impact of Numbers on Personal Welfare* (New York: Basic Books, 1980).

55. Steven Mintz, e-mail correspondence with author, December 5, 2009; the last portion of this essay has benefited greatly from Mintz's comments on an earlier draft.

56. Ann Gibbons, "The Birth of Childhood," *Science* 322, 5904 (November 14, 2008): 1040–43.

57. Joan W. Scott, "Gender: A Useful Category of Analysis," *American Historical Review* 91 (December 1986): 1075.

58. See, e.g., Peter Laslett's musing on the rising significance of what he and others refer to as the "third age" (fifty to seventy-five) in *A Fresh Map of Life: The Emergence of the Third Age* (London: Weidenfeld and Nicolson, 1989).

Chapter 5

1. *Calvert v. Johnson*, 5 Cal. 4th 84, 851 P.2d. 776.

2. Mary Ann Mason, *From Father's Property to Children's Rights: A History of Child Custody in the United States* (New York: Columbia University Press, 1994), 4, 5.

3. Ibid., 162, 163.

4. *Mercein v. People ex. Re. Barry*, 25 Wnd. 64, 101 NY 1840.

5. All divorce settlements, including custody of the children, were under the juris-

diction of the court; only a small percentage of custody determinations were decided by the judge at trial, the remainder were agreed upon by the parties.

6. Demographers predicted that at least half of American marriages entered into in the 1980s would end in divorce. Lenore Weitzman, *The Divorce Revolution: The Unexpected Social and Economic Consequences for Women and Children in America* (New York: Free Press, 1985), xiv.

7. National Organization for Women "Statement of Purpose," in Aileen S. Kraditor, ed., *Up From the Pedestal: Selected Writings in the History of American Feminism* (Chicago: Quadrangle, 1970), 368.

8. Weitzman, *The Divorce Revolution*, 231.

9. National Women's Law Center, http://www.nwlc.org/pdf/WorkingMothers-March2008.pdf.

10. Margaret Mead, "Some Theoretical Considerations of the Problems of Mother-Child Separation," *American Journal of Orthopsychiatry* (1954): 24, quoted in *State ex rel. Watts v. Watts*, 350 NYS 2d. 285 (1973).

11. Joseph Goldstein, Anna Freud and Albert Solnit, *Beyond the Best Interests of the Child* (New York: Free Press, 1973).

12. For a thorough discussion of father parenting studies, see Michael E. Lamb, ed., *The Father's Role: Cross Cultural Perspectives* (Hillsdale, N.J.: Erlbaum, 1986), chap. 3.

13. *Taylor v. Taylor*, 306 Md. 290, 508 A.2d. 964, 975 (1986).

14. Frank. F. Furstenberg, Jr., S. Philip Morgan, and Paul D. Allison, " Paternal Participation and Children's Well-being after Marital Dissolution, "*American Sociological Review* 52, 5 (October 1987): 700.

15. *Zummo v. Zummo*, 394 Pa. Super. Crt. 44, 574 A. 2d. 1130, 1137.

16. Hugh McIsaac, "Court-Connected Mediation," *Conciliation Courts Review* 21 (December 1983): 3.

17. See, e.g., Randy Klaff, "The Tender Years Doctrine: A Defense," *California Law Review* 70 (1982): 335.

18. MSNBC, March 18, 2009. http://www.msnbc.msn.com/id/29754561/ns/health-womens_health/, accessed April 18, 2011.

19. *Michael U. v. Jamie B.*, 218 Ca. Rptr.39 (1985).

20. Ruth Padawer, "Losing Fatherhood," *New York Times Magazine*, Nov. 22, 2009, 38–44, 58–62.

21. Frank Furstenberg, "The New Extended Family: The Experience of Parents and Children After Remarriage," in Kay Pasley and Marilyn Ihinger-Tallman, eds., *Remarriage and Stepparenting: Current Research and Theory* (New York: Guilford Press, 1987), 185–86.

22. *Howell v. Gossett*, 214 S.E. 2d 882 (1975).

23. *Bottoms v. Bottoms* 249 Va. 10, 457 S.E. 2d. 102, 107 (1996).

24. Same-Sex Adoption Laws by State, http://www.lc.org/profamily/samesex_adoption_by_state.pdf. (2008)

25. *Nancy S. v. Michele G.*, 228 Cal. App. 3d, 279 Cal. Rptr. 212, 218 (1991).

26. *Troxel v. Granville*, 530 US 57 (2000).

27. Mary Ann Mason and Nicole Zayac, "Rethinking Stepparent Rights: Has the ALI Found a Better Definition?" *Family Law Quarterly* 36 (2002): 232.

28. Mary Ann Mason, *The Custody Wars: Why Children Are Losing the Legal Battles and What We Can Do About It* (New York: Basic Books, 1999), 204.

29. *Davis v. Davis*, 842 S.W. 2d 588 (1992).

30. Ibid., 589.

31. Ibid., 604.

32. 1986 L. Acts R.S. 9:121 et seq.

Chapter 6

1. Barack Obama, "What I Want for You—And Every Child in America," *Parade*, Sunday, January 18, 2009, 4–5.

2. For examples of this interpretation of U.S. history, see Eric Foner, *The Story of American Freedom* (New York: Norton, 1999); and Alan Dawley, *Struggles for Justice: Social Responsibility and the Liberal State* (Cambridge, Mass.: Belknap Press of Harvard University Press, 1991).

3. Kriste Lindenmeyer, *"A Right to Childhood": The U.S. Children's Bureau and Child Welfare, 1912–1946* (Urbana: University of Illinois Press, 1997), 10–27; U.S. Senate, 62nd Cong., 2nd sess., Congressional Record, 11573–79; "Brief History of the U.S. Children's Bureau," U.S. Department of Health, Education and Welfare Social Security Administration, Children's Bureau publication 357 rev. 1962.

4. Lindenmeyer, *"A Right to Childhood"*, 179–95; many scholars note racial discrimination and other weaknesses in the 1935 act; for example see Judith Sealander, *The Failed Century of the Child: Governing America's Young in the Twentieth Century* (New York: Cambridge University Press, 2003), 111–12.

5. U.S. Census Bureau, *Income, Poverty, and Health Insurance Coverage in the United States: 2008* (Washington, D.C.: Government Printing Office, 2009), 14–18, http://www.census.gov/prod/2009pubs/p60-236.pdf, accessed December 12, 2010.

6. The official federal poverty rate in the United States in 2009 was $25,991 annual income for a family of five, $21,954 for a family of four, $17,098 for a family of three, and $13,991 for a family of two; U.S. Bureau of the Census, Poverty Thresholds 2009, http://www.census.gov/hhes/www/poverty/data/threshld/thresh09.html accessed January, 2, 2011; Julia Cass, "'Held Captive': Child Poverty in America" (Washington, D.C.: Children's Defense Fund, 2010), 5–7, http://www.childrensdefense.org/child-research-data-publications/data/held-captive-child-poverty.pdf, accessed January 4, 2011.

7. Bureau of Labor Statistics, *100 Years of U.S. Consumer Spending: Data for the Nation, New York City, and Boston*, BLS Report 991 (Washington, D.C.: Government Printing Office, 2006), 21–26, http://www.urban.org/UploadedPDF/411699_kids_share_08_report.pdf, accessed October 29, 2009; First Focus, *The Children's Budget, 2009* (Washington, D.C.: First Focus, 2009), http://www.firstfocus.net/Download/

CB2009.pdf, accessed December 28, 2009; U.S. Census Bureau, *Current Population Reports*, Series P60–222, Detailed Poverty Tables, Table 1 http://pubdb3.census.gov/macro/032006/pov/new01_100_01.htm, accessed May 15, 2009; "The Wealth Divide: An Interview with Edward Wolff," *Third World Traveler*, http://www.thirdworldtraveler.com/America/Wealth_Divide.html, accessed April 10, 2009; Alister Bull, "America's Rags-to-Riches Dream An Illusion: Study," http://today.reuters.com, April 26, 2006, accessed May 30, 2009; Bureau of Labor Statistics, "The Employment Situation, March 2010," Press Release, USDL-10-0394, April 2, 2010, http://www.bls.gov/news.release/pdf/empsit.pdf, accessed December 9, 2010.

8. James Truslow Adams, *Epic of America* (Boston: Little, Brown, 1931), 214-215.

9. National Commission on Children, *Beyond Rhetoric: A New American Agenda for Children and Families* (Washington, D.C.: Government Printing Office, 1991); Michael Katz, *In the Shadow of the Poor House: A Social History of Welfare in America* (New York: Basic Books, 1986); Sealander, *The Failed Century of the Child*, 1–2.

10. For overviews of the break up of the Children's Bureau see "Brief History of the U.S. Children's Bureau"; Drexel Godfrey, Jr., *The Transfer of the Children's Bureau* (New York: Harcourt, Brace, 1952), 20–22; Lindenmeyer, *"A Right to Childhood"*, 250–52.

11. Adam Carasso et al., *Kids Share 2008: How Children Fare in the Federal Budget* (Washington, D.C.: Urban Institute, New Foundation, 2008), 1–4, http://www.urban.org/UploadedPDF/411699_kids_share_08_report.pdf, accessed November 10, 2009.

12. Ibid. Thomas F. Schaller estimates that in 2009 the federal government spent two-fifths of its resources on elderly Americans, who constitute only one-seventh of the population. Only Japan's ratio of spending on the elderly compared to the non-elderly is wider than that of the United States; Schaller, "Backward Looking Nation," *Baltimore Sun*, November 30, 2010, 13.

13. The exception is a federal law requiring states to pay the out-of-pocket expenses for very low-income seniors (incomes below approximately $432 per month), Medicare Improvements for Patients and Providers Act enacted in July 2008; U.S. Census Bureau, *Current Population Survey, People in Families by Family Structure, Age, and Sex, Iterated by Income-to-Poverty Ratio and Race: 2007: Below 100% of Poverty—All Races*, http://pubdb3.census.gov/macro/032008/pov/new02_100_01.htm, accessed January 6, 2010.

14. On children as the property of fathers see Mary Ann Mason, *From Father's Property to Children's Rights: The History of Child Custody in the United States* (New York: Columbia University Press, 1994), 49–120.

15. For a good overview of orphans and dependency see Leroy Ashby, *Endangered Children: Dependency, Neglect, and Abuse in American History* (New York: Twayne, 1997). Michael Grossberg, *Governing the Hearth: Law and the Family in Nineteenth-Century America* (Chapel Hill: University of North Carolina Press, 1985), 1–17.

16. Ibid.

17. Sealander, *The Failed Century of the Child*; Congressional Record, 60th Cong., 2nd sess., February 15, 1909.

18. For a more detailed overview of state and federal policies for children up to

1932 see Robert H. Bremner, ed., with John Barnard, Tamara K. Hareven, and Robert M. Mennel, *Children and Youth in America: A Documentary History*, vol. 1, *1660–1865*, vol. 2, *1866–1932* (Cambridge, Mass.: Harvard University Press, 1974); on the establishment of the U.S. Children's Bureau, see Dorothy E. Bradbury, "Four Decades of Action for Children: A Short History of the Children's Bureau, 1903–1946," Children's Bureau pub. 358 (Washington, D.C.: Government Printing Office, 1956), 1; and Lindenmeyer, *"A Right to Childhood,"* 8–29.

19. On shifts in minimum-age-at-marriage laws see Mary E. Richmond and Fred S. Hall, *Child Marriages* (New York: Russell Sage, 1925); and Kriste Lindenmeyer, "For Adults Only: The Anti-Child Marriage Campaign and Its Legacy," in Andrew Kersten and Kriste Lindenmeyer, eds., *Politics and Progress: American Society and the State Since 1865* (Westport, Connecticut: Praeger, 2001), 31-44.

20. Lindenmeyer, *"A Right to Childhood"*; Molly Ladd-Taylor, *Mother Work: Women, Child Welfare, and the State, 1890–1930* (Urbana: University of Illinois Press, 1994).

21. On the effects of the Great Depression and the New Deal on children see Kriste Lindenmeyer, *The Greatest Generation Grows Up: American Childhood in the 1930s* (Chicago: Ivan R. Dee, 2005), esp. 9-109, 206-46.

22. Sealander, *The Failed Century of the Child*, esp. 234–37, 156–67; Richard Reiman, *The New Deal and American Youth: Ideas and Ideals in a Depression Decade* (Athens: University of Georgia Press, 1992).

23. On discriminatory structures built into SSA programs for children see Linda Gordon, *Pitied But Not Entitled: Single Mothers and the History of Welfare* (New York: Free Press, 1994); Joanne L. Goodwin, *Gender and the Politics of Welfare Reform, 1911–1929* (Chicago: University of Chicago Press, 1997); Premilla Nadasen, Jennifer Mittelstadt, and Marissa Chappell, eds., *Welfare in the United States: A History with Documents, 1935–1996* (New York: Routledge, 2009).

24. Lindenmeyer, *The Greatest Generation Grows Up*, 238–40.

25. For an overview of how the shift affected child welfare policy in the twentieth century see Sealander, *The Failed Century of the Child*; on the motivations behind acceptance of federal responsibility for dependent children in the 1930s see Lindenmeyer, *The Greatest Generation Grows Up*; on the early evolution of Social Security, see Larry W. DeWitt, Daniel Beland, and Edward D. Berkowitz, *Social Security: A Documentary History* (Washington, D.C.: CQ Press, 2008), 93–140; Roosevelt's quotation is from Franklin D. Roosevelt, Radio Address to the Young Democrat Clubs of America, August 24, 1935, reprinted in *Public Papers and Addresses of Franklin D. Roosevelt* (New York: Random House, 1938-[50]), 4: 336.

26. Cassandra Clifford, "The United States and the Rights of the Child," Foreign Policy Association, March 12, 2007, http://children.foreignpolicyblogs.com/2007/03/12/the-united-states-and-the-rights-of-the-child/, accessed June 5, 2009.

27. U.S. Census Bureau, "Historical National Population Estimates," http://www.census.gov/population/www/popclockus.html, accessed December 26, 2009.

28. United States, Army Service Forces, Information and Education Division, *The*

GI Bill of Rights and How It Works, (Washington, D.C.: Government Printing Office, 1945); Dennis W. Johnson, *The Laws That Shaped America: Fifteen Acts of Congress and Their Lasting Impact* (New York: Routledge, 2009), 202-28.

29. Mary R. Jackman, "The Subjective Meaning of Social Class Identification in the United States," *Public Opinion Quarterly* 43, 4 (1979): 443–62; on the correlation between fathers' education and adolescent health, see Elizabeth Goodman et al., "Adolescents' Perceptions of Social Status: Development and Evaluation of a New Indicator," *Pediatrics* 108, 2 (August 1, 2008): e31, http://pediatrics.aappublications.org/cgi/content/full/108/2/e31, accessed December 2009.

30. A good case study on race, ethnicity, and housing is Antero Pietila, *Not in My Neighborhood: How Bigotry Shaped a Great American City* (Chicago: Ivan R. Dee, 2010).

31. "Levittown, Pennsylvania: The Most Perfectly Planned Community in the World," http://www.levittowners.com/Default.htm, accessed October 2009.

32. On the history of life in Levittowns see Victor D. Brooks, *Boomers: The Cold-War Generation Grows Up* (Chicago: Ivan R. Dee, 2009), 27–29; Levittown Historical Society, Levittown, N.Y., http://www.levittownhistoricalsociety.org/history.htm, accessed December 8, 2009; Robert Griswold, *Fatherhood in America: A History* (New York: Basic Books, 1993).

33. Diana B. Elliott, Tavia Simmons, and Jamie M. Lewis, "Evaluation of Marital Events Items on the ACS," U.S. Census Bureau website, http://www.census.gov/hhes/socdemo/marriage/data/acs/Evaluation_paper.pdf, accessed December 27, 2010.

34. Brooks, *Boomers*, 7–42; Johnson, *The Laws That Shaped America*, 202–28, 261–92; Janny Scott and David Leonhardt, "Class Matters: The Shadowy Lines That Still Divide," *New York Times*, May 24, 2005; this essay was part of an eleven-part series examining class in the United States that ran in the *New York Times* in May and June 2005.

35. *Brown v. Board of Education, Topeka, Kansas*, 347 U.S. 463 (1954), reprinted in Bremner, *Children and Youth in America*, 1703–79; Johnson, *The Laws That Shaped America*, 292–32.

36. Rebecca de Schweinitz, *If We Could Change the World: Young People and America's Long Struggle for Racial Equality* (Chapel Hill: University of North Carolina Press, 2009), 151–90; Lloyd New, "The Failure of National Policy: A Historical Analysis," in U.S. Senate Committee on Labor and Public Welfare, Special Subcommittee on Indian Education, Indian Education: A National Tragedy—A National Challenge, 91st. Cong., 1st sess. (1969), Report 91-501 (Washington, D.C.: Government Printing Office, 1969), 152–56; Sara Evans argues that the Women's Liberation Movement also followed the lead of the Black Civil Rights Movement, *Personal Politics: The Roots of Women's Liberation in the Civil Rights Movement and the New Left*, (New York: Vintage, 1980).

37. de Schweinitz, *If We Could Change the World*, 93–99.

38. Robert Francis Saxe, "Scottsboro Case," in Robert S. McElvaine, *Encyclopedia of the Great Depression* (New York: Macmillan, 2004), 870–72; for an overview of media coverage of the case see Dan T. Carter, *Scottsboro: A Tragedy of the American South* (Delanco: N.J.: Notable Trials Library, 2000); on vulnerability of adolescents in the 1930s

see Errol Lincoln Uys, *Riding the Rails: Teenagers on the Move During the Great Depression* (New York: TV Books, 1999).

39. Bremner, "Desegregation of the Schools," in *Children and Youth in America*, 1830–68.

40. Carroll Van West, "Clinton Desegregation Crisis," in *Tennessee Encyclopedia of History and Culture*, online version (Knoxville: University of Tennessee Press, 2002), http://tennesseeencyclopedia.net, accessed October 20, 2009.

41. Julian Bond quotation from his, "The Media and the Movement: Looking Back from the Southern Front," in Brian Ward, ed., *In Media, Culture, and the Modern African American Freedom Struggle* (Gainesville: University Press of Florida, 2001), quoted in de Schweinitz, 206.

42. Virginia Historical Society, "The Civil Rights Movement in Virginia: The Closing of Prince George County Schools," http://www.vahistorical.org/civilrights/pec.htm, accessed October 10, 2009; Desegregation in Public Schools," *Encyclopedia of Virginia* (Virginia Foundation for the Humanities), http://www.encyclopediavirginia.org/, accessed November 2, 2009;

43. de Schweinitz, *If We Could Change the World*, 218.

44. *Four Little Girls*, Spike Lee, Director, USA Films, 1997; for an example of the transformation of public high school as a pathway to the mainstream see Paula S. Fass, *Outside In: Minorities and the Transformation of American Education* (New York: Oxford University Press, 1989).

45. For an overview of the history of the Department of Education see http://www.ed.gov/about/overview/fed/role.html, accessed December 28, 2009.

46. For a case study on school debates in the post-*Brown* era see Howell Baum, *Brown in Baltimore: School Desegregation and the Limits of Liberalism* (Ithaca, N.Y.: Cornell University Press, 2010).

47. Bremner, "Head Start," in *Children and Youth in America*, 1816–30.

48. Patrick J. Mcguinn, *No Child Left Behind and the Transformation of Federal Education Policy*, Studies in Government and Public Policy (Lawrence: University of Kansas Press, 2006); Linda Perlstein, *Tested: One American School Struggles to Make the Grade* (New York: Holt Paperback, 2008).

49. Sarah Burd-Sharps, Kristen Lewis, and Eduardo Borges Martins, *The Measure of America: American Human Development Report, 2008-2009* (New York: Columbia University Press, 2008), 91, 101–2; on the failures of the *Brown* decision to desegregate the nation's schools over the long term see Gary Orfield and Susan Eaton, *Dismantling Desegregation: The Quiet Reversal of Brown v. Education* (New York: New Press, 1997).

50. U.S. Census Bureau, *America's Children: Key National Indicators of Well-Being, 2009* (Washington, D.C.: Government Printing Office, 2009); ChildStats.gov, http://www.childstats.gov/americaschildren/glance.asp, accessed December 26, 2009.

51. "America the UnEducated," *Business Week*, November 21, 2005, ttp://www.businessweek.com/magazine/content/05_47/b3960108.htm, accessed June 2009.

52. U.S. Census Bureau, "PC Generation," http://www.census.gov/population/www/pop-profile/files/1999/chap10.pdf, accessed December 26, 2009; "Computer Adoption," *Popular Mechanics* (May 9, 2007), http://www.popularmechanics.com/blogs/technology_news/4216501.html, accessed December 26, 2009.

53. Lindenmeyer, *"A Right to Childhood,"* 232–34; James Gilbert, *A Cycle of Outrage: America's Reaction to Juvenile Delinquency in the 1950s* (New York: Oxford University Press, 1986).

54. Congress became increasingly concerned with the influence of new digital technologies on children's behavior in the 1990s; for example see U.S. Senate, Committee on Commerce, Science, and Transportation, "Technology," Senate 619 (Washington, D.C.: Government Printing Office, 1998); on how new technologies may be changing the ways children learn and think see the documentary, "Digital Nation," Frontline, PBS, Written and Directed by Rachel Dretzin and Douglas Rushkoff; Rachel Dretzin, Producer; 2010, http://www.pbs.org/wgbh/pages/frontline/digitalnation/, accessed December 10, 2010.

55. Joseph Hawes, The Children's *Rights Movement: A History of Advocacy and Protection* (Boston: Twayne, 1991), 96–121; U.S. Supreme Court, *In re Gault,* 387 U.S. 1 (1967) reprinted in The Oyez Project, http://oyez.org/cases/1960-1969/1966/1966_116, accessed March 25, 2011.

56. U.S. Supreme Court, www.supremecourtus.gov, accessed December 27, 2010; Adam Liptak, "Justices Limit Life Sentences for Juveniles," *New York Times,* May 17, 2010.

57. Keith S. Goldfield, *TANF at Ten: Retrospective* (Washington, D.C.: Woodrow Wilson School of Public and International Affairs, 2007).

58. "Immigrants Make Paths to Suburbia, Not Cities, Census Data Show," *New York Times,* December 15, 2010, A14.

59. Cass, "'Held Captive': Child Poverty in America,"6.

60. "Immigrants Make Paths to Suburbia."

61. Nancy Gibbs, "How Obama Rewrote the Book," *Time,* November 5, 2008.

62. Pew Research Center, *Between Two Worlds: How Young Latinos Come of Age in America* (Washington, D.C.: Pew Hispanic Center, 2009), http://pewhispanic.org/reports/report.php?ReportID=117, accessed December 27, 2009.

63. Centers for Disease Control, "Trends in Childhood Obesity," various reports, http://www.cdc.gov/obesity/childhood/trends.html, accessed January 4, 2011.

64. Janet Golden, Richard Meckel, and Heather Prescott Monroe, eds., *Children and Youth in Sickness and in Health: A Historical Handbook and Guide* (Westport, Conn.: Greenwood Press, 2004), 121–23; Lawrence R. Jacobs and Theda Skocpol, *Health Care Reform and American Politics: What Everyone Needs to Know* (New York: Oxford University Press, 2010).

65. Burd-Sharps, Lewis, and Borges Martins, *The Measure of America,* 16.

66. Perlstein, *Tested.*

67. Burd-Sharps, Lewis, and Borges Martins, *The Measure of America,* 10–13, 44–79, 120–49, 74–77, 197; the UN human development model uses "the economic, social,

legal, psychological, cultural, environmental, and political processes" to measure the "broader everyday experiences of ordinary people," 2.

68. Obama, "What I Want for You—And Every Child in America," 4–5.

Chapter 7

1. Ellen Key, *Barnets århundrade* (Stockholm: ABF, 1995).

2. For different interpretations, see Jens Qvotrup, "Varieties of Childhood," in Jens Qvotrup, ed., *Studies in Modern Childhood, Society, Agency, Culture* (London: Palgrave Macmillan, 2005); Ann-Sofie Ohlander, *Det bortträngda barnet: uppsatser om psykoanalys och historia* (Uppsala: Historiska institutionen, 1993); Bengt Sandin and Gunilla Halldén, eds., *Barnets bästa: en antologi om barndomens innebörder och välfärdens organisering* (Eslöv: B. Östlings bokförlag Symposion, 2003); Therborn Göran, "The Politics of Childhood," in Göran Therborn and Francis G. Castles, eds., *Families of Nations: Patterns of Public Policy in Western Democracies* (Aldershot: Dartmouth, 1993); Jan Kampmann, "Societalization of Childhood: New Opportunities? New Demands?" in Helene Brembeck, Barbro Johansson, and Jan Kampmann, eds., *Beyond the Competent Child: Exploring Contemporary Childhoods in the Nordic Welfare Societies* (Frederiksberg: Roskilde University Press, 2004); Margit Palmær, *Svenska Barn i Bild* (Stockholm: Redaktionskommittén for Svenska Barn i Bild, 1942). Astri Andresen et al., *Barnen och välfärdspolitiken. Nordiska barndomar 1900-2000* (Stockholm: Dialogos förlag, 2011).

3. Francisco Ramirez, "Reconstituting Children: Extension of Personhood and Citizenship," in David Kertzer and K. Warner Schaie, eds., *Age Structuring in Comparative Perspective* (Hillsdale, N.J.: Erlbaum, 1998), 143–66.

4. Henrik Berggren and Lars Trägårdh, *Är svensken människa?: gemenskap och oberoende i det moderna Sverige* (Stockholm: Norstedt, 2006); Lars Trägårdh, "The 'Civil Society' Debate in Sweden: The Welfare State Challenged," in Lars Trägårdh, ed., *State and Civil Society in Northern Europe: The Swedish Model Reconsidered*, (New York: Berghahn, 2007), 9–36.

5. Andreas Bergh, *Den kapitalistiska välfärdsstaten: om den svenska modellens historia och framtid* (Stockholm: Ratio, 2007); Peter Flora and Sven E. O. Hort, eds., *Growth to Limits: The Western European Welfare States Since World War II*, vol. 1, *Sweden, Norway, Finland, Denmark* (Berlin: de Gruyter 1986);

6. Yvonne Hirdman, *Att lägga livet till rätta: studier i svensk folkhemspolitik* (Stockholm: Carlsson, 1989); Diane Sainsbury, "Gender and the Making of Welfare States: Norway and Sweden," *Social Politics* 8 (2001): 113–43; Sven E. O. Hort, *Social Policy and the Welfare State in Sweden* (Stockholm University, 1990): Thom Axelsson, Rätt elev i rätt klass: skola, begåvning och styrning 1910-1950 (Linköping University, 2007).

7. Christina Florin, Elisabeth Elgán, and Gro Hagemann, eds., *Den självstyrande medborgaren?: ny historia om rättvisa, demokrati och välfärd* (Stockholm: Institutet för framtidsstudier, 2007). Trägårdh, "The 'Civil Society' Debate in Sweden"; Klas Åmark, *Hundra år av välfärdspolitik: välfärdsstatens framväxt i Norge och Sverige* (Umeå: Boréa 2005).

8. Sandin and Halldén, eds., *Barnets bästa;*

9. Hort, *Social Policy and the Welfare State in Sweden*; Anne-Li Lindgren, *Att ha barn med är en god sak': barn, medier och medborgarskap under 1930-talet* (Linköping University, 2000); Ann-Sofie Ohlander, *More Children of Better Quality?* *Aspects on Swedish Population Policy in the 1930s* (Uppsala: Almqvist and Wiksell, 1980); Ann-Katrin Hatje, *Befolkningsfrågan och välfärden: debatten om familjepolitik och nativitetsökning under 1930- och 1940-talen* (Stockholm University, 1974); Ann-Katrin Hatje, *Från treklang till triangeldrama: barnträdgården som ett kvinnligt samhällsprojekt under 1880–1940-talen* (Lund: Historiska media, 1999). Astri Andresen et al., *Barnen och välfärdspolitiken.*

10. Gena Weiner, *De räddade barnen: om fattiga barn, mödrar och fäder och deras möte med filantropin i Hagalund 1900–1940* (Linköping University, 1995); Maria Sundkvist, *De vanartade barnen: mötet mellan barn, föräldrar och Norrköpings barnavårdsnämnd 1903–1925* (Linköping University, 1994).

11. Eva Gullberg, *Det välnärda barnet: föreställningar och politik i skolmåltidens historia* (Linköping University, 2004); Ulf Jönson, *Bråkiga, lösaktiga och nagelbitande barn: om barn och barnproblem vid en rådgivningsbyrå i Stockholm 1933–1950* (Linköping University, 1997); Ann-Charlotte Münger, *Stadens barn på landet: Stockholms sommarlovskolonier och den moderna välfärden* (Linköping University, 2000).

12. Yvonne Hirdman, *Att lägga livet till rätta: studier i svensk folkhemspolitik* (Stockholm: Carlsson, 1989). Sainsbury, "Gender and the Making of Welfare States"; Hort, "Social Policy and the Welfare State in Sweden."; Stefan Svallfors, *Välfärdsstatens moraliska ekonomi: välfärdsopinionen i 90-talets Sverige* (Umeå: Boréa, 1996).

13. Sandin and Halldén, eds., *Barnets bästa*; Andreas Bergh, Den *kapitalistiska välfärdsstaten.*

14. The Swedish state, a centralized government constructed at a national level, controls a body of national and regional government agencies as well as different regional and local political governments. The electorate votes for a national parliament, which appoints the cabinet but also a regional and local political body. The national government regulates the forms and general framework for decision making at the local level. The political majority is often different in local, regional, and central levels. The responsibility for child care and social policy is divided between these separate bodies in different ways during different periods, and the system of governance may shift from a focus on centrally issued directives or more general legal frameworks to offering local governments greater leeway in forming independent policies. The political interaction between these different levels forms the core of Swedish political culture.

15. Margit Palmær, *Svenska Barn i Bild.*

16. Ann-Sofie Ohlander, *More Children of Better Quality?*; Ann-Katrin Hatje, *Från treklang till triangeldrama;* Ann-Katrin Hatje, *Svensk välfärd, genus och social rationalism under 1900-talet: mikro- och makroperspektiv på offentlig sektor, den svenska modellen och kvinnors politiska agerande* (Umeå: Institutionen för idé- och samhällsstudier, Umeå universitet, 2009); Helena Bergman and Peter Johansson, eds., *Familjeangelägenheter: modern historisk forskning om välfärdsstat, genus och politik* (Eslöv: Östlings bokförlag. Symposion, 2002); Barbro Nordlöf, *Barnets rätt och bästa: en studie i barnavårdsmanna-*

verksamheten i Stockholm (Stockholm: Stockholmia 1997); Astri Andresen et al.,*Barnen och välfärdspolitiken.*

17. Jacques Donzelot, *The Policing of Families: Welfare Versus the State* (London: Heinemann, 1980); Yvonne Hirdman, *Att lägga livet till rätta.*

18. Torsten Husén, *Vad har hänt med skolan?: perspektiv på skolreformerna* (Stockholm: Verbum Gothia, 1987), 12–14.

19. *Barnstugor, Barnavårdsmannaskap, Barnolycksfall,* Statens Offentliga Utredningar 1967:8 (Stockholm: E. Kihlströms tryckeri, 1967), 46.

20. Karin Zetterqvist Nelson, "När Bowlby kom till Sverige. Från motstånd till erkännande: anknytningsteori i Sverige 1950–2000," in Ann-Marie Markström, Maria Simonsson, Ingrid Söderlind, and Eva Änggård, eds., *Barn, barndom och föräldraskap* (Stockholm: Carlssons, 2009).

21. Ulf Jönson, *Bråkiga, lösaktiga och nagelbitande barn:* Karin Zetterqvist Nelson, "När Bowlby kom till Sverige."

22. Judith Lind (Areschoug), *Det sinneslöa skolbarnet: undervisning, tvång och medborgarskap 1925–1954* (Linköping University, 2000). Gullberg, *Det välnärda barnet.*

23. Kerstin Thorsén, Läroplan *för grundskolan,* Lgr 69 (Stockholm: Utbildningsförl, 1969–1978).

24. Johanna Schiratzki, *Mamma och pappa inför rätta* (Uppsala: Iustus, 2008), 46–52.

25. Svallfors, *Välfärdsstatens moraliska ekonomi;* Åmark, *Hundra år av välfärdspolitik.*

26. Trägårdh,"The 'Civil Society' Debate in Sweden."

27. Jonas Qvarsebo, *Skolbarnets fostran: enhetsskolan, agan och politiken om barnet 1946–1962* (Linköping University, 2006).

28. Johanna Schiratzki, *Barnrättens grunder* (Lund: Studentlitteratur, 2006); Anna Singer, *Föräldraskap i rättslig belysning* (Uppsala University, 2000).

29. *Betänkande om barnkostnadernas fördelning med förslag angående allmänna barnbidrag m. m. Bilagor,* 1941 års befolkningsutredning (Stockholm, 1946); Olof Bergholtz and Åke Bylander, eds., *Barnbidrag och bidragsförskott: kommentar till lagarna om barnbidrag och om förskottering av underhållsbidrag till barn.* (Stockholm: Norstedt, 1940).

30. Ingrid Söderlind Ingrid and Kristina Engwall, eds., *Barndom och arbete* (Umeå: Boréa, 2008), chap. 7: Elisabet Näsman, & Christina von Gerber, *Från spargris till kontokort: barndomens ekonomiska spiraltrappa* . (Institutionen för tematisk utbildning och forskning, Linköpings universitet, Norrköping, 2003).

31. Olof F. Lundquist, *Studiestöd för vuxna: utveckling, utnyttjande, utfall* (Dissertation Göteborg University, 1989); Sven-Eric Reuterberg, *Studiemedel och rekrytering till högskolan* (Göteborg University, 1984).

32. Riksförbundet Hem och skola, *Föräldrarna och SIA: ur betänkandet Skolans arbetsmiljö,* Statens Offentliga Utredningar 1974: 53 (Stockholm: Riksförb. Hem och skola, 1974); Mats Sjöberg, "Att fostra ett skolbarn: Den nya skolan och barndomens förändring. 1950–1970," in Sandin and Halldén, eds., *Barnets bästa.*

33. Ingrid Söderlind and Kristina Engwall, *Var kommer barnen in? barn i politik, vetenskap och dagspress* (Stockholm: Institutet för framtidsstudier, 2005), 29 n.23.

34. Utredningen om skolans inre arbete, *Rapporter från undersökningar genomförda av Utredningen om skolans inre arbete*, vol. 1, *Skolan som arbetsplats* (Stockholm, 1974)

35. Sven Persson, *Förskolan i ett samhällsperspektiv* (Lund: Studentlitteratur, 1998); Sven Persson, *Föräldrars föreställningar om barn och barnomsorg* (Lund University, 1994); Gunilla Halldén, *Förhållandet till tid: en föräldragrupps reflektioner över utveckling och uppfostran* (Stockholm, 1988); Gunilla Halldén, *Föräldrars tankar om barn: uppfostringsideologi som kultur* (Stockholm: Carlsson, 1992).

36. Kampmann, "Societalization of Childhood."

37. Statens kulturråd, *Kulturpolitik i praktiken: statliga kulturinsatser: en översikt*, 9. (Stockholm: Statens kulturråd, 1997); Kulturutredningen, *Tjugo års kulturpolitik 1974–1994: en rapport från Kulturutredningen* (Stockholm: Fritze; Kulturutredningen 1995). *Tjugo års kulturpolitik 1974–1994: en rapport från Kulturutredningen. Tabellbilaga* (Stockholm: Fritze; Statens kulturråd, 1972); *Ny kulturpolitik: [betänkande]*. vol. 1, *Nuläge och förslag* (Stockholm: Statens kulturråd, 1972); Eva Änggård, *Bildskapande— en del av förskolebarns kamratkulturer* (Linköping University, 2005).

38. Kulturutredningen, *Tjugo års kulturpolitik 1974–1994*.

39. Joakim Palme, *Welfare in Sweden: The Balance Sheet for the 1990s* (Stockholm: Fritzes offentliga publikationer, 2002), *Barnomsorg och skola under 1990-talet: underlag till ett välfärdsbokslut* (Stockholm: Statens skolverk 1999); *Barns och ungdomars välfärd: antologi från kommittén Välfärdsbokslut*, Statens Offentliga Utredningar (Stockholm: Fritzes offentliga publikationer 2001), 55; Åke Bergmark and Marta Szebehely, eds., *Välfärdstjänster i omvandling: antologi från Kommittén Välfärdsbokslut* (Stockholm: Fritzes, 2001)

40. Vicki Paskalia, *Free Movement, Social Security and Gender in the EU* (Oxford: Hart, 2007); Seth Koven and Michel Sonya, eds., *Mothers of a New World: Maternalist Politics and the Origins of Welfare States* (New York: Routledge, 1993). Schiratzki, *Mamma och Pappa*, 53–59; Roger Klinth, *Göra pappa med barn: den svenska pappapolitiken 1960–95* (Linköping University, 2002).

41. Thomas Johansson and Roger Klinth, "De nya fäderna: om pappaledighet, jämställdhet och nya maskulina positioner," *Tidskrift för genusvetenskap: konst—scen, film, forskning* 1, 2 (2007): 143–66; Roger Klinth, "The Man and the Equal Family: A Study of the New Images of Masculinity in the Educational Radio and TV Programmes in Sweden, 1946–1971," in Rolf Torstendahl, ed., *State Policy and Gender System in the Two German States and Sweden, 1945–1989* (Uppsala: Historiska institutionen, Uppsala University, 1999), 169–97; Roger Klinth, "The Best of Both Worlds?" *Fathering* 6, 1 (Winter 2008): 34.

42. Föräldraförsäkringsutredningen, *Reformerad föräldraförsäkring: kärlek, omvårdnad, trygghet: betänkande* (Stockholm: Fritze; 2005), 13–20; www.forsakringskassan.se, April 11, 2011.

43. See, for example, Thomas Johansson. *Faderskapets omvandlingar: frånvarons socialpsykologi* (Göteborg: Daidalos, 2004); Johan Cullberg, *Kris och utveckling*, 5, Statens Offentliga Utredningar 2005: 73 (Stockholm: Natur och kultur, 2005), 143; Anders Bro-

berg, *Anknytningsteori: betydelsen av nära känslomässiga relationer*, 1. utg. (Stockholm: Natur och kultur, 2006); Magne Raundalen, *Empati och aggression: om det viktigaste i barnuppfostran* (Lund: Studentlitteratur, 1997).

44. Lucas Forsberg, *Involved Parenthood: Everyday Lives of Swedish Middle-Class Families* (Linköping University; 2009), 11–42, http://urn.kb.se/resolve?urn=urn:nbn:se: liu:diva-18680 (April 11, 2011)

45. Anita Nyberg, "From Foster Mothers to Child Care Centers: A History of Working Mothers and Child Care in Sweden," *Feminist Economics* 6, 1 (2000): 5–20; Marie Sallnäs, *Barnavårdens institutioner: framväxt, ideologi och struktur* (Stockholm University, 2000), http://urn.kb.se/resolve?urn=urn:nbn:se:su:diva-1029, April 11, 2011; Bo Vinnerljung, *Fosterbarn som vuxna* (Lund University, 1996); Bo Vinnerljung, *Svensk forskning om fosterbarnsvård: en översikt* (Stockholm: Centrum för utvärdering av socialt arbete (CUS), 1996).

46. Cecilia Lindgren, *En riktig familj: adoption, föräldraskap och barnets bästa 1917–1975* (Linköping University, 2006); Anna Kaldal, *Parallella processer: en rättsvetenskaplig studie av riskbedömningar i vårdnads- och LVU-mål* (Stockholm: Jure Förlag; 2010).

47. Jan Qvist and Bo Rennermalm, *Att bilda familj: samboende, äktenskap och barnafödande bland kvinnor födda 1936–60* (Stockholm: Statistiska centralbyrån, 1985); *Varför föds det så få barn?: resultat av en enkätundersökning om vad som påverkar beslutet att få barn* (Stockholm: Statistiska centralbyrån, 2001); Disa Bergnéhr, *Timing Parenthood: Independence, Family and Ideals of Life* (Linköping University, 2008).

48. Karin Zetterqvist Nelson, "Att vara pappa i homofamiljer: berättelser om barn, mammor och familjeliv," *Socialvetenskaplig tidskrift* 13, 1 (2006): 66–86; Karin Zetterqvist Nelson, *Mot alla odds: regnbågsföräldrars berättelser om att bilda familj och få barn* (Malmö: Liber 2007).

49. Gunilla Halldén, *Den moderna barndomen och barns vardagsliv* (Stockholm: Carlssons, 2007), 174–86; Gunilla Halldén, *Naturen som symbol för den goda barndomen* (Stockholm: Carlsson 2009).

50. Vivi Edström, *Astrid Lindgren: Vildtoring och lägereld* (Kristianstad: Raben & Sjögren, 1992).

51. Ann Solberg, " Negotiating Childhood: Changing Constructions of Age for Norwegian Children," in Allison James and Alan Prout, eds., *Constructing and Reconstructing Childhood: Contemporary Issues in the Sociological Study of Childhood* (London: Falmer, 1997).

52. Donzelot, *Policing of Families.*

53. For an expression of the latter, see *Bilaga till betänkandet: Lag om stöd och skydd för barn och unga (LBU)*, Statens Offentliga Utredningar 2009: 68 (Stockholm: Fritze, 2009), 70–73; Kampmann,"Societalization of Childhood."

54. Johanna Schiratzki, *Vårdnad och vårdnadstvister* (Stockholm University, 1997); Anna Singer, *Föräldraskap i rättslig belysning*, Juridiska fakulteten 85 (Uppsala: Iustus, 2000).

55. Alan Prout makes the point that the old dichotomy between children and

adults no longer has any value as an analytical tool, as childhood and adulthood are thus blurred. Alan Prout, *The Future of Childhood: Towards the Interdisciplinary Study of Children* (London: Routledge Falmer, 2005).

56. Gunilla Halldén, *Föräldrars tankar om barn: uppfostringsideologi som kultur* (Stockholm: Carlsson, 1992).

57. Kampmann,"Societalization of Childhood."

58. Schiratzki, *Vårdnad och vårdnadstvister*, 54–55, 68; Singer, *Föräldraskap i rättslig belysning*, chap.1: Anna Kaldal, *Parallella processer.*

59. Johanna Schiratzki, *Barnets bästa i ett mångkulturellt Sverige: en rättsvetenskaplig undersökning* (Uppsala: Iustus, 2005).

60. Söderlind and Engvall, *Var kommer barnen in?*, 47.

61. Lindgren, *Att ha barn med är en god sak*; Weiner, *De räddade barnen*; Sundkvist, *De vanartade barnen*; Gullberg, *Det välnärda barnet*; Jönson, *Bråkiga, lösaktiga och nagelbitande barn* (Münger: Stadens barn på landet).

62. Lindgren, *En riktig familj*; Gunvor Andersson, *Adoption som barnavårdsinsats*, in *Bilaga till betänkandet.*

63. http://spraakbanken.gu.se, search for barndom, barn, barns, barns bästa, barn perspektiv, barns röst. Jan Kampmann places this transformation between the 1970s and the 1990s, while I argue for longer processes of historical change. Kampmann, "Societalization of Childhood."

64. Statens Offentliga Utredningar 1997:116; LVU 2007: 1312: Regeringens proposition 1997/98:182 *Strategi för förverkligande av FN:s konvention om barnets rättigheter i Sverige* (Stockholm: Socialdepartementet).

65. Statens Offentliga Utredningar 1991: 70, 23; Bodil Rasmusson, *Barnperspektiv: Reflektioner kring ett mångtydigt och föränderligt begrepp* (Stockholm: Barnombudsmannen, 1994).

66. Dagens Nyheter, April 16, 2006.

67. Statens Offentliga Utredningar 1997: 116, 138–39; LVU 2007: 1312.

68. Statens Offentliga Utredningar 2001: 55.

69. Karin Zetterqvist Nelson, *Att mäta barns psykiska hälsa med självskattningsenkäter: en kunskapsöversikt* (Linköping: Folkhälsovetenskapligt centrum 2001); see also Kommittén Välfärdsbokslut and Palme, *Welfare in Sweden* (2002), http://www.regeringen.se/sb/d/108/a/885, April 11, 2011.

70. Anna Kaldal, *Parallella processer.*

71.   http://www.fhi.se/sv/Aktuellt/Nyheter/50-miljoner-till-lokalt-folkhalsoarbete-for-barn-och-unga, April 11, 2011; see also Peter Adamson and John Bennett, *The Child Care Transition: A League Table of Early Childhood Education and Care in Economically Advanced Countries*, Innocenti Report Card 8 (Florence: UNICEF Innocenti Research Center, 2008). Camilla Löf, *Med livet på schemat: om skolämnet livskunskap och den riskfyllda barndomen* (Lund: Lunds universitet, Malmö, 2011).

Contributors

Paula S. Fass is Margaret Byrne Professor at the University of California at Berkeley and Distinguished Scholar in Residence at Rutgers University, New Brunswick.

Michael Grossberg is Sally M. Reahard Professor of History and Professor of Law at Indiana University, Bloomington.

Stephen Lassonde is Deputy Dean of the College and Adjunct Assistant Professor of History at Brown University.

Kriste Lindenmeyer is Professor and Chair, Department of History at the University of Maryland, Baltimore County.

Mary Ann Mason is Professor and Codirector of the Center, Economics & Family Security at the University of California, Berkeley, School of Law.

Steven Mintz is Director of the Graduate School of Arts and Sciences Teaching Center, Columbia University.

Bengt Sandin is Professor and Chair, Department of Thematic Studies-Child Studies at the University of Linköping, Sweden.

Index

Acknowledgments

The collaboration that resulted in this volume and that brought colleagues together from many different parts of the United States and from Sweden has led us through years of joyous interdependence. The book has also been the result of much dependence on the generous support of others and we are delighted to acknowledge our debt here. Especially important to the project as a whole and to three of us in particular, Steven Mintz, Bengt Sandin, and Paula Fass, was the year in residence that we shared as Fellows at the Center for Advanced Study in the Behavioral Sciences at Stanford (CASBS) during academic year 2006–7. Anyone who has spent any time there knows that it is as close to paradise as most of us will ever get. We would especially like to acknowledge the support and assistance of Claude Steele (then director), and Linda Jack. The Center for Child and Youth Policy at the University of California at Berkeley started the project on its way by funding the initial conference on the History of Childhood and the Social Sciences held in October 2005. This allowed the members of the group to get together and begin our collaborative efforts. We are very pleased to acknowledge with deep thanks Neil Gilbert and Jill Duerr Berrick for their unwavering support. The University of Maryland, Baltimore County, the California Wellness Foundation, and the William T. Grant Foundation sponsored the conference at the University of Maryland, Baltimore County, and the John and Rebecca Moores Chair supported us at the University of Houston, the two other sites that hosted our preliminary attempts to bring history together with the other social sciences.

Since we are all affiliated with and terrifically proud of the work being done by the Society for the History of Children and Youth in promoting the serious study of children's history and encouraging genuine fellowship among scholars, we would like to acknowledge the importance of that organization, where we presented earlier versions of these essays at its biannual conference in Berkeley in July 2009. We were also privileged to hold a seminar on our work with an extremely appreciative audience at the American Historical

Association meeting in San Diego in January 2010. It is very important for new fields of inquiry to have organizations and individuals available to succor those efforts and we feel extraordinarily fortunate to have found just such support among these wonderful groups and organizations.

The University of Pennsylvania Press, its editorial board, and especially Peter Agree have been staunch supporters of this book and we are deeply grateful for Peter's assistance at all stages of its progress. Two excellent readers, one of whom, Julia Grant, identified herself to us, helped to strengthen and fine-tune the volume as a whole.

Finally, our children are always on our minds as we write about the history of childhood, not only because we are devoted to their welfare but because they stimulate us to imagine other people's children, their history and their future. We, therefore, dedicate this book to our children with gratitude and love.